# LARGE BELLS
# OF
# AMERICA

Neil Goeppinger

First Edition: August 2016
Printed in the United States of America
ISBN: 978-1-939237-44-6
Published by Suncoast Digital Press, Inc.
Sarasota, Florida, USA
Library of Congress Cataloging-In-Publication Data
Library of Congress Control Number: 2016942859

# DEDICATION

I dedicate this book to Ginny, my wife of 49 years, my two children, Tauri and Cole, my four grandchildren, Maddie, Bella, Sam and Lou, my friends and my God. Because of them, my life has been fun and well worth living.

# ACKNOWLEDGMENTS

First, I must thank Carl Scott Zimmerman for his many notes emailed to me when he would discover new information on large bell foundries, and for his advice and early editing of my foundry information dating back quite a few years. He supplied me with more bell foundry information than anyone else.

Second, I would never have discovered the fun of bell research without the welcoming and encouragement of then Editor of the *Bell Tower Magazine*, Louise Collins. She was the "Grand Old Lady" of the American Bell Association, International, Inc. for decades, and knew everyone who ever had anything to do with the Association. When I first discovered the organization and wrote to them about joining, back came a letter from Louise, and once she knew what information I was seeking, she published a note in the magazine for members to pass along any information they had on bell foundry history. On the wall of my office I have a picture of her dancing with me at the Fairlee, Vermont convention, to remind me of her. Louise started and encouraged many of us in the bell collecting hobby.

Thanks to Joseph Rayzor for helping move my data into Access. It was a more complicated process than I anticipated.

Finally, I want to thank Barbara Dee of the Suncoast Digital Press for her help in bringing my information together and putting it in logical form. Only those who have written a book know the importance of a good editor/publisher.

# CONTENTS

## PART I

## PART II

# PART I

# INTRODUCTION

## A Tale of Two Bells

I grew up on a sprawling Iowa farm which had two creeks. My mother called my brother and me from work or play with an 18-inch iron dinner bell (approximately 80 pounds). This system worked so well that when my wife and I moved to the country in 1978, I thought it would be good to have a similar bell for summoning our two children. I ran an ad in our local newspaper for a "large bell." A man answered my ad, and I became the owner of a 30-inch iron fire bell (approximately 350 pounds, fig. 1). That same week, a friend who knew I was looking for a large bell saw another 30-inch bell for sale at a salvage yard and told me about it. I thought I might like it better and the price was reasonable. That is how I started collecting.

*fig. 1: Iron Fire Bell with Anchor Shaped Clapper*

I limited my collection to bells made in the United States, and I tried to get bells from different foundries, rather than just from various churches. I found I loved the sound of church bells. Nothing else sounds so much like *church*. At my peak as a collector, I had acquired over 60 large bells. I might add that through this hobby, my wife, Ginny, and I have collected many wonderful friends in America and abroad over the years. (You may be surprised to learn how many bell enthusiasts there are!)

## American Bell Association International, Inc.

As I collected, I learned about bells and researched the foundries which made them. Eventually I learned there was an association for bell collectors and joined the American Bell Association International, Inc. (ABAII) in 1983. That was the gem of my collecting. The American Bell Association® was organized in 1940 for educational and scientific purposes related to the collection, study, preservation, restoration and research of all kinds of bells. It is an all-volunteer, non-profit organization, has chapters in nearly every state plus several other countries, and holds annual conventions. I learned from other bell collectors and they helped me in my research, often sending me old bell foundry catalogs or other bits of foundry history to add to my research.

Soon, any large bell inquiries which came into the ABAII by mail or phone were directed to me for answer (this was before the Internet). Anyone who was researching a bell for a church, historical museum, or antique shop and went to a library usually found their way to me through the ABAII. My research launched in response to these inquiries often helped fill in information for me about when a particular foundry was in operation, or when it changed its name. We both benefited. I even consulted the Smithsonian and the National Park Service regarding bells for which they were seeking information. With the Internet, research is much easier today, although much of what is in old foundry catalogs and books is not on the Internet. Eventually, I partially repaid the American Bell Association International, Inc. by serving as its President.

The first job I held with the ABAII was as a Welcome Letter Writer. The names and addresses of new members were distributed to several of us, and we wrote letters telling the new member what the organization had to offer and welcoming them as a member. Early one Saturday morning I received a phone call from Japan in broken English and it took me a bit to decipher it was a new member to whom I had written, Dr. Takanori Sasaki. I learned he lived in Iwaki

Shi, Fukushima Ken, Japan, about 110 miles north of Tokyo. Soon gifts of table bells were crossing the Pacific, going both ways. Dr. Sasaki had a relationship with a museum procurer who was gathering artifacts from Tibet, and when Dr. Sasaki got more than one of a particular kind of bell, he would give me the duplicate. Thus I obtained a fine collection of bells from Tibet, likely the best in the US. This led to visits by me, my wife and me, and our children to Japan to see bell collectors and stay in their homes (fig. 2). There were a number of trips, and it also led to visits by Dr. Sasaki, some of his friends, his daughter and a friend of hers, who all stayed with us, and the son of a friend of his who stayed with us off and on for two years while going to school in Iowa. We took him to an ABAII convention in San Antonio, Texas, as well as fishing in Canada. It was a wonderful relationship which all started with the bell collecting hobby. Ginny and I also took a cruise with four other bell collecting couples and we all had a wonderful time. In these and many other ways, the ABAII is truly an "Association" of its "International" membership (https://americanbell.org).

*fig. 2, Ginny and Rieko in Kimonos*

### The Pleasure of Matchmaking

As I became more well-known as a collector, I was often offered bells, and inevitably some were duplicates to ones I already owned—so I kept a list of bells available, and every so often someone would contact me looking for a bell and I could connect them with someone with the type of bell they were seeking. I found this very fulfilling. One great story involved a Missouri foundry which made very few bells. David Caughlan had made bells in the area of St. Louis, Missouri, prior to the Civil War (fig. 3). He was strongly against slavery and made speeches against it. One night, a pro-slavery mob broke into his foundry and burned it. He then started a newspaper and continued to speak out against slavery until a mob burned his newspaper business. He took this as a calling from God and entered the ministry, but still spoke out against slavery. David Caughlan had a church in central Illinois and Abraham Lincoln came there and delivered a well-known anti-slavery speech. Fast forward to my lifetime—I had the opportunity to acquire one of David Caughlan's bells. The history and rarity of this bell made it a very exciting find for me. A few years later, the bellmaker's great-grandson, also named David Caughlan, found out about my bell. As he and his wife, Edith, were traveling to St Louis to see some of his great-grandfather's bells, they stopped by to see me (or, rather, my bell) and we had a nice afternoon together (fig. 4). He had managed to obtain one bell cast by his great-grandfather, but he had two daughters and both wanted the bell, so he was looking for another and wanted to know if I would sell mine. I chose to keep it in my collection, at least for the near future.

*fig. 3, David Caughlan Bell*

But the story of the quest for a David Caughlan bell does not end there. A couple of years went by and I received a call from a missionary who was home on leave from New Guinea. He told me he had a large bell in his garage and wanted to know if I could tell him its worth. It so happened that he had a David Caughlan bell and was intent on trading it to his neighbor for some ham radio equipment. While in New Guinea, his only contact with family or friends was through using another missionary's ham radio when he visited him. I told him about David Caughlan wanting to buy a bell by his ancestor, but the bell owner was not interested. It was not money he wanted, it was ham radio equipment. A couple of months went by and I was curious, so I called him and found that he was dejected. The neighbor had sold the ham radio equipment to someone else before he could get back to him. I then called David Caughlan and told him I knew where he could get a second bell, but it would cost him—he would have to pay whatever the ham radio equipment cost new. The end result? The missionary returned to New Guinea with his radio equipment, and David Caughlan had his second bell made by his great-grandfather.

## Organizing My Research Findings for Future Generations

The bell foundry research was always a part of my collecting, and was most often what inquirers were seeking. The Bell Foundry Directory in Part II of this book contains a listing of those foundries. There are over 400 of which I have knowledge. I can't put every detail and piece of data in the directory or it would be the size of a file drawer—still, it passes to future generations most of my basic bell foundry information. Much of this was obtained before the days of the Internet by contacting state Historical Societies, hiring a researcher to go through the Society's business records, then send me photocopies of their listings. Even today, few of the old foundry catalogs are on the Internet, and I have collected many of those.

The first part of this book gives general large bell information—history, uses, metals used, early foundry locations, nomenclature—in other words, an overview of big bells. If you are researching one or more large bells made in the United States, this book will help you. If you are curious about one of America's earliest manufactured products and how large bells figured in the lives of Americans before and since its formation as a nation, this book may inspire you to learn even more by beginning your own collection.

*fig. 4, David and Edith Caughlan under his Great Grandfather's Bell*

Courtesy of Massachusetts Historical Society

*fig. 6, Revere Bell with Iron Clamps for Wood Yoke*

*fig. 7, Revere Advertisement Showing Bell and Cannon*

*fig. 8, Revere Bell with heavy Reeds 2,2,3,2 plus 2 on top*

*fig. 9, Revere Bell with Raised Top Above Top Reeds*

*fig. 10, Revere Bell with Square Cannons and Square Argent with Steps*

*fig. 11, J. Warner and Sons, London bell, Studied by Revere*

# Chapter 1

# EARLY HISTORY

While large bells have a relatively long history, smaller bells are known to have been cast since 3,000 BC. They have been found in evidence from many civilizations including Nishapur, Luristan, Babylonia, Nineveh, Phoenicia and Egypt. They are mentioned in the Bible in Exodus 28:33, 34 & 35, Exodus 39:25 & 26, and Zechariah 14:20.

Large bells have been calling people to Christian worship services since 400 AD. As the years went on, they were used to call people for many other gatherings as well, including a fire in the community. By the time North America was discovered, large bells were in widespread use in Europe. Within 100 years after Columbus sailed in 1492, Peter Hemony had discovered how to tune large bells to specific musical notes so groups of tuned bells could be used to play music. If there were 23 or more tuned bells in a group, it was called a *carillon*, and if fewer than 23, it was called a *chime*.

By the time of the American Revolutionary War (1776), large bells were in general use in the colonies for church, fire, and meetings. At this point, most large bells were made of bronze and imported from England. A few foundries in the colonies had cast some large bells for use in their immediate area prior to the Revolutionary War, but I don't believe any of these made more than four or five bells. Post-war, one of the first established manufacturers in America was none other than Paul Revere.

*fig. 5, Paul Revere*
*Painting by John Copley*

Revere (1734-1818) was a patriot, a prominent Boston silversmith, and manufacturer (fig. 5), with his main product being sheet copper to cover ships' hulls to prevent barnacles. He also made survey instruments, and is well-known for his devoted service to help defeat the British during the Revolutionary War. In fact, according to Blake Valleau, a modern-day bell caster, Revere cast cannon for the Revolutionary Army at his foundry (fig. 7). When the war ended, he was owed a lot of money for this work and the young government was short of funds, so they gave him part of the cannon as payment. There being no market for cannon in the colonies, but knowing that cannon and church bells are both made of low bronze (approximately 20 to 22 percent tin and 78 to 80 percent copper), he decided to convert the cannon to bells and sell them.

The nearest foundry casting church bells at the time was at Abington, Massachusetts, where Colonel Aaron Hobart had hired a British Navy deserter named Gillimore who had worked in an English bell foundry. Revere contacted Hobart, who then sent Gillimore as well as his own son to Boston to teach Paul Revere how to cast church bells (fig. 6).

The question arises, why would Colonel Aaron Hobart help Paul Revere go into competition with his own foundry? I believe the answer lies in the comradery of men who had faced the enemy together. Had they lost the war, both Revere and Hobart would certainly have been executed. These were men for whom money was viewed with greater objectivity, and Revere needed to be paid for extending the army credit for the casting of cannon during the war.

Revere's early church bells were not melodious, but rather harsh in tone (figs. 8, 6, 9, 10). As relations with England improved, he sent his son Joseph to England to learn bell-casting, including how to improve the sound. Joseph bought a bell by John Warner of London to use as a model (fig. 11). Later, in 1795, Revere sold the Warner bell to the North Congregational Society of Newburyport, Massachusetts, and they have retained the bill of sale.

# LINEAGE OF SOME AMERICAN BELLFOUNDERS

(dates refer to the casting of bells)

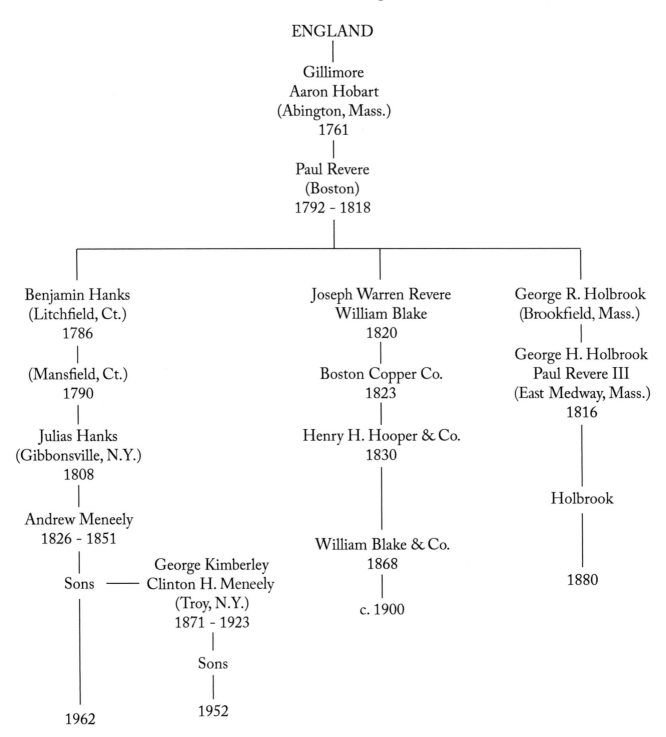

ENGLAND
|
Gillimore
Aaron Hobart
(Abington, Mass.)
1761
|
Paul Revere
(Boston)
1792 - 1818

Benjamin Hanks
(Litchfield, Ct.)
1786
|
(Mansfield, Ct.)
1790
|
Julias Hanks
(Gibbonsville, N.Y.)
1808
|
Andrew Meneely
1826 - 1851
|
Sons ——— George Kimberley
Clinton H. Meneely
(Troy, N.Y.)
1871 - 1923
|
Sons
|
1962       1952

Joseph Warren Revere
William Blake
1820
|
Boston Copper Co.
1823
|
Henry H. Hooper & Co.
1830
|
William Blake & Co.
1868
|
c. 1900

George R. Holbrook
(Brookfield, Mass.)

George H. Holbrook
Paul Revere III
(East Medway, Mass.)
1816
|
Holbrook
|
1880

*fig. 12, Lineage of Some American Bell Founders by William De Turk*

Being a leader and success-minded businessman, Revere took on apprentices to learn the various trades he was conducting. The bell foundry linage chart was prepared by William De Turk and published in the Guild of Carillonneurs of North America "Bulletin" in April, 1978 (fig. 12). On the right you will see one of these apprentices was Major George R. Holbrook who was apprenticed to Paul Revere to learn clock-making. However, Holbrook preferred to make bells, and learned that trade instead. According to Winthrop Warren, author of the article "Bell Founders of New York and Beyond" in a journal published by the American Clock & Watch Museum, Inc., Holbrook completed his bell-making apprenticeship in 1800. He then split off with Paul Revere Jr. and they formed and operated their own bell foundry until 1813 when Paul Revere Jr. died. Holbrook then quit due to health reasons, but started up again three years later in 1816 in Brookfield, Massachusetts, with his son, Colonel George H. Holbrook (fig. 13). Later, the foundry was run by his

grandson, Edwin H. Holbrook; the foundry lasted until 1880, producing around 10,000 bells, most of which are in New England.

In 1786, Colonel Benjamin Hanks started casting bells in Litchfield, Massachusetts. According to William De Turk, he had apprenticed with Paul Revere prior to that. In 1790, he moved the foundry to Mansfield, Connecticut, and in 1808 he brought his son Julius in with him (fig. 14) and they started a bell foundry in Gibbonsville, New York (later named West Troy in 1836, and still later named Watervliet in 1896). (The reason for listing the town name changes will become apparent later.) The foundry was located near the Hudson River. Benjamin Hanks and his son Julius were relatives of Nancy Hanks, the mother of US President Abraham Lincoln.

*fig. 13, George Holbrook Bell 1837*

Andrew Meneely was apprenticed to Julius Hanks in 1817 and in 1826 he married his boss's niece, Philena Hanks, and took over the Gibbonsville foundry. Julius Hanks moved across the river to Troy, New York, and started another Hanks

*fig. 14, Julius Hanks Bell 1829*

foundry. These foundries on the Hudson River had cheap water transportation to New York City, the Atlantic Ocean, and thus the entire east coast of the country. Starting in 1825, the Erie Canal connected them to the Great Lakes and the west, while Eastern Canada could be reached by the Champlain Canal and the St. Lawrence River. The Hanks Foundry continued in Troy until at least 1859 under Julius Hanks' son, Oscar.

Andrew Meneely (fig. 15), who had taken over the Gibbonsville (or West Troy) foundry from Julius Hanks, turned out to be a very skilled bell-maker and greatly advanced the art of bell-making in America

fig. 15, Andrew Meneely

fig. 16, Meneely and Co West Troy 1882

(fig. 16). He had a musical ear and experimented with bell designs. Eventually, the firm was able to produce both chimes and carillons. The Meneely Foundry of West Troy, later called Meneely and Company (fig. 17), grew to be one of the seven major foundries supplying bronze bells in North America. Andrew Meneely and Philena Hanks had five children, three of whom were sons, and all three worked at the foundry. Edwin and George were older, and Clinton Hanks Meneely was the youngest. By the time the Civil War broke out Andrew was dead, but his young son, Clinton Hanks Meneely, went off to war. This is significant. He was in many battles including Gettysburg and was, remember, related to President Lincoln. He served on the personal staffs of both General McClellan and General Wadsworth, and by the end of the war had advanced to Colonel.

Unlike the war comradery of Revere and Hobart, when Colonel Clinton Meneely returned to West Troy, his brothers Edwin and George informed him that the business was not sufficiently prosperous to support three families, so in 1870, Clinton Meneely (after selling army surplus and metal for a time) formed a partnership with his brother Edwin's brother-in-law, George Kimberly. They opened the Meneely and Kimberly Bell Foundry across the river in Troy (fig. 18). The brothers, fearful of losing business to the new competition, sued to stop him from using the Meneely name. The Appellate Court held that "a person cannot make a trademark of his own name and thus debar others, having the same name, from using it in their business." That court case is still cited to this day as it set an important precedent.

The rift caused the two sides of the family not to speak to each other until they went out of business during the Korean War more than 80 years later. After Kimberly dropped out, it became the Clinton H. Meneely Foundry, and still later operated under the name The Meneely Bell Company (fig. 19). They too became one of the seven major foundries producing bronze bells in the United States (figs. 20 & 21). Both the Meneely Foundries produced chimes, demonstrating their ability to tune bells to each other so songs could be played on them (figs. 22 & 23). The Troy name became synonymous with quality bells. After the name of West Troy was changed to Watervliet, Meneely and Company continued to advertise their location as West Troy, with Watervliet in parentheses, or vice versa, to not give their relative an advantage. They did the same on their letterhead.

To follow these early American bell founders, William De Turk provides key historical information in "Linage of Some American Bellfounders." (De Turk was carillonneur at the University of Michigan from 1981 to 1987 and worked at Bok Tower Carillon in Lake Wales, Florida, from 1993 to 2011, first as Assistant Carilloneur, then for the last seven years as Head Carilloneur.) In this linage summary, there should be another sidebar in 1852 just under Andrew Meneely.

James H. Hitchcock had worked for Andrew Meneely, and the two men had married sisters. Phelena Hanks (wife of Andrew Meneely) and Juliaette Hanks (wife of James H. Hitchcock) were relatives of President Lincoln through his mother, Nancy Hanks Lincoln. Perhaps due to the tension and discord among the three Meneely brothers,

fig. 17, Meneely and Co Bell Foundry

fig. 18, Meneely and Kimberly Bell 1878

fig. 19, Meneely Bell Co Troy, N.Y. Foundry

MENEELY BELLS

CHURCH BELLS

Church Bells, fully warranted as to excellence of tone, purity of composition, and strength of casting; mounted in the most approved manner; of weight, dimension, and tone, noted in the accompanying table. The mountings consist of our "Conical Rotary Yoke", described on page 19, and for which Letters Patent have been granted, so arranged as to firmly sustain the bell, greatly

fig. 21, Clinton H. Meneely Bell 1883

fig. 20, Meneely Bell Co Troy, N.Y. Church Bell

fig. 22, Meneely Bell Co, 20 Bell Chime,
Grace Church, N.Y.

## CHIME AND PEAL BELLS

There is no limit to the number of bells necessary to constitute a chime or peal, except that which is suggested by the necessarily constant decrease of weight and the consequent shrillness of tone ; but in this country a *chime* is generally said to consist of eight bells, attuned to the eight tones of the octave, or diatonic scale.   In nearly every case a bell, attuned to the flat seventh tone of the scale, is added, thus rendering the chime capable of producing music in two keys.   The finest chimes in this country were manufactured in our foundry, and we can furnish them of any weight and number, with or without mountings, and adapted to any position.

fig. 23, Meneely Bell Co Troy N.Y. Chime

fig. 25, Jones and Hitchcock Troy Bell Foundry

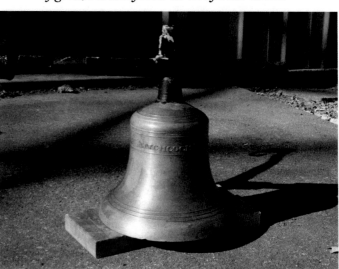

fig. 24 Jones and Hitchcock 1856

fig. 26, Jones and Co Troy Bell Foundry
1871, 53-inch bell

fig. 27, Jones and Co Troy Bell Foundry

James H. Hitchcock left the firm and started another company in 1852, the year after Andrew (the father) died. He had as his partner Eber Jones, and the firm was known as Jones and Hitchcock (figs. 24 & 25). They made quite a few bells—I would estimate a few hundred, over five years. In 1857, Hitchcock withdrew and the name became The Jones and Company Troy Bell Foundry, continuing until 1887, last run by Octavous Jones (figs. 26, 27 & 28). While in operation, it was a major manufacturer of bells selling nationwide, one of the seven major US foundries to fill North American church steeples (figs. 29 & 30).

Now you may wonder, "so Hitchcock worked for Meneely, or Meneely for Hanks, or Hanks and Holbrook for Revere, so what? Do they really trace their bell founding back to Paul Revere?" Absolutely. Like farming or auto-making, each generation built upon what had been discovered or perfected before.

Some of America's earliest "trade secrets" included the hard-earned intricacies of superior bell-making: what proportion of horse manure, sand, and clay went into the mold mix, the thickness of the bell at each point, the bell's shape (and there were many arguments and experiments on that topic), the percent of copper and tin, what temperature to heat the copper and tin before mixing them, how to mix them, how long to cool a given sized bell, and even how to place the letters in the mold for the inscription. There was a lot a young man could learn from the master tradesman to whom he was apprenticed. It took several generations of bell makers before bells as fine as those from the two Meneely foundries were produced toward the end of the 1800s (figs. 16 & 21).

We have now accounted for Holbrook, Hanks, the two Meneely foundries, and Jones, but what happened to the Revere foundry? Paul Revere's son, Joseph, who had been sent to Europe to study bell founding, joined first with two of Paul

fig. 28, Octavous Jones

Revere's grandsons, Paul Revere III and Thomas Eayres Jr., until 1818 when Eayres died. Later, Paul Revere III joined with a former Revere employee, William Blake, to produce bells, and even after the Revere firm was incorporated as the "Revere Copper Company" (the same firm making cookware today), bells were still produced in the 1830s with the inscription "Revere Boston," but no date.

William Blake partnered with several people making bells. According to William De Turk and Edward Stickney (author and expert on Revere bells), those partners included both Joseph Revere and Paul Revere III. In 1830, William Blake, Thomas Richardson, and Henry N. Hooper formed the Henry N. Hooper & Company Foundry (fig. 31) and produced

fig. 29, Jones and Co. 1870 Catalogue Church Bell

fig. 30, Jones and Co. Troy Bell Foundry

fig. 31, Henry N. Hooper Foundry and Chime

fig. 32, Henry N. Hooper Bell 1852

bells until around 1868 (fig. 32) when the name was changed simply to William Blake and Company (Hooper had died three years earlier in 1865). The firm closed in 1888. That was the last of the foundries which could trace their lineage directly from Paul Revere (figs. 33, 34, 35, & 36).

The Stickney's research shows the Revere Foundry made a total of 958 bells. The Holbrook name was on an estimated 10,000 large bells, while the two Meneely Foundries and the Jones and Company Troy Bell Foundry turned out thousands of bells each year. Although research has not

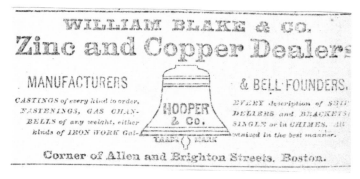

*fig. 33, William Blake and Co Advertisement, 1876*

revealed exactly how many bells they made, few towns of any size in the US and Canada do not have a bell by each of them. Certainly Paul Revere was the original and notable founder of the church bell industry in the United States, his influence seemingly immortal, and continues to ring to this day.

*fig. 34, William Blake and Co
formerly H. N. Hooper and Co*

*fig. 35, William Blake and Co*

As the population of the US grew, new churches were formed and each wanted a bell. The settlement of new lands in the west reached its peak in the 1880s with more new congregations formed during that decade than at any other time. This was the peak of church bell production in the United States. As congregations grew larger in succeeding decades, they built larger churches, but kept their old bell both because it was still serviceable, and because they had a historical and nostalgic attachment—it was *their* church bell. In fact, every large bell has a distinctive tone, and then as well as now in my own community, one can tell which of the church bells are being rung just by the sound, certainly an important part of the church's identity.

*fig. 36, Left Bell is by William Blake*

## How Bells Were Used In Early Communications

Large bells were rung in different locations and in different ways for different messages.

Church Bells: The bell of a church was often the reference point people used to know the time of day. Also, the bell summoned the community to come to church services. During church, the Lord's Prayer was often accompanied by the quiet ringing of the church bell with the tolling hammer (fig. 37). The bell was usually struck softly three times, at three different points during the prayer. The church bell was rung loudly by swinging to call people to church. Deaths were announced in different ringing series in different communities, and often it was different for a man, a woman or a child. In a small community, if they knew who was ill, the people could usually figure out who had passed, i.e., "for whom the bell tolls." In some communities, if it was a prominent man, they rang out his age. In other communities, they rang out the age for everyone who died.

fig. 37, Tolling Clapper or Tolling Hammer        fig. 38, Bronze Fire Bell with Eye on Clapper

Fire Bells: Fire alarm bells were rung rapidly and the bell did not swing (figs. 38 & 1). The fire bell was mounted high above the ringer and had an eye on the bottom of the clapper (fig. 39). Two ropes were attached to this and ran left and right (the width of a person's shoulders) to pulleys. Then, the ropes ran through these, down to the ringer below. Thus the fire bell could be rung rapidly with a rope in each hand. Often the fire bell was mounted in its own tower in front of the fire station.

School: A school day's beginning and ending were announced by a bell which was twenty to twenty-eight inches in diameter and cast thinner than a church or fire bell, so its sound was higher and unmistakable. These bells were normally cast in two-inch increments of diameter (fig. 40) and were almost always made of iron or steel.

Town Meetings: For meetings they simply rang the bell at a time when they wouldn't be having a church service, such as in the evening.

Other Uses Of Bells: Other uses of bells on the "smaller end" of large bells include:

Plantation bells to call workers to and from work.

Dinner (also known as farm) bells to call people for meals.

Ship and riverboat bells to announce they were coming into port or river landings, and to mark time.

Buoy bells to warn ships of reefs and rocks.

*fig. 39, Eye for Ropes on*        *fig. 40, 26 inch School Bell*
*Fire Bell Clapper*

Lighthouse bells accompanied a light to increase effectiveness for alerts and guidance.

Bridge bells to warn people there was a bridge ahead.

Fire engine bells to warn that the fire engine was approaching at high speed.

(Note the life-and-death value of using bells in many cases, such as in a thick fog where lights would not be noticed as early as a warning sound.)

## Locations of American Bell Foundries

Bell foundries were located in many areas of the US, but most were in the eastern half of the country as this was the area which was first settled, and most industry was located there. Bells were heavy and bulky, so transportation distance increased the expense of a bell to the buyer. Because water transportation was cheaper than other means, many of the large bell foundries were located on water. Troy and West Troy, New York, New York City, Cincinnati and Saint Louis all became major centers of bell founding activity with multiple firms in each of those cities. The Troy and West Troy (later re-named *Watervliet*) area was connected to the Great Lakes by the Erie Canal and to the Atlantic Ocean by the Hudson River. Similarly, New York City was connected to the same bodies of water. The Atlantic gave water access to all the eastern seaboard cities of the country as well as several of the large cities of Canada by way of the St. Lawrence Seaway and Lake Ontario. Cincinnati and St. Louis had access to the Ohio, Mississippi, and Missouri River systems and all the lands and cities close to them. Competition among the large bell foundries was keen, as exemplified by the two Meneely foundries, so a transportation cost advantage was important.

## Dates and Eras of Large Bell Production in America

I had read that although more bells were produced in the US in the 1880s, and my own observation over the past thirty-eight years bears that out, *more firms* were making bells in the *1820s* than in the 1880s. That would be predictable with consolidation, as happened in the auto industry—far more cars were made from 1950 to 1970 than in the 1900 to 1920 period, but there were many more firms making cars from 1900 to 1920. The data did not support this.

In compiling the Bell Foundry Directory for this book, which is the heart of the book and has the information on individual foundries, it was possible to record what firms were in business during each decade. There were some surprises. First, I knew that prior to 1800 there were no large foundries making large quantities of bells. Those firms working then were usually foundries serving a local area which were asked to produce a bell for local use. They would then make a few, perhaps five or six, for local churches or schools. The surprise was that so many did this prior to 1800 (thirty firms have been discovered which operated in the 1700s). The second surprise was discovering that so many firms operated after 1920—I had assumed the industry was pretty well shut down by then. There were 35 firms which operated after 1920. I also thought there would be zero firms during the 1940s due to WWII and the necessary use of copper for shell casings instead of bells. I forgot the military still needed bells, especially for naval ships, and for other uses where electricity was not available for sirens. After the end of the war, many firms which had been dormant restarted their operations. There were ten firms which produced bells during that decade.

Since iron and steel bells were not dated, unless historical records were discovered, many of the smaller firms which made only iron or steel bells are presumably not represented in the data. Dates of operation were obtained through research of state historical records, business directories, and through family historical data, providing an overall conclusion which should be correct as to which decades represented the operation of the most bell-making firms.

My observation that more bells were produced during the decade of the 1880s as the US settled the western agricultural lands is substantiated by the number of firms (111) operating during that decade. The breakdown follows:

| ESTIMATED NUMBER OF LARGE BELL FOUNDRIES IN AMERICA (THROUGH 2015) | | | | | |
|---|---|---|---|---|---|
| 1717 | 1 | 1820s | 30 | 1920s | 20 |
| 1730s | 2 | 1830s | 40 | 1930s | 12 |
| 1740s | 5 | 1840s | 58 | 1940s | 10 |
| 1750s | 3 | 1850s | 69 | 1950s | 11 |
| 1760s | 6 | 1860s | 80 | 1960s | 8 |
| 1770s | 6 | 1870s | 74 | 1970s | 8 |
| 1780s | 6 | 1880s | 111 | 1980s | 4 |
| 1790s | 14 | 1890s | 54 | 1990s | 7 |
| 1800s | 15 | 1900s | 48 | 2000–2015 | 4 |
| 1810s | 14 | 1910s | 24 | | |

## The Most Famous Bell In The United States

Our nation's most famous bell is called "The Liberty Bell," though few people know much about its origin and complex history.

In Colonial times, the bell was ordered from England in November, 1751, by the State Assembly of the Province of Pennsylvania for the statehouse in the city of Philadelphia. It was to be cast in 1752, and have as part of its inscription, "Proclaim liberty throughout all the land unto all inhabitants thereof. Leviticus XXV:10."

The bell was first cast by Thomas Lester and Thomas Pack of Whitechapel (a suburb of London), later to be known as the Whitechapel Bell Foundry. It was shipped to Philadelphia where it was to be installed in the assembly house. The night before it was to be hung in the new building, the workmen rang it and it cracked. The incident was described by Isaac Norris, one of three men who signed the order for the bell, as he wrote in a letter, "it was cracked by a stroke of the clapper without any other violence as it was hung up to try the sound." It has been postulated that perhaps the workmen had a few beers and were a little too enthusiastic in their swinging of the clapper. In any case, the new bell was broken and it would take a very long time to send it round-trip by sailing ship back to England for recasting.

Two Pennsylvania men, John Pass and Charles Stow, Jr., stepped forward and offered to recast it, since they could use the bell as a model to make the needed inner and outer molds. That solution was discussed and decided on. Pass and Stow thought the bell had cracked because it had too much tin in the bronze, making it too brittle (bronze metal is a mix of copper and tin), so they added more copper when they melted the bell.

After the bell cooled and the molds were broken away, the new bell was a dud—it had too much copper, so Pass and Stow started over again, made new molds, re-melted the metal, and added more tin. Voilà! The new bell rang. The original bell's inscription from Leviticus was cast on the new bell, but now the words "Pass and Stow, Philadelphia, Pennsylvania" were also on it.

Most people believe the bell became famous when it rang for the signing of the Declaration of Independence, but many church and assembly house bells rang for that event. This second version of the bell was cracked sometime between 1824 and 1835. There are differing stories as to exactly when it was cracked, but the most likely year is 1835, based on research by Justin Kramer who wrote a book about the bell in 1975 (*Cast In America*). At the time it was cracked, it was still not a well-known bell.

At some point prior to the Civil War, the abolitionists decided the inscription on the bell characterized their movement and they put a likeness of the bell on the front of their antislavery pamphlets with the inscription below it: "Proclaim liberty unto all the land and unto all the inhabitants thereof. Leviticus XXV:10." They named the pamphlet "The Liberty Bell." This use of the icon (as a logo for the abolitionist mission) made the bell famous. Furthering its status as an icon of "liberty," during the Centennial of 1876 it was featured as THE national symbol of American independence.

From 1885 to 1915, the bell traveled over 20,000 miles by train, on its own railroad car, exhibited at expositions and in large cities across America. In 1904, 75,000 school children in San Francisco signed a petition for the bell to travel to their city, which it did. For many years the bell was on public display in Independence Hall in Philadelphia. Around 1976, it was moved to its present site, Liberty Bell Center, Independence National Historic Park, at 6th and Market Streets in downtown Philadelphia, just across from its original home, Independence Hall. Millions of people have seen the bell, and it is still one of the most visited sites in America (fig.40A & 40B). See Wilbank Foundry entry on page 167 for more information.

*fig. 40A, The Liberty Bell*

*fig. 40B, The Liberty Bell Toured America 1885-1915 on its own rail car*

TOP
SHOULDER
WAIST
REEDS
HIP
SOUND BOW
LIP
MOUTH
CLAPPER

*fig. 41, Bell Parts*

CROWN
CANNON
ARGENT IN CENTER

WHEEL
YOKE
GUDGEON
A-FRAME STAND

*fig. 42, Bell Parts*                 *fig. 43, Bell Parts*

# Chapter 2

# PHYSICAL FACTS ABOUT LARGE BELLS

## Components of a Bell

Please refer to figs. 10, 41 & 42 as we identify the parts of a large bronze bell. The bell has a TOP, which may be surmounted by a CROWN, which is a holdover from European town bells which were mounted high in towers. The crown had loops which were normally chained to a stationary timber, and the clapper was moved to strike the bell with the sound emanating from the MOUTH, which was pointed straight down. These crowns were often decorative.

The crown is made up of a center post called the ARGENT, and outer loops which connect the top of the bell to the top of the argent, called CANNONS. Both the argent and cannons can be either round or square. In North America, swinging bells were used in which the bell moved and the clapper hung loose. There was no pull-rope attached to the clapper. When the bell swung, the inside wall of the bell struck against the clapper. At the time of the strike, the mouth of the bell pointed horizontally, resulting in the sound carrying much further than that of a bell designed to ring with the sound directed straight down to the ground. In Europe the people lived in the towns, congregated for protection, while in North America the farmers lived on large tracts of land so the sound needed to travel much further, which it did when emitted at the horizontal angle.

The curve at which the outer surface of the bell goes from horizontal on the top and curves down to almost vertical on the side, is called the SHOULDER. It is shaped like the shoulder of a human, and the area below it where the vertical surface starts to flair outward is called the WAIST. The most vertical surface on the bell near the top is also the thinnest. When exposed to extreme heat such as in the event of a fire, this is the most likely place for a bell to crack.

The outer surface then continues downward and outward, and at the point at which it starts to round and head downward toward the lip (or outer rim) of the bell, one can feel inside and outside the bell and find that this is the thickest portion of the bell. This thickest part of the bell is the part which the clapper strikes and is called the SOUND BOW. This is the portion which holds the reverberation after the bell is struck and produces what is called the HUM NOTE. The STRIKE NOTE (when the clapper first strikes the bell) is one octave higher, but as one hears the bell reverberate afterwards, one hears the hum note—the vibrations of the sound bow. The point at which the concave of the waist meets the convex of the sound bow is the HIP of the bell. The MOUTH is the opening of the bell from which the sound emanates. The LIP of the bell is the edge that would rest on the floor if the bell were placed with its mouth down.

Did you realize you can know at a glance where one of these types of bells was made? On the outside of most bronze bells are thin rings which are decorative and are called REEDS. They are the fingerprint of each bell foundry. The size of each reed, their spacing, quantity, and location were unique to each foundry, and they are one of the ways in which a foundry can be identified. Each foundry established one given set of placements for the reeds and stuck with it for all sizes of their bells. Like a company logo works today, the manufacturer wanted their excellent products to be identifiable and recognized.

The iron piece to which the bell is bolted at its top, and which generally is shaped like an upside down letter "C," is called the YOKE (fig. 43). On bells made prior to 1830, many had a wooden yoke as did our Liberty Bell. The two pegs which stick out each end of the yoke and upon which the bell yoke swings or fulcrums are called GUDGEONS (sometimes called TRUNCHEONS). These gudgeons rest in the A-FRAME STANDS (so named because they are shaped like the letter "A").

fig. 44, Clevis attached to bolt

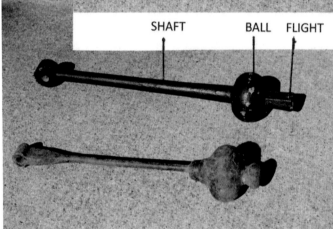

SHAFT    BALL    FLIGHT

fig. 46, Clapper parts                    fig. 45, Bolt, Clevis, Limiting Springs, Washers, and Nuts

Attached to the end of the yoke, but located inward of one of the gudgeons, was usually a cast iron disk with holes which allowed for attaching either a wood or cast iron WHEEL. The wheel had a concave outer rim allowing for a rope to run around it, and a hole through which the rope would go with a knot on the inside of the rim to secure the rope. With the rope hanging off the opposite side from the knot, the bell ringer could turn the wheel and thus swing the bell by pulling on the rope.

Inside the bell is a piece called the CLEVIS, and this is the piece which has a bolt or pin through it from which the clapper is suspended and from which it swings (figs. 44 & 45). The clevis can be a separate piece, or it can be part of the bolt which holds the bell and yoke together. The CLAPPER is the part which hangs inside the bell and strikes the bell to make it ring. It includes the BALL, which is the part which makes contact with the bell when ringing occurs; the SHAFT, which is the part above the ball; and the FLIGHT, which is the short bar extending below the ball (usually one-and-a-half to two inches long) (fig. 46). Clappers for bronze bells usually have a flight, and clappers for iron and steel bells usually do not. The clapper swings from the clevis, which is mounted inside the bell on the underside of the top.

Inside most large bells are LIMITING SPRINGS which restrict the contact of the clapper with the bell to keep the sound from trailing off when the ringer quits pulling on the rope to swing the bell. The limiting springs are approximately two thirds of the length of the clapper, located opposite each other on either side of the shaft of the clapper. These springs normally had leather on the lower ends to silence them when they made contact with the shaft of the clapper. This way the clapper gives one last good strike on the side of the bell so the sound doesn't trail off as the clapper makes lighter and lighter strikes on the bell. When the bell swings a smaller arc, the clapper simply bounces off the limiting springs, rather than making lighter contact with the bell (fig. 45). There are different methods of attaching the clevis inside the bell, and also for attaching the limiting springs.

Many church bells have a second clapper called either a TOLLING or FUNERAL CLAPPER (fig. 37). Sometimes it is referred to as a TOLLING HAMMER instead of clapper. This is an iron ball or cylinder mounted on a pivoting arm which allows it to strike either the inside or outside of the bell. Some of these have massive hollow balls which provide space for a round wood insert which makes the contact with the bell. These tolling clappers are used to make measured, soft ringing of the bell possible. In some churches, the bell is tolled three times during recitation of the Lord's Prayer. A century ago it was common to toll the age of the deceased with this clapper.

Cast iron and cast steel bells generally do not have reeds cast into them, and I have never seen one with a crown, but all other parts are similar to what has been described above.

## Composition and Sound

Big bells are made of iron (fig. 47), steel (fig. 48), bronze (fig. 18), and brass (fig. 49). There is little difference between the sound of an iron bell and a steel bell, but there is a big difference between the sound of a bronze bell and a brass bell. There is also a big difference from an iron bell to that of either a bronze or brass bell. The ring of iron and steel bells is not as pleasing as that of a bronze bell and the reverberation does not last as long, but they cost far less. This is both because bronze metal costs more and because there is much more labor involved in making a bronze bell than for an iron or steel bell. Bronze is denser than iron or steel with a cubic inch of bronze weighing more than either of the two ferrous metals. Brass bells are much more shrill and not very pleasing, but make great attention-getters. Thus they are used for railroad engines, fire engines, and small ships' bells (figs. 50 & 51).

*fig. 47, Cincinnati Bell Co, 48-inch Bell*

Brass bells are a mix of copper and zinc, with the zinc ranging from 5 to 40 percent.

Iron bells are made of iron.

Steel bells are made of iron and tin.

Bronze bells are usually 78 to 80 percent copper, and the remainder tin. Exceptions to this are very small bronze bells which can go down to 75 percent copper, and very large ones which can go up to 82 percent copper. The copper and tin in a bronze bell do not completely amalgamate (combine to form one alloy). Thus a broken piece of bell bronze will show shiny flecks of tin which did not completely mix with the copper (fig. 53).

## Patina

A bronze bell starts its life gold-colored (fig.54). After about 80 years, a silver patina will usually appear on the outside of a bronze bell (fig. 55), especially if it has been in an unheated bell tower or completely exposed to the weather. As the copper component has oxidized and

*fig. 48, C. S. Bell Co, Pre Civil War Shape Left, Post Civil War Shape Right*

*fig. 49, Howard Brass Locomotive Bell*          *fig. 50, Fire Engine Bell*

*fig. 51, USN Brass Bell*          *fig. 52, Ship Bell, Dallas, Bronze*

*fig. 53, Broken Bronze Bell*          *fig. 54, Polished Bronze Bell*

*fig. 55, Author with his favorite bell – 39-inch McShane*

turned green, condensation and/or rain have kept washing this off. A bell gets wet most nights because the mass of bronze changes temperature more slowly than the air, thus forming condensation. In the process, the flecks of tin are left exposed on the surface because they don't oxidize as much, until the bell looks to be silver or nickel-plated. You can polish a bell hard enough to remove this thin tin covering, after which the process starts all over again. If you polish the bell lightly, it will gleam like a tin can. Helen Gelman reported in her article in *The Bell Tower* (November/December 1978), "Copper and Its Alloys, Bronze and Brass," that carbon and sulfur in the air affect copper and cause it to tarnish, but moisture is the catalyst. Thus, condensation plus exposure to air cause bronze to tarnish. If a bronze bell stays indoors where the temperature is controlled and thus there is little condensation, it will first turn brownish yellow, then get more brown with age, never attaining the bright tin-colored patina of an outdoor bronze bell. This brown coloration usually occurs with small bronze table bells, not large bells.

Brass bells normally remain gold-colored all their lives, and can be polished. Low-zinc-content brass is gold-colored, while brass with a high zinc content is a bright yellow. A brass bell may have quite a different outside appearance, too. For example, some fire engine brass bells are plated with either nickel or chrome (fig. 50).

It does not hurt the sound of a steel or iron bell to paint it. That is how they came from the foundry. Without paint, they rust.

Size/Weight Ratio

I read in an old issue of *The Bell Tower* (the magazine published by the American Bell Association International, Inc.) that when the diameter of the mouth of a bronze bell is doubled, the weight is multiplied eight times. I looked this up in old bronze bell foundry catalogs and it was basically true. This made me wonder why this would be true for bronze bells, but not for iron or steel bells. I then went to old iron and steel bell foundry catalogs and made the same comparison and found that the same still holds true, but not quite as exactly as for bronze bells.

fig. 56, Largest C. S. Bell Co Bell (54 inches)

fig. 57, Largest Bell made in US

fig. 58, USLHS Buoy Bell

fig. 59, Broken Top on McShane Bell
From Not Removing Clapper

fig. 60, German shaped sound bow

fig. 61, Sound Bow

## Largest Bells Made in the US

The largest steel or iron bell made in the United States was 54 inches in diameter, and with mountings weighed 3,150 pounds. It was made of steel by the C. S. Bell Co. of Hillsboro, Ohio (fig. 56). At least one other firm made a 54-inch diameter bell, but its name does not appear on the bell.

The largest bronze bell made in the US was 9 feet in diameter, seven feet tall, and weighed 35,000 pounds. It was cast by Vanduzen of Cincinnati, Ohio, for the Francis de Sales Church of that city. The story is told that the first time they rang it in the church it shattered so many windows in the blocks around it they could never ring it full-throat again (fig. 57).

Brass bells are rarely made larger than 18 inches in diameter as their main uses are as railroad and fire engine bells, and bells larger than that would be too heavy. Also, the sound does not get any better with size, whereas with bronze bells, for example, the larger the bell the deeper the tone and better the sound.

## Thickness of Bells

The thinnest part of a bell is between the shoulder and the waist. The United States Light House Service buoy bell (fig. 58) has two pocks and one hole about evenly spaced apart, all being a half-inch in diameter, and in a straight line. Apparently some navy men decided to ring the bell with a 50-caliber machine gun. Since a normal machine gun belt has three standard rounds, one tracer and one armor-piercing, then repeats the sequence, the hole was caused by the armor-piercing round striking the bell at its thinnest point.

What would you guess was the cause if you saw a bell with a hole broken in the top? The second thinnest part of a bronze bell is the top. When a bell is lowered to the ground by a crane, if the clapper was not first removed it will strike the ground first since the clapper extends below the mouth of the bell (fig. 59). This causes the clapper to jam upward and often breaks the top out of the bell.

## Form Follows Function for a Bell's Sound

The thickest part of a bell is the sound bow. It is located a few inches just above the lip of the bell. If the bell is suspended, running one hand on the inside of the bell and the other hand opposite it on the outside, one can readily find it. This is where the clapper makes contact with the bell when it is rung (figs. 60 & 61). When the clapper strikes it, it gives off the "strike note." When a carillonneur plays music on a carillon, it is the strike notes which are heard. After the clapper has struck the sound bow, the note which continues to resonate for many seconds (up to a minute in a well-made bronze bell) is called the hum note and is exactly one octave below the strike note. These notes are produced by the bell in five major locations along the side called the major overtones, and there are also minor overtones, but they are hard to pick out.

In iron and steel bells, the school bells (20- through 28- inch diameter) were cast thinner than the church and fire bells (30 through 54 inches) so there was no mistaking the call of the school bell from that of the church and fire bells. The school bells had a higher more shrill tone (fig. 40).

## How Bells are Tuned

Only bronze bells are tuned to specific musical notes. Iron and steel bells keep the tone they have when they are cast and this is determined by the bell's shape, its diameter, its thickness, and the temperature the day it was cast (affecting how long it took to cool).

Bronze bells can be tuned to a specific musical note, but it is much more complicated than just that. The tuning is done by placing the bell upside down on a turning table and shaving metal off the inside of the bell at different points (fig. 90). When the clapper strikes the bell, it sounds the strike note. We hear five major overtones which are produced from five different locations along the inside surface of the bell. These must be in tune to each other for the sound to be pleasing and this is the job of the bell tuner. It requires someone with a keen ability to pick out the major overtones, but tuning gets much more complicated if the bell is to be used to play music in either a carillon (23 bells or more) or a chime (less than 23 bells). In this case, the bell tuner not only has to tune the major overtones within the bell, but must tune them to the bell above it and the bell below it in the chime or carillon so they "agree" with each other and the music is pleasing.

### Shapes of Bells

Bronze bells made in the US have basically two shapes. In the Germanic shape (fig. 62), there is a ridge around the outside of the sound bow with a straight surface running from that ridge to the lip of the bell (fig. 60). There is a corresponding ridge on the inside of the sound bow also with a straight surface running from it to the lip, forming a wedge shape with the edge of the wedge being the lip of the bell. All other bronze bells have a curve from the thickest part of the sound bow to the lip (figs. 63 & 61). Each bronze bell foundry had their own unique bell shape which helped determine the unique sounds of each firm's bells.

*fig. 62, H. Stuckstede 1890 Bell*

Iron and steel bells are shaped the same, but are different from the shape of bronze bells. They are shorter from the lip to the top as a percentage of the diameter of their mouth. Iron and steel bells have a rougher finish than bronze bells because they come from molds which are used over and over again, while a bronze bell mold is only used once. Large iron and steel bells were made in basically the same shape until the time of the US Civil War (fig. 64). Around that time (1865), someone discovered that by adding a little more metal to make the bell taller and slightly larger in diameter at the top, the sound was improved (fig. 65). In bells over 30 inches in diameter, the difference was significant and very soon no one wanted to buy a bell of the old shape. This forced all makers of iron or steel bells to change the shape of their bells. The sound improvement was not as noticeable in dinner bells (12 to 18 inches in diameter), and as a result some firms continued to make them in the older shape until the 1880s.

The makers of some dinner bells also added a decorative band around the outside of the bell (fig. 66) but by the 1880s this had basically been dropped. I have never come across a dinner bell made after 1880 with this band, so when one finds an iron or steel dinner bell with it, the date of its casting can at least be generalized as being made prior to 1880. Iron and steel bells are almost always undated due to the way they are cast. Unlike bronze molds, the iron and steel molds are made of sand and iron casks, and so it is not practical to put type (made of wax) between the inner and outer mold.

*fig. 63, McShane 39 inch Bell*          *fig. 64, On right, C. S. Bell Co Pre Civil War Shape Bell*

### Bell Wheels

Smaller bells had iron wheels for the rope, while large bells had wooden wheels. There were two reasons for this. Large iron wheels were heavy which increased shipping costs, and the spokes were thin and easily broken, again adding to shipping problems. Smaller iron wheels didn't weigh as much and were less subject to breakage (figs. 40 & 43).

## Swinging Versus Stationery Bells

Stationery bells are mounted to a beam or some sort of mount so the bell does not move (fig. 67). Instead, the clapper is swung to strike the non-moving bell. A swinging bell is attached at the top to a yoke which then revolves back and forth so the bell swings with its mouth pointing first one direction, then the opposite direction. Early European bells were mounted stationery and high in the towns. The towns were walled for protection and the people went out to the fields to work during the day, but came into the walled city or town at night. Since the sound of a bell comes out its mouth, this directed the sound down to the people gathered together in the town. Another reason the people came into the town at night was because the farmland belonged to the nobility and the peasants did not have the right to build houses on it.

*fig. 65, Post Civil War Shape Iron Bell*

In the United States, the people settled on the farms and lived on them outside the towns. The ability to own their own farmland was a big draw, bringing immigrants from Europe to America. Many of the churches and schools were located in the country. This made the use of swinging bells much more practical as the mouth of the bell was first pointed horizontally one way, then pointed horizontally in the opposite direction, sending the sound out as far as possible to the rural population. Even the churches in town wanted this method of ringing.

## Mounting Bells to the Yoke

Most iron and steel bells are mounted with a large bolt going up through a clevis from which the clapper swings, then up through a hole in the top of the bell, through a hole in the center of the yoke, then secured with a large cast washer and nut.

*fig. 66, L.E.B. MFG Co.*

Bronze bells are mounted in a number of ways. The method used for the most bronze bells was to have a tapered cone cast into the top of the bell with a hole through it, and also cast a matching tapered hole in the bottom of the iron yoke. A large bolt then went through a clevis from which the clapper swung, through the hole in the tapered cone on top of the bell, through the yoke and was again secured with a large cast washer and nut on top. McShane, both Meneely foundries, Jones and Rumsey all used this method (figs. 68 & 69).

Vanduzen used a large hole in the top of their bronze bells (approximately 4 to 5 inches in diameter) with a large stepped down washer (about a half-inch thick) with two holes in it the size of the mounting bolts. This washer was slightly bigger in diameter than the hole in the top of the bell, and was inserted inside, on the underside of the bell's top. The mounting bolts then went up from the inside through the clevis from which the clapper swung, through the stepped down washer, and finally through the yoke, and it was secured with two large nuts on top of the yoke. The yoke had a large circular washer cast into the bottom center and this was thus clamped to the top of the bell (fig. 70). If you see a church bell with two bolts with nuts protruding from the top of the yoke, you know it was made by Vanduzen. This is often handy identifying the maker of a bell in an open steeple using binoculars and thus saving a climb up a rickety dirty ladder.

*fig. 67, Stationary Bell Mounting*

fig. 68, Rumsey Bell Top

fig. 69, Meneely Bell Top

fig. 70, Vanduzen Bell Mounting

fig. 71, Stuckstede Bell Mounting

fig. 72, G. W. Coffin Bell 1851

fig. 73, Chaplin Fulton Bell Crown with Yoke

The two Stuckstede foundries in St. Louis had a ring of holes for bolts in the top of their bells and they cast a matching ring of iron on the bottom of their yoke. Bolts came up through the holes in the bell and went through bronze pawls which were "L" shaped. These pawls went over the ring of iron on the bottom of the yoke, so when nuts were tightened on top of the pawls, the bell was clamped to the yoke (fig. 71).

G. W. Coffin had a flat top on their bells with a single bolt going up through the bell and yoke with a nut on top, similar to an iron bell mounting (fig. 72). This bell could easily be rotated.

fig. 74, Julius Hanks Bell Crown with Yoke

All these bronze bell mountings described so far have one thing in common. They allowed the mounting bolt or bolts to be loosened and the bell rotated, with the bolts then re-tightened so the clapper would strike a new location on the sound bow. The ball of the clapper was iron and harder than the bronze of the bell, so the bronze would be smashed in with use, creating a stress point where the bell could crack. Bronze bells were delivered with instructions to rotate the bell periodically. In practice they rarely were rotated. When originally mounted, the inscription was centered between the two A-frame mounting stands. Almost always if you climb a steeple, that is where the inscription is still located, indicating the bell has never been rotated, and there are two smashed-in spots inside the bell where the clapper still strikes.

Bronze bells cast with crowns as part of the bell top were sometimes mounted to yokes, but it was much more difficult to rotate the bell. The bell would have to be lowered to the ground or floor of the bell room in the steeple, the yoke detached and rotated, then reattached and the assembly raised back up on the A-frame stands. It would be a hard and dangerous job since the bell would weigh from 400 to 3,000 pounds (figs. 73 & 74). Crowns on bells were usually used to mount stationary (non-swinging) bells and a yoke was not used.

Another method of mounting smaller bronze bells included a round bronze cylinder as part of the top of the bell with a horizontal hole through it. It was mounted to a yoke with a matching hole the same shape and diameter as the cylinder, with a matching horizontal hole for a pin to attach the two together (figs. 32 & 75). In this case, rotation could only be done 180 degrees, which would result in the clapper striking in the same two places, so there was no point rotating the bell.

A mounting method usually used with wooden yokes on early bronze bells was a vertical flat tang which was cast into the top of the bell. The tang was usually about a half-inch thick, and had a square hole through it. A matching vertical rectangular hole was made in the bottom of the wood yoke for the bronze tang, then a cross hole was made in the wood for an iron bar which went horizontally through both the wood yoke and the square hole in the bronze tang holding them together. Georg H. Holbrook used this mounting method. The bell could not be rotated, except 180 degrees (fig. 13).

I've come across two examples of the most unique mount I've seen. Both were on smaller iron bells with a ratcheting mechanism on top which included a round gear with teeth. When the bell was rung, the ratcheting mechanism automatically rotated the bell. Why they did that on an iron bell where the clapper ball and the bell were the same hardness and the bell was not going to be smashed in causing a stress point, I don't know.

fig. 75, Henry N. Hooper Mounting

## Ornamentation on the Outside of Bells

The most ornate bells made in the US were made by G. W. Coffin of Cincinnati, Ohio (forerunner of Vanduzen), and by W. Garratt of Indiana (figs. 72, 76, & 77). Coffin made more designs and more bells than Garrett. I have seen artistic designs of dancing girls with veils trailing all the way around the bell, and designs with grapes, Christ, large harps, cherubs and/or putti on Coffin bells. W. Kaye of Louisville, Kentucky, also made bells which were ornate, but his detail was rough and unrefined compared to the other two (fig. 78). The rings around the outside of bronze bells were discussed in the earlier section on parts of a bell. They are called *reeds*.

*fig. 76, Garratt and Co Madison IA*

Bronze bells normally had the name of the foundry, its city and state, and the year the bell was made cast into the side of the bell itself. An exception to this was smaller bronze bells, which were to be kept on hand for orders for plantations, river boats, bridge bells, etc. These often had the name of the foundry, its city and state, but not the year, so if the bell was carried over to the next year for sale it wasn't outdated. Iron and steel bells rarely had any lettering or reeds cast on the outside of the bell itself. Normally, the name of the foundry appeared on the yoke of the cast iron bell, but the year of manufacture did not. If a date appeared on the A-frame stands for an iron or steel bell, it was a patent date and didn't change from year to year. Iron bells with no name on the yoke were bells sold by Sears Roebuck, Montgomery Ward, or Henry Field Seed Company (fig. 79). If it was inscribed, "Steel Alloy Church Bell," but with no foundry name, it was made by the C. S. Bell Company of Hillsboro, Ohio, and sold through one of the three above retailers. Another firm which made bells for those three firms was the American Bell Company of Northville, Michigan, and it is probable the companies ordered from other foundries as well.

*fig. 77, J Garratt & Son, Madison I*

## Size and Use of Iron and Steel Bells

Iron and steel bells are broken into three basic groups based on size and use. They were generally made in 2-inch increments of diameter. Some firm's bells were slightly under the 2" increments – 11 ½", 13 ½", 15 ½" etc. This is because they measured the molds instead of the bells (12", 14", 16" etc.) and the bell metal shrank as it cooled. Most firms oversized the molds so the bells came out

*fig. 78, W. Kaye Bell*

at even sizes after cooling. Iron and steel bells under 20 inches of diameter were considered dinner bells (also called farm bells). Most firms made them in 12-, 14-, 16- and 18-inch diameters. Bells with diameters of 20, 22, 24, 26, and 28 inches were cast thinner than the larger bells, and these were made to be school bells. Because they were thinner, their tone was higher and thus the listener could tell it was the call to school. I did, however, come across one 28-inch-diameter bell cast thicker, which was a church bell. Church and fire bells are from 30 inches up through whatever was the foundry's largest bell (usually the largest cast was between 44 and 54 inches in diameter). Again, these were normally made in two-inch increments. These were considered church bells if they were mounted to swing, but were also sold as fire alarm bells when outfitted with a special clapper and mounted stationary so the clapper swung to strike the bell. In the case of fire bells, the clapper had an eye at the bottom for two ropes to be attached for rapid ringing as described earlier (figs. 1 & 39. There was no mistaking the sound of the fire bell. Some fire bells had a triangular-shaped clapper with two balls at the lower points so the clapper moved a shorter distance and thus rang even more rapidly.

*fig. 79, Sears Robuck Bell*

*fig. 80, Treating Limiting Spring Pads*

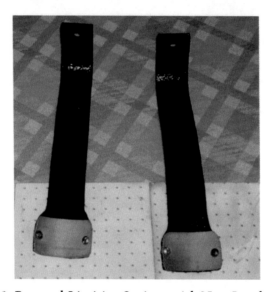

*fig. 81, Restored Limiting Springs with New Leather Pads*

*fig. 82, Restored Limiting Springs and Clapper inside Bell*

# Chapter 3

# LARGE BELL RESTORATION
# AND MAINTENANCE

## Iron and Steel Bell Restoration

Restoration of iron or steel bells is the same. Both are made of ferrous metal and thus are subject to rust. Whether a dinner bell, school bell, or church bell, the restoration process is the same:

Disassemble the yoke, clapper and clevis from the bell, along with limiting springs if it has them, and remove any leather from the limiting springs;

Have all parts sandblasted, then paint (with spray or brush) all the parts with a high quality primer at once (when the metal is absolutely bare from sandblasting, it can start to rust from moisture in the air within 24 hours);

After the primer is dry, apply a good quality top coat—use outdoor paint for metal, and glossy paint will last longer than flat paint if the bell is to be outside. An alternative is to have the bell and parts powder-coated—outside, this finish will last longer than paint, but costs considerably more. Iron and steel bells were normally painted black when they left the foundry. What color the bell is painted is dependent on your tastes and the use to which you want to put the bell. Paint does not harm the function or sound of these bells.

If the bell had limiting springs, make new leather pieces the size of the large area at the end of each spring where the shaft of the clapper will make contact. Treat the leather with Lexol or neatsfoot oil;

Usually, the leather was attached with rivets. I usually drill these out and replace them with small bolts and washers (figs. 80, 81 & 82);

Finally, reassemble all the parts.

If the bell is mounted in A-frame stands, before mounting the bell, put some grease in the U-shaped cups on the top of the stands so the gudgeons rotate easily.

## Bronze Bell Restoration

Bronze bells should be restored in a different manner. Some restoration firms sandblast bronze bells, often to the point of removing the inscriptions cast on the outside of the bells. This is done so the bell can be resold to a new owner who doesn't want the name of a prior church or city on their bell. I have a certain reverence for the historic value of bells, so I do not encourage this practice. Sandblasting also removes the tin flecks which have been exposed on the bell surface over time by the washing away of the oxidized copper, leaving the bell gold-colored instead of silver- or pewter-colored. The change of color process takes about 80 years to produce the beautiful patina, and sandblasting removes that in minutes. Also, if the inscriptions are left on the outside of the bell, sandblasting will dull the lettering.

I will describe the methods I have settled upon for restoration of my bronze bells. I will not describe methods I tried and abandoned in the past. First, disassemble the bell. If the yoke is stuck on the bell (often the case on bells made with a tapered bronze cone fit into a tapered hole in the yoke—McShane, Rumsey, both Meneely foundries and Jones all used this method), try soaking the surfaces with penetrating oil and tapping it lightly with a small hammer. This may take several days of allowing it to soak, then applying new penetrant and tapping again each day. If this doesn't work, it may be necessary to rig up a puller. On a large bell, this can be done with a short piece of I-beam above the bell, two strong chains around it and the arms of the yoke just inches from the center part of the yoke, then placing a hydraulic jack between the top of the yoke center and the I-beam. You may need a round spacer on top of the bronze cone—a three-quarter-inch or one-inch drive socket of the largest diameter which will fit against the top of the bronze cone often works well, with a steel plate on top of the socket for the hydraulic jack to push against (fig. 83). Again use penetrating oil and jack the yoke off the bell. In one case, I had a Jones bell that was on so tight it took a week of applying penetrating oil, tapping, and increasing the pressure from the jack before it came loose. I also have to admit one defeat at the hands of a large Meneely bell which I never could get loose. You have to use some judgment as to how much pressure to exert with the hydraulic jack so as not to break the yoke. I never broke one, but I had a 100-ton hydraulic jack, so it was capable of breaking practically any yoke.

I am not trained in metallurgy, but I suspect the reason these tapered cone mounting arrangements become so tight is because the two different metals (bronze and iron) set up an electrolysis which corrodes the two metals at the point of union and practically cements them together. Once the bell is disassembled, you can proceed with its restoration.

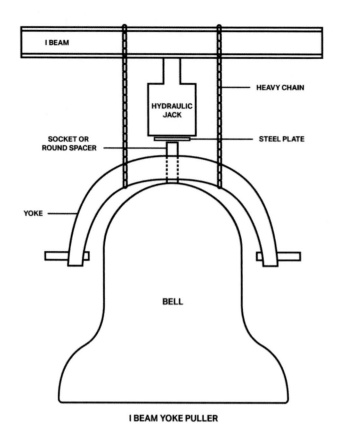

*fig. 83, I Beam Yoke Puller*

If the bell is covered with dirt or bird manure, a stiff bristle nylon brush with hot water and liquid detergent followed by a hose will take care of it, or use a pressure washer.

If the bronze bell has been painted, the paint can be removed with paint-stripper from a paint or hardware store. Follow the instructions. It is usually hard work. I use putty knives (both plastic and metal) and scrub brushes (both stiff nylon and brass, the latter are sold for cleaning barbecue grills).

Next, if the oxidation has left a hard black surface, this is hard to remove, but Naval Jelly from a hardware store will take it off. Use rubber gloves, glasses or goggles to protect your eyes, and old clothes. Apply this pink acid containing jelly to one area at a time, not larger than 12 by 12 inches. Allow the time to pass as instructed on the container, then scrub

*fig. 84, Cleaning Two Bells*

it with a brass bristle brush until the black surface is soft. Using water, remove it with a hose with a solid stream nozzle. Dry the next area and repeat the process until the whole surface is cleared of the black crud (fig. 84).

Now you are down to the silver-colored tin surface (patina). It will normally be a dull color like pewter. If you want it to shine, use a high-speed buffing polisher with a sheep's wool (or synthetic) cloth attached. Next, buy a gallon jug of 3M® brand liquid auto polishing compound available from auto parts stores. This cream-colored liquid is easy to work with and burns less than other brands. Pour some in a baking pan, dip part of the polishing head in the liquid and polish an area of the bell using the highest speed the polisher will run. If it burns and turns black, the polishing head is running too slowly. If this happens, and it often does, remove it with a stiff bristle scrub brush dipped in gasoline. I finally researched and purchased a high speed grinder with a large polishing wheel made by the commercial division of Black & Decker®. It runs at 6,000 rpm and works very well, but it was expensive.

Once the bell is cleaned and shiny, use a quality auto polish like Turtle Wax® to protect it from the elements. Just follow the directions on the package.

The iron mounting parts, including the A-frame stands, can be sandblasted, painted with a good quality primer, and top-coated with an outdoor enamel (fig. 85). If it has limiting springs they will need new leather pads attached to them after they are painted. If they had rivets holding the leather to the ends of the springs, an easy way around this is to drill the rivets out and attach the leather pads with small bolts, washers and nuts (figs 80, 81 & 82). On a very few bells (I have personally only restored one of each of these) you will find either a leather or wooden disk between the bell and yoke. In this case, recreate a duplicate of what you find if it cannot be reused (fig. 86).

When you reassemble the bell, a good precaution (and favor to someone in the future) is to coat the bronze cone with any of several products which will inhibit future corrosion of the two metals. Two of these are *Never Seize*, and *Anti-Seize* (by Permatex®). They are available at auto parts stores. An even better one, but harder to find, is LanoCote Marine Grade Rust & Corrosion Protection®. This product is specifically formulated to retard oxidation where different metals come in contact with each other. It is available from marine supply stores, but usually has to be ordered.

### Brass Bell Restoration

Brass bells are normally used for fire engines, smaller ship bells, and railroad bells. Disassemble the mountings from the bell, polish the bell using the 3M® polishing liquid described in the bronze bell restoration section above, sandblast any iron or steel mountings, paint them as described in the bronze bell section, and reassemble the bell to the mountings. Lubricate the moving parts. Brass bells polish beautifully (figs. 51 & 87). Some fire engine bells were nickel- or chrome-plated. In this case, use a polish designated for that metal, and then apply the automobile polish as described in the bronze bell section above (fig 50).

fig. 85, Restored Mounting Parts

fig. 86, New Leather Washer between Bell and Yoke

That all sounds easy enough, until you try to disassemble a steam locomotive bell that is in a cradle and yoke made so the bell can swing (figs. 49 & 88). These usually have tight tolerances and are very hard to get apart. First try penetrating oil and tapping with a light hammer to vibrate the oil through the corrosion. Do this each day for several days until the joints come free and the parts can be disassembled. If this does not work, try using an acetylene torch with a rosebud tip to heat the two parts of the metal until they are cherry red. Be sure to heat the rest of the yoke and cradle but not

*fig. 87, Bell from first USS Iowa Battle Ship*

until they are cherry red. This will avoid cracking due to too great a difference in heat. Then let them cool, and follow this with the penetrating oil. This does two things: It often breaks the corrosion loose so the penetrating oil can get through the tight fit, but it also produces a gap and increases the tolerance. When the metal expands with heat, it has to move someplace. Since it can't move closer to the other metal piece because it is already tight against it, it has to expand by moving away from the other piece. When the metal cools, it contracts, leaving an increased gap. I had a railroad bell cradle which was frozen so the yoke would not rotate, so I asked a machinist for any suggestions and he told me about this trick. It worked perfectly.

**Obtaining Missing Bell Parts**

At the writing of this book, bell parts for dinner bells can be obtained from the Internet web site of Prindle Station, at www.prindlestation.com. This firm obtained the mold patterns from the C. S. Bell Company and now sells cast steel dinner bells and dinner bell parts.

Lower Bells at www.lowerbells.com casts parts for larger bells including A-frame stands, wheels, clappers, yokes, etc. Todd Lower is the owner and the quality is good.

Church Specialties LLC (www.churchspecialtiesllc.com) has a selection of used bell parts available.

Another source is the Verdin Company in Cincinnati, www.verdin.com. You would need to call them to see what they have available.

Finally, sometimes bell parts are offered on the huge Internet buy-sell site, www.ebay.com.

**Bell Maintenance**

About once each year the U-shaped troughs in the tops of the A-frame stands where the yoke pivots should be oiled or greased. When the paint on the mounting parts of bronze bells, and those parts plus the bell itself in the case of iron and steel bells, starts to show age, they should be re-painted. My bells are displayed outside and I have repainted the first bells I acquired three times in 36 years, so that is approximately once every 12 years for outdoor bells.

Finally, for bronze bells being rung every week, they should be rotated on their yoke about every 30 or 40 years to reduce the stresses in the metal which can cause the bell to crack. If rung half that often, double the years, and so forth. For most collector bells, they will never need to be rotated once the first rotation is done. Iron and steel bells do not need to be rotated as the bell is made of metal with the same hardness as the clapper, so the bell metal does not get smashed in, causing stresses in the metal.

*fig. 88, Steam Locomotive Railroad Bell*

*fig. 89, Vanduzen Bell Foundry Making Core Mold*

# Chapter 4

# HOW BIG BELLS ARE BORN

This will only be a simplified description of the processes used to create large bells. There are other books listed in the bibliography which give much more detail.

Iron and steel bells are much simpler to make than bronze. A large iron mold, the shape and size of the inside of the bell, is coated with a material to keep the melted iron or steel from sticking to the mold. Then a second larger iron cask, the inside of which is the size and shape of the outside of the bell, is clamped over the first mold leaving a space between them the thickness of the bell to be produced, but allowing a little extra thickness for shrinkage of the metal as it cools. The inside of the larger, outer mold is also coated with a material to keep the molten metal from sticking to the mold, and it is perforated with many small holes to allow hot gases from the liquid metal to escape. There is an opening at the top and when all is ready, the melted iron or steel is poured into this opening until it completely fills the cavity between the two iron molds.

After the metal has cooled, the clamps are removed and the new bell is born. There will be some clean-up of the material which lined the inner and outer mold from both the molds and the bell. Once the molds are clean, they can be used again to make the next bell. Another more complex method uses sand molds, but this is for smaller bells.

When a bronze bell is made, the inner and outer mold are destroyed, thus only one bell can be made from each set of two molds. First, fire bricks are stacked in the general shape of the inside of the bell. Next, a mixture of clay and horse manure is packed against the bricks and a device called a *strickle board* is revolved around a vertical axis which is centered on the mold being made. This is a silhouette of the shape of the inside of the bell. As it is revolved, it shaves off any high spots and reveals any places which are not yet thick enough, to which more of the clay and horse manure mixture are applied until the strickle board makes complete contact. The strickle board is removed and a fire is built in the center of the firebricks to dry out the inner mold (fig. 89).

The use of horse manure may seem odd, but it burns out in the heat and allows porosity so the gases can escape without causing an explosion.

Next, an outer mold is made using a similar process, but with the mold upside down so the workmen can use a revolving strickle board on the inside of the mold. Because this mold will produce the outside of the bell, it is finished much smoother than the inner mold. The outside of the outer mold is usually an iron cask. Next, if there is to be lettering or ornamentation on the bell, these are usually made of hard wax and pressed into the clay manure mixture. When, after the strickle board and its axis have been removed, the outer mold is heated to make it hard, the wax melts out, leaving space for the metal to flow when the bell is poured.

Once the inner and outer molds are dried by heat, they are coated with a graphite powder and the outer mold is inverted and placed over the inner mold and both are clamped in place. Again there is an opening at the top. In large bells, the molds are buried in the ground with the opening at the top being ground level. This allows the bell to cool more slowly after pouring so it is less likely to crack, and also is a safety measure should an explosion occur. If the bell is to have a crown, a separate mold for it is attached to the larger mold at its top and both the bell and crown can be poured at the same time so they are attached.

Next, the copper and tin in the correct proportions are heated to approximately 2,000 degrees F and then mixed together. In early days a green sapling was used as 1) it would not burn immediately due to the moisture in it, and 2) the moisture in the sapling would turn to steam and cause the mixture to mix more completely. The proportion of copper and tin in a bronze bell is normally 78 to 80 percent copper and 20 to 22 percent tin. Once the two metals are mixed and any floating slag is skimmed off, the molten metal is poured into the opening at the top of the mold until the cavity is full. The bell is then allowed to cool with the time required increasing with the size of the bell. A very large bell can be left for several days.

After the bell is sufficiently cool, if it was buried in the ground, they must dig out around the mold. Next, the outer mold is broken off with hammers and the inner mold is broken out as well. Next comes cleaning and polishing, and finally attaching the iron hangings to support the bell or allow it to swing. If the bell is flawed due to an air pocket in the molten metal, the entire process has to start over, except that they can re-use the bronze for the next bell.

Bronze bells were the Cadillacs and iron and steel bells were the Fords. The sound of the bronze bells was much more melodious, but as described, they were much more expensive, not only because the metal cost more, but because of the amount of labor involved.

*fig. 90, E. W. Vanduzen Bell on Tuning Table*

# Chapter 5

# LARGE BELL VALUES

What is a large bell worth? The value of existing older large bronze bells is heavily dependent on the value of bronze, and the cost of new bronze bells. An Internet search will give websites with the price of scrap bronze. At the writing of this book, a web site, www.answers.yahoo.com, gave a value of $6 per pound for bronze. Thus bells containing 600 or 800 pounds of bronze would have scrap values of $3,600 or $4,800. That establishes an estimated bottom value.

Next, the current sources of large bronze bells available should be consulted. On the Internet, Lower Bells at www.lowerbells.com lists their bells for sale. Brasamer's Bells Inc. lists theirs at www.brasamersbells.com, and Church Specialties LLC lists theirs at www.churchspecialtiesllc.com. You may need to call these firms for prices on some of their bells as not all bells are priced on the Internet. They list their phone numbers on their web pages. There are usually bronze bells for sale on ebay and that should also be checked.

As an example, at the writing of this book, a 47-inch diameter bell by Meneely & Co of West Troy, New York, was offered for $14,000, while a 55-inch diameter bronze bell was offered for $30,500, and a 17-inch diameter Vanduzen bronze bell was offered for $2,800. The 55-inch bell sounds expensive, but at $6 per pound, the scrap value alone is $25,800.

Since iron and steel bells larger than dinner bells are no longer being made, their value is dependent on the price to which a buyer and seller are willing to agree. Again, the Internet locations listed above for bronze bells can be checked for current market iron or steel bell prices. At this writing, a 32-inch diameter iron church bell is offered on Ebay for $2,800 (or best offer), and Brasamers Bells website lists their iron bells starting at $1,900.

If you have a bell for which you want a value, another option is to get an appraisal. Todd Lower of Lower Bells offers this service, as does Brosamers Bells.

# PICTURES OF MY HOBBY

*2003 Bell Convention*

*Author Standing Below 48 inch Iron Bell*

*The Author with a Semi Load of Bells*

*...and another Semi Load of Bells*

*Two Sets of I Beams*

*A Set of I Beams*

*The Author Standing Among His Bells*

*Loading a Bell in Pa.*

*The Author's Collection c. 1980*

*Removing the Bell from a Church*

*The Author's Bell Collection*

*The Author's Bell Collection*

*A Semi Load of Bells*

*The Author with G. W. Coffin Bell*

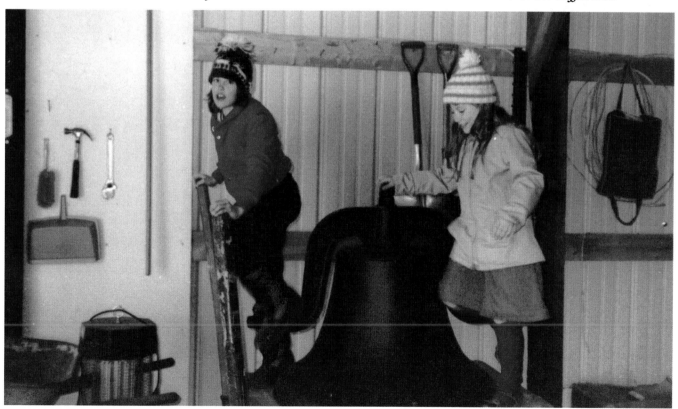

*The Author's Daughter and Friend Playing Among Bells*

# PART II

# TIPS FOR THE USE OF THIS
# BELL FOUNDRY DIRECTORY

Different names used by the same foundry over time are included to facilitate looking up a bell foundry based on the inscription on a particular bell.

If there is a SUCCESSOR to the firm at the same address, the YEAR CLOSED is actually the year of the name change, as the foundry continued to make bells.

The Large Bell Foundries are basically listed alphabetically.

When there are a number of names for the same firm, they are listed chronologically as the names were used, rather than alphabetically (e.g. the three Vanduzen firms are listed together in the order the names were used, not alphabetically).

When the ending of a foundry name is "& Company," it means there were other owners, unnamed.

While not every entry here has an accompanying image or photograph, many do, so check the pages before and after the listing if you do not find one on the entry's page.

At the end of this list of foundry information is a list of large bell foundries by state.

# BELL FOUNDRY DIRECTORY

## Alcor & Company

*Address:* New York, New York; *Year Established:* No Data; *Year Closed:* No Data; *Years Known In Operation:* No Data; *Founder:* No Data; *Predecessor:* No Data; *Successor:* No Data; *Source:* No Data; *Other Facts:* Made bell for ship "Atlantic"

## Cyrus Alger

*Address:* South Boston, Massachusetts; *Year Established:* No Data; *Year Closed:* No Data; *Years Known In Operation:* 1817; *Founder:* No Data; *Predecessor:* No Data; *Successor:* No Data; *Source:* List of Sydney J. Shepp of Mississauga, Ontario, Canada; *Other Facts:* No Data

## James P. Allaire

*Address:* Cherry Street, New York, New York; *Year Established:* No Data; *Year Closed:* No Data; *Years Known In Operation:* 1830; *Founder:* James P. Allaire: *Predecessor:* No Data; *Successor:* No Data; *Source:* George Matthew, Jr., ABA large bells post of 7 - 20 - 2013 by "locallyn," in 1994 a 12" diameter bell belonging to Pete Jones of Arlington, Texas, and Wikipedia; *Other Facts:* Carillonneur Jim Sanger of Washington, D.C. says he saw a bell by this firm in a church in New York (phone conversation with Mr. Matthew). Above ABA post says the person acquired a bell with "James P. Allaire" on it. It further states that James P. Allaire founded a town called Allaire Village, Howell Iron Works, where today Allaire State Park in Monmouth County, New Jersey is located. He also built ships and was an acquaintance of Paul Revere and Robert Fulton. The Jones bell has a square shoulder, fairly vertical waist, and quick flare to the sound bow. Wikipedia states James Peter Allaire (July 12, 1785 - 1858) was a noted master mechanic and steam engine builder and founder of the Allaire Iron Works, the first marine steam engine company in New York City, and

*Allarie Works Bell*

later Howell Works in Wall Township New Jersey. He also built parts for Fulton's steam ships, and with partner Charles Soutinger, built the engine for Fulton's last steamship design, The Chancellor Livingston, as well as the air cylinder for the first steam powered vessel to cross the Atlantic (the Savannah).

# G. T. Allamby & Son

***Address:*** Bangor, Maine; ***Year Established:*** No Data; ***Year Closed:*** No Data; ***Years Known In Operation:*** No Data; ***Founder:*** No Data; ***Predecessor:*** No Data; ***Successor:*** No Data; ***Source:*** Bell belonging to Micki and Marie Varian of Maine; ***Other Facts:*** Above bell is 10" in diameter, bronze, with nice detail, a tang mount, and the name is on the top.

# American Bell Company

***Address:*** 30 Liberty St & W. 33rd (117 Liberty in 1868 & 1869), New York City, New York; ***Year Established:*** No Data; ***Year Closed:*** No Data; ***Years Known In Operation:*** 1863 -1869; ***Founder:*** Brown & White; ***Predecessor:*** No Data; ***Successor:*** No Data; ***Source:*** Wayne E. Morrison of Ovid, N.Y. & Russell Frehse of Kendallvelle, Indiana, a bell belonging to Todd Lower then of Toledo, Ohio, and a letter from the Rochester, N.Y. Public Library to L. Elsinore Springer; ***Other Facts:*** A 42" bell by this firm is on a pedestal in front of the Green Chapel, Wesleyan Church, La Grange County, Indiana with the following inscription "American Bell Co New York City 1863". This is an iron or steel bell. This is one of the few iron church bells I know of made in the U.S. with an inscription on the outside of the bell. Some like this were made in England and Germany. The Lower bell was iron and had a gear as part of the yoke so the bell rotated so it would strike in different places. The inscription read American Bell Co N. Y. City 1863 and was on the bell itself.

# American Bell Foundry Company

***Address:*** Northville, Michigan; ***Year Established:*** No Data; ***Year Closed:*** No Data; ***Years Known In Operation:*** 1895 to 1926; ***Founder:*** Frank S. Harmon; ***Predecessor:*** No Data; ***Successor:*** No Data; ***Source:*** Eugene P. Burns, Troy, N.Y., and Mr. Wayne E. Morrison, Sr. of Ovid, N.Y., various bells, Springer's research papers, 1982 Mill Race Quarterly of Northville Historical Society; ***Other Facts:*** A 36" cast iron bell by this firm with unique squirrel cage style roller bearings in the stands was purchased by Neil Goeppinger 1 - 22 - 85 in Ollie Ia. It came from the Methodist church at Pekin, Iowa (1 mile south of Dickies Prairie Home S.W. of Ollie, Ia). A 38" by this firm is also owned by Neil Goeppinger. A 38" one is in the Oto United Church of Christ, Oto, Ia. It has cast into the bell itself "Presented by Nellie E. Cutting to First Congregation Church Oto, Ia. American Bell Foundry Northfield, Mich." They purchased the molds and patterns from the Globe Furniture Co after a fire in 1899. They sold bells to Sears Roebuck, Montgomery Ward and American Seating Co. They made 17,000 bells in 1908, 14,500 in 1915, 12,697 in 1916, 12,000 in 1918 and 18,000 in 1919. They made bells up to at least 48" diameter. The firm also made cast iron school desks.

# American Casting Company

***Address:*** Birmingham, Alabama; ***Year Established:*** No Data; ***Year Closed:*** No Data; ***Years Known In Operation:*** 1904 to 1910; ***Founder:*** Daniel B. & Harry V. Dimick, George H. Harris, Julian E. Dow. (1904); ***Predecessor:*** No Data; ***Successor:*** No Data; ***Source:*** Research papers of Lois Springer, Birmingham Public Library, R.L. Polk Directory of 1910, Birmingham City Directory of 1904, and post by "holly" on the ABAII website big bells forum on May 27, 2015; ***Other Facts:*** In 1904 this firm was owned by Daniel B. and Harry V. Dimick, George H. Harris and Julian E. Dow. In 1910 F.T. Dow was president and general manger and J.E. Dow was secretary and treasurer. A bell exists which is dated 1904 and has Number 4 on it.

# Ames Company

*Address:* Chicopee, Massachusetts; *Year Established:* 1834; *Year Closed:* No Data; *Years Known In Operation:* 1834 to 1863; *Founder:* Nathan Peabody Ames & brother James Tyler Ames; *Predecessor:* No Data; *Successor:* No Data; *Source:* That Vanishing Sound and December 15, 1964 Springfield Union Paper, Springfield, Massachusetts (research papers of Lois Springer); *Other Facts:* Cast 8,000+ lb. bell for City Hall in New York which stood 6' tall. They also made cannon for the civil war.

*Ames Company Bell*

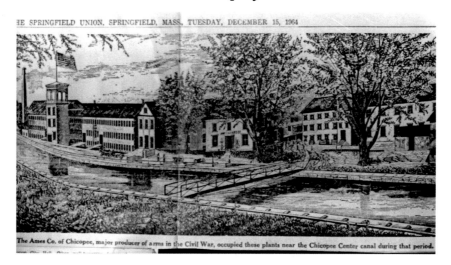

*Ames Company Foundry*

# Ames Manufacturing Company

*Address:* Cabotville (later a part of Chicopee), Massachusetts; Year Established: No Data; *Year Closed:* No Data; *Years Known In Operation:* No Data; *Founder:* No Data; *Predecessor:* No Data; *Successor:* No Data; *Source:* Bell owned by Mickey & Marie Varian of Maine; *Other Facts:* Bell reads Ames Mfg. Co.

# C. W. Arnold

*Address:* No Data; *Year Established:* No Data; *Year Closed:* No Data; *Years Known In Operation:* No Data; *Founder:* No Data; *Predecessor:* No Data; *Successor:* No Data; *Source:* ABAII website Inquiry by Ray Grodecki on April 14, 2004; *Other Facts:* Mr. Grodecki saw a cast iron farm bell with the above inscription.

# G. W. Arnold & Sons

*Address:* Ionia, Michigan; *Year Established:* No Data; *Year Closed:* No Data; *Years Known In Operation:* No Data; *Founder:* No Data; *Predecessor:* No Data; *Successor:* No Data; *Source:* Bell belonging to Carol who inquired about it on ABAII website on July 17, 2003; *Other Facts:* The above bell is 20" in diameter made of cast iron. Carol's father bought the bell in the early 1970s at an auction.

# L. Aspinwall

*Address:* Albany, New York; *Year Established:* No Data; *Year Closed:* No Data; *Years Known In Operation:* 1831 - 1839; *Founder:* No Data; *Predecessor:* No Data; *Successor:* No Data; *Source:* Joe Connors of Albany, N.Y. on 2 - 12 - 94 and Carl Scott Zimmerman of St Louis, Mo. On 3 - 9 - 97; *Other Facts:* A 4,000 lb bell by this firm dated 1836 is in St. Mary's Church, Lodge St., Albany, N.Y. Zimmerman reports a bell dated 1831 in Christ Church, Raleigh, N.C. inscribed L. Aspinwall.

# John Bailey

*Address:* No. 20 Little Dock Street, New York, New York; *Year Established:* No Data; *Year Closed:* No Data; *Years Known In Operation:* 1794; *Founder:* John Bailey; *Predecessor:* No Data; *Successor:* No Data; *Source:* Photo of bell supplied by Gary A. Trudgen of Endwell, N.Y. in 1994. Photo was in The Colonial Newsletter of Huntsville, Alabama dated July 1990; *Other Facts:* Above bell dated 1794 has crown.

*John Bailey Bell*

# Baker, Holmes & Brown

*Address:* Baltimore, Maryland; *Year Established:* No Data; *Year Closed:* No Data; *Years Known In Operation:* 1856; *Founder:* William Baker, Robert S. Holmes and John Brown; *Predecessor:* No Data; *Successor:* No Data; *Source:* Research of city directories by Carl Scott Zimmerman of St Louis, Mo; *Other Facts:* No Data

# Baltimore Plow Company

*Address:* Howard Street, Baltimore, Maryland; *Year Established:* No Data; *Year Closed:* No Data; *Years Known In Operation:* No Data; *Founder:* No Data; *Predecessor:* No Data; *Successor:* No Data; *Source:* Todd Lower then of Toledo, Ohio, and a bell owned by Neil Goeppinger of Boone, Iowa; *Other Facts:* Goeppinger bell is an iron dinner bell.

# Bartholomew & Brainard

*Address:* Hartford, Connecticut; *Year Established:* No Data; *Year Closed:* No Data; *Years Known In Operation:* 1828; *Founder:* No Data; *Predecessor:* No Data; *Successor:* No Data; *Source:* List of Sydney J. Shepp, Mississauga, Ontario, Canada L4Y 3N3; *Other Facts:* No Data

# The Barton Bell Company

*Address:* East Hampton, Connecticut; *Year Established:* No Data; *Year Closed:* No Data; *Years Known In Operation:* 1888 - 1889; *Founder:* No Data; *Predecessor:* No Data; *Successor:* No Data; *Source:* Zell's U.S. Business Directories of 1888 and 1889; *Other Facts:* No Data

# Basler-Goe

*Address:* No Data; *Year Established:* No Data; *Year Closed:* No Data; *Years Known In Operation:* No Data; *Founder:* No Data; *Predecessor:* No Data; *Successor:* No Data; *Source:* Star Clark of Oshkosh, Wisconsin; *Other Facts:* ABA member Star Clark reported a 24" to 30" diameter bronze school bell at Read School in the 1100 block of Algoma Blvd., Oshkosh, Wisconsin in March of 1995. The school was built in the 1860's to 1880's period. Basler-Goe is the only inscription on the bell so we don't know where it was made, but Star Clark said there are many people in the Oshkosh area with the last name Basler.

# Bates & Blymyer Co.

*Address:* Mansfield, Ohio; *Year Established:* No Data; *Year Closed:* No Data; *Years Known In Operation:* 1860; *Founder:* John S. Blymyer; *Predecessor:* No Data; *Successor:* No Data; *Source:* ABAII website posting by Todd Lower on April 13, 2004; *Other Facts:* No Data

# Bay City Foundry

*Address:* Wilmington, California; *Year Established:* 1926; *Year Closed:* Approximately 1976; *Years Known In Operation:* No Data; *Founder:* Julio E. Azpeitia; *Predecessor:* No Data; *Successor:* No Data; *Source:* Louise Springer (feature article in the Long Beach Press Telegram - 1978),; *Other Facts:* The above article attributes many church, U.S. Navy and public building installations of his bells over a 50 year span. His first and largest bell was a 755 lb. bell cast in 1926 for an Arizona boom town church.

# Beecher Gibbs

*Address:* Canton, Ohio; *Year Established:* No Data; *Year Closed:* No Data; *Years Known In Operation:* No Data; *Founder:* No Data; *Predecessor:* No Data; *Successor:* No Data; *Source:* Ad for bell auction in Center Junction, Iowa north of Cedar Rapids, July 28, 2001; *Other Facts:* This was a #3 iron dinner bell. It may have been a misspelling of the Bucker-Gibbs foundry, or Mr Gibbs may have had different partners and used different names in different years.

# Barton Beelzebub

*Address:* Cairo, New York; *Year Established:* No Data; *Year Closed:* No Data; *Years Known In Operation:* Early 1800's; *Founder:* Barton Beelzebub; *Predecessor:* No Data; *Successor:* No Data; *Source:* Louise Springer letter of 3/4/1985, her source: History of Greene County, New York, 1884; *Other Facts:* Quote from above history: "for casting church-bells, sleigh bells, and other goods of character... One of his bells has for years hung in Presbyterian Church of Cairo."

# Bell & Brass Founder

*Address:* Walnut between Front and Second Streets, Cincinnati, Ohio; *Year Established:* 1841; *Year Closed:* No Data; *Years Known In Operation:* 1841; *Founder:* No Data; *Predecessor:* No Data; *Successor:* No Data; *Source:* Mrs. G. Lyle Ringland of Norwood, Ohio; *Other Facts:* No Data

# C. H. Bell Co.

*Address:* No Data; *Year Established:* No Data; *Year Closed:* No Data; *Years Known In Operation:* No Data; *Founder:* No Data; *Predecessor:* No Data; *Successor:* No Data; *Source:* 48" diameter cast iron bell of Neil Goeppinger of Boone, Iowa; *Other Facts:* The mountings and inscription are definitely not similar to those of the C. S. Bell Company of Hillsboro, Ohio.

# C. S. Bell

*Address:* Hillsboro, Ohio; *Year Established:* No Data; *Year Closed:* No Data; *Years Known In Operation:* 1858 - 1882; *Founder:* Charles Singleton Bell; *Predecessor:* No Data; *Successor:* C. S. Bell & Co; *Source:* Towerbells.org website of Carl Scott Zimmerman of St Louis, Mo and C. S. Bell company pamphlets; *Other Facts:* When Charles S. Bell took in his son, Charles E. Bell, the name changed to C. S. Bell & Co.

*(On right) C. S. Bell Company - Pre Civil War Shape Bell*

*C. S. Bell Company, Pre Civil War Shape Bell On Left, Post Civil War Shape Bell On Right*

# C. S. Bell & Company

*Address:* Hillsboro, Ohio; *Year Established:* No Data; *Year Closed:* No Data; *Years Known In Operation:* 1882 - 1894; *Founder:* No Data; *Predecessor:* C. S. Bell; *Successor:* C. S. Bell Co; *Source:* Bell reported by Carl Scott Zimmerman of St Louis, Mo; *Other Facts:* This name was used when Charles Singleton Bell brought his son, Charles E. Bell, into the business. It was last run by a family member when Virginia Bell (Charles' granddaughter) sold the firm in 1974.

# C. S. Bell Company

*Address:* Hillsboro (now Tiffin), Ohio; *Year Established:* 1894; *Year Closed:* No Data; *Years Known In Operation:* 1894 - 1974; *Founder:* Charles Singleton Bell; *Predecessor:* C. S. Bell & Company; *Successor:* No Data; *Source:* *That Vanishing Sound* and a reprint of a C.S. Bell Co catalogue, Mrs. G. Lyle Ringland, and the Towerbells.org website of Carl Scott Zimmerman of St Louis, Mo; *Other Facts:* The name was changed to this when the firm was incorporated in 1894. Present mailing address is P.O. Box 291, Tiffin, Ohio 44883. The firm was owned by the bell family until 1974 when it was sold to an attorney and a banker. They quit making church bells in 1974 and then made dinner and boat bells. The largest bells the firm made were 48" and 54" diameter. All their large bells were made from "tempered steel" rather than bronze or cast iron. Another firm using this material was located in Sheffield, England. C. S. Bell Company sold 1,000 bells its first year of making bells, and sales had grown to 20,000 a year by 1889. This firm was the largest producer of steel or iron bells in the U.S.

# John Benson

*Address:* New York, New York; *Year Established:* No Data; *Year Closed:* No Data; *Years Known In Operation:* 1848 - 1850; *Founder:* No Data; *Predecessor:* No Data; *Successor:* No Data; *Source:* Bell owned by Joe Russo of Sands Point, New York, and ABAII website inquiry dated around September 29, 2005; *Other Facts:* From photo of bell, outside appeared to be a rough casting with two reeds around top of sound bow, and a small rise just above the shoulder. It has an unusual mounting to the yoke.

# Joseph Bernhard

*Address:* No 78 N 6 St, Philadelphia, Pennsylvania; *Year Established:* No Data; *Year Closed:* No Data; *Years Known In Operation:* 1845 - 1880; *Founder:* No Data; *Predecessor:* No Data; *Successor:* No Data; *Source:* That Vanishing Sound and a 45 1/2" diameter buoy bell at Great Lakes Marine Hall of Fame in Sault Ste. Marie dated 1856, a 40" diameter bronze fire bell dated 1857 listed for sale on Ebay 9/9/2013 with photos, an 1851 bell located in Miami Beach, Florida, The Saint Thomas Bell by Adam Sawicki (Internet posting of "The Friends of Old Saint Thomas", and bell from the courthouse, Union County, Monroe, S. C. dated 1857; *Other Facts:* They made bronze bells of the Germanic shape. The Miami Beach bell has the foundry street address cast in the bell.

*J. Bernhard Bell 1850*

*Joseph Bernhard 1857 Bell on ebay*

# C. & A. G. Bevin

*Address:* East Hampton, Connecticut; *Year Established:* 1832; *Year Closed:* 1838; *Years Known In Operation:* 1832 - 1838; *Founder:* No Data; *Predecessor:* No Data; *Successor:* Bevin Bros and Bevin Bros Mfg Co; *Source:* Zell's U.S. Business Directories of 1888 and 1889, and company catalogue # 125A belonging to Benjamin Koenig of Plainfield, Vermont, and Thomas' Register 1905 - 1906; *Other Facts:* See Bevin Brothers Manufacturing Company

# Bevin Brothers

*Address:* E. Hampton, Conn.; *Year Established:* 1838; *Year Closed:* 1868; *Years Known In Operation:* 1838 - 1868; *Founder:* No Data; *Predecessor:* C. & A. G. Bevin; *Successor:* Bevin Brothers Manufacturing Company; *Source:* Zell's U.S. Business Directories of 1888 and 1889, and company catalogue # 125A belonging to Benjamin Koenig of Plainfield, Vermont, and Thomas' Register 1905 - 1906; *Other Facts:* See Bevin Brothers Manufacturing Company.

# Bevin Brothers Manufacturing Company

*Address:* East Hampton, Connecticut; *Year Established:* 1868; *Year Closed:* No Data; *Years Known In Operation:* 1832 - 1906; *Founder:* No Data; *Predecessor:* C. & A. G. Bevin (started in 1832, Bevin Bros (1838), this name (1868); *Successor:* No Data; *Source:* Zell's U.S. Business Directories of 1888 and 1889, and company catalogue # 125A belonging to Benjamin Koenig of Plainfield, Vermont, and Thomas' Register 1905 - 1906, and research letters of L. Elsnore Springer from the Bevin Brothers firm; *Other Facts:* Advertised gongs and sleigh bells, academy, factory and ships bells as well in catalogue #125A from 8 1/2" (12 1/2 lbs.) to 21" (210 lbs.). A Bevin Brothers bell sank with the Battleship Maine in Havana Harbor in 1898, and one opens the New York Stock Exchange each day. They also made bells for fire engines.

*Bevin Brothers Letterhead 1944*

# Arthur Lynds Bigelow

*Address:* Princeton, New Jersey; *Year Established:* No Data; *Year Closed:* No Data; *Years Known In Operation:* Later than 1920; *Founder:* No Data; *Predecessor:* No Data; *Successor:* No Data; *Source:* George Matthew Jr of Stamford, Connecticut, and 1995 Vol XLIV Bulletin of Guild of Carillonneurs in North America, and May 2, 1949 Life Magazine; *Other Facts:* Quote of Mr. Matthew's letter of 4/4/1990, "There is an extensive collection of his letters and writing at Princeton. Unfortunately, it is only organized by date (mostly year) and so material dealing with bell founding is mixed in with carillon music, which is in turn mixed in with acoustics research, etc." Bells by Bigelow are in House of Hope Presbyterian Church in St. Paul, Minn., and St. Vincent's Seminary, Philadelphia. 1949 Life Magazine told about casting bells at Princeton. Photo of one of his bells is in GCNA Bulletin.

# M. C. Bignall & Company

***Address:*** St Louis, Missouri; ***Year Established:*** No Data; ***Year Closed:*** No Data; ***Years Known In Operation:*** No Data; ***Founder:*** No Data; ***Predecessor:*** No Data; ***Successor:*** Bignall & Ostrander and Goulds & Ostrander; ***Source:*** Carl Scott Zimmerman of St Louis, Mo; ***Other Facts:*** No Data

# Bignall & Ostrander

***Address:*** 806 & 808 N. 2nd, St Louis, Missouri; ***Year Established:*** No Data; ***Year Closed:*** No Data; ***Years Known In Operation:*** 1879; ***Founder:*** Ernest Bignall and John J. Ostrander; ***Predecessor:*** M. C. Bignall & Company; ***Successor:*** Goulds & Ostrander; ***Source:*** St Louis Directory of 1879 (through Missouri Historical Society), and Carl Scott Zimmerman of St Louis, Mo; ***Other Facts:*** No Data

# William Blake

***Address:*** Brighten at Allen Streets, Boston, Massachusetts; ***Year Established:*** 1820; ***Year Closed:*** No Data; ***Years Known In Operation:*** 1820 to 1890's; ***Founder:*** William Blake; ***Predecessor:*** H. N. Hooper & Co; ***Successor:*** Boston Copper Company, Henry N. Hooper & Company, Hooper, Blake & Richardson, W. Blake & Co, Blake Bell Co; ***Source:*** *That Vanishing Sound*, pages 43 - 46, a bell belonging to Micki and Marie Varian of Maine, and an excerpt from the book "Blake Bell Co., Successors to William Blake and Co., Bronze Bell - Founders, Boston Mass, Established 1820"; ***Other Facts:*** William Blake is listed as a separate name although bells may never have been made with only his name on them. Through his life he operated under many company names, and in a number of partnerships and his name was included in several of them. A number of them overlapped in years of operation. It is hard to discern what bells were made under which name in some cases. William Blake was an apprentice of Paul Revere's, and he operated in partnership with Paul Revere's son, Joseph Warren Revere, and later in partnership with Paul Revere's grandson, Paul Revere III. He made 2 chimes of bells (one of 8 bells with the tenor weighing 2,000 lbs cast in 1825 and one of 11 bells with the tenor bell weighing 3,000 lbs for which a silver medal was awarded at the 1850 Mechanic's Fair in Boston). He claimed his 8 bell chime of 1825 was the first set of chime bells cast in the U.S. They also made a bell weighing 21,612 pounds for the city of New York. The Varian bell is 30" in diameter and bears the inscription "Cast by William Blake & Co. Formerly H. N. Hooper & Co Boston Mas 1877"

# Blake Bell Company

***Address:*** Brighten and Allen Streets, Boston, Massachusetts; ***Year Established:*** 1890; ***Year Closed:*** No Data; ***Years Known In Operation:*** 1890 until later in the 1890's; ***Founder:*** William Blake; ***Predecessor:*** Charles T. Richardson & Company, William Blake & Company, Hooper & Company; ***Successor:*** No Data; ***Source:*** *That Vanishing Sound*, and Winthrop Warren of Fairfield, Connecticut; ***Other Facts:*** Another of William Blake's firm names during the period he made and sold bells under the "Hooper & Co" name (total period of 1820 to mid 1890's). See William Blake for more information. As far as I know, this was the last firm name he used. They operated under this name until later in the 1890's.

# William Blake & Company

*Address:* Brighten and Allen Streets, Boston, Massachusetts; *Year Established:* 1868; *Year Closed:* 1888; *Years Known In Operation:* 1868 to 1888; *Founder:* William Blake; *Predecessor:* Hooper, Blake & Richardson (1830 - 1831), Henry N Hooper & Co (1830 - 1890); *Successor:* No Data; *Source:* That Vanishing Sound and Zell's U.S. Business Directory and Edward Stickney of Bedford, Massachusetts and Winthrop Warrant of Fairfield, Connecticut, Robert Cowie of Paris, Ark. and many bells; *Other Facts:* Another of William Blake's firms which made bells and sold them under this name and the Hooper & Co name. When it first started it was known as "William Blake & Co. Formerly Henry N. Hooper & Co. Boston Massachusetts." A bell dated 1870 is in Greenland, New Hampshire. About 1890 the name changed to "Blake Bell Company Boston Massachusetts". William Blake was an apprentice under Paul Revere and later a partner of Paul Revere 3rd, grandson of the patriot. Earlier he partnered with Joseph Warren Revere, son of Paul Revere. Robert Cowie of Paris, Ark. has a 48" bell.

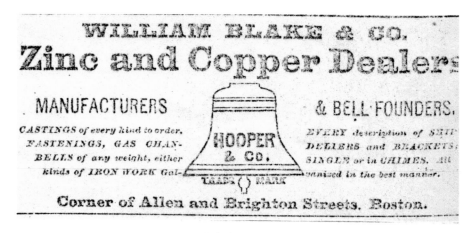

1876

*William Blake and Company Advertisement*

*William Blake and Company formerly H. N. Hooper and Company Bell*

*William Blake and Company Bell*

*William Blake Bell On Left*

## Blake, Lamb & Company

***Address:*** Waterbury, Connecticut; ***Year Established:*** No Data; ***Year Closed:*** No Data; ***Years Known In Operation:*** 1881; ***Founder:*** No Data; ***Predecessor:*** No Data; ***Successor:*** No Data; ***Source:*** Zell's United States Business Directory of 1881; ***Other Facts:*** No Data

## W. Bleedorn

***Address:*** Watertown, Minnesota; ***Year Established:*** No Data; ***Year Closed:*** No Data; ***Years Known In Operation:*** 1888; ***Founder:*** No Data; ***Predecessor:*** No Data; ***Successor:*** No Data; ***Source:*** Zell's U.S. Business Directory of 1888; ***Other Facts:*** No Data

# Bleymeyer Foundry

*Address:* Spring Grove Avenue, Cincinnati, Ohio; *Year Established:* 1915; *Year Closed:* No Data; *Years Known In Operation:* 1915 - 1935; *Founder:* No Data; *Predecessor:* No Data; *Successor:* No Data; *Source:* Mrs. G. Lyle Ringland of Norwood, Ohio, and verified by Mr. Eugene P. Burns of Troy, New York; *Other Facts:* Winston Jones of Evergreen, Co. had a bell by this firm in his collection. This foundry was purchased in 1920 by The Morris Tool and Machinery Co located at Court and Harriet Streets, Cincinnati, Oh. They quit casting bells in 1935.

# Henry Bloemker

*Address:* 6th and Myrtle, St. Louis, Missouri; *Year Established:* 1863; *Year Closed:* 1893; *Years Known In Operation:* 1863 - 1893; *Founder:* Henry Bloemker; *Predecessor:* J. G. Stuckstede & Co. (partner); *Successor:* No Data; *Source:* 1866 St. Louis City Directory & 1875 Gould's City Directory (thru Missouri Historical Society), and Carl Scott Zimmerman of St Louis, Mo. ; *Other Facts:* Address was 6th and Myrtle in 1866 and 14 Myrtle in 1875.

# Blymyer & Brothers Company

*Address:* Mansfield, Ohio; *Year Established:* No Data; *Year Closed:* No Data; *Years Known In Operation:* 1877; *Founder:* No Data; *Predecessor:* No Data; *Successor:* No Data; *Source:* ABAII website posting by Todd Lower on April 13, 2004; *Other Facts:* No Data

# Blymyer Day & Company

*Address:* Mansfield, Ohio; *Year Established:* No Data; *Year Closed:* No Data; *Years Known In Operation:* 1874; *Founder:* No Data; *Predecessor:* No Data; *Successor:* No Data; *Source:* ABAII website posting by Todd Lower on April 13, 2004; *Other Facts:* This firm was bought by Mansfield Machine Works in 1874.

# Blymyer Manufacturing Company

*Address:* 664 W. 8th, Cincinnati, Ohio; *Year Established:* 1873; *Year Closed:* No Data; *Years Known In Operation:* 1873 - 1880; *Founder:* No Data; *Predecessor:* Blymer Norton & Co; *Successor:* Cincinnati Bell Co; *Source:* Wayme E. Morrison Sr of Ovid, N.Y., and Zell's United States Business Directory of 1888. Note difference in spelling of Blymyer. 48" diameter cast iron bell which belonged to Winston Jones of Evergreen, Colorado, and a 48" diameter located along highway 30 at the Harrison County Iowa Historical Village Museum S. W. of Logan, Iowa, and ABAII website inquiry by Steve Allen of the Courtland Oakfield United Methodist Church in Rockford, MI; *Other Facts:* I do not know if this is a misspelling of Blymer, the other foundry, or if it is a coincidence, but there are more than one reference to each firm spelling so it is likely there were two different firms. There were also Blymyer bell firms in Mansfield, Ohio.

# Blymyer Norton & Company

*Address:* Cincinnati, Ohio; *Year Established:* 1867; *Year Closed:* 1873; *Years Known In Operation:* 1867 - 1873; *Founder:* No Data; *Predecessor:* No Data; *Successor:* Blymyer Mfg Co. of Cincinnati, Ohio; *Source:* 32" bell described below, and ABAII inquiry by Steve Allen of the Courtland Oakfield United Methodist Church of Rockford, MI. dated 10/17/2006; *Other Facts:* In June, 1984 Leonard Fleisher of Columbus, Nebraska bought a 32" cast iron bell from Don Moreland of Farrar, Iowa and I transported it to Boone for shipment to Columbus. The bell came from the Methodist Church in Allerton, Iowa. The Courtland Oakfield United Methodist Church bell is 40" in diameter.

# B. N. & Company

***Address:*** Cincinnati, Ohio; ***Year Established:*** No Data; ***Year Closed:*** No Data; ***Years Known In Operation:*** No Data; ***Founder:*** No Data; ***Predecessor:*** No Data; ***Successor:*** No Data; ***Source:*** Bell owned by Leonard Fleischer of Columbus, Nebraska, and Carl Scott Zimmerman of St Louis, Mo; ***Other Facts:*** The above bell is cast iron and has a very unusual iron wheel with 6 spokes merging into 3 spokes in a curved "V" fashion. This might be another name for the Blymer Norton & Co. firm of Cincinnati, but I have no way of knowing. The inscription reads "B.N. & Co Cin. O." Carl Scott Zimmerman states that "the distinctive shapes of the bell, yoke, and wheel are all common to Blymer, Norton and Cin Bell Co in all variants that I have seen." Thus it appears there is either a tie between the two firms, or they operated one foundry but sold bells under different names.

# Bogue & Mills Manufacturing Company

***Address:*** Chicago, Illinois; ***Year Established:*** No Data; ***Year Closed:*** No Data; ***Years Known In Operation:*** 1892; ***Founder:*** No Data; ***Predecessor:*** No Data; ***Successor:*** No Data; ***Source:*** Bell at Evergreen Farm, Eminence, Indiana; ***Other Facts:*** Small iron dinner bell. "Crystal Metal" on yoke.

# Alex. Borrowman

***Address:*** 16th and 3rd Avenue, Brooklyn, New York; ***Year Established:*** No Data; ***Year Closed:*** No Data; ***Years Known In Operation:*** 1870; ***Founder:*** No Data; ***Predecessor:*** No Data; ***Successor:*** No Data; ***Source:*** N.Y. State Directory for 1870 (thru N.Y. St. Historical Association); ***Other Facts:*** No Data

# Boston & Braintree

***Address:*** Boston, Massachusetts; ***Year Established:*** 1825; ***Year Closed:*** 1825; ***Years Known In Operation:*** 1825; ***Founder:*** Paul Revere 3rd, William Blake and John Sullivan (same as predecessor); ***Predecessor:*** Paul Revere & Company; ***Successor:*** Boston Copper Company; ***Source:*** Edward and Evelyn Stickney of Bedford, Massachusetts; ***Other Facts:*** Name was changed the same year (1825) to Boston Copper Company. The bells were dated.

# Boston Copper Company

***Address:*** Boston, Massachusetts; ***Year Established:*** 1820; ***Year Closed:*** 1830 see other facts; ***Years Known In Operation:*** 1820 - 1830; ***Founder:*** Paul Revere 3rd (grandson of Paul Revere), William Blake, and John W. Sullivan; ***Predecessor:*** Boson & Braintree, Paul Revere & Company; ***Successor:*** Henry N. Hooper & Co; ***Source:*** Edward & Evelyn Stickney of Bedford, Massachusetts, and bell in Portsmouth, N.H. church dated 1828, *That Vanishing Sound*, and Winthrop Warren of Fairfield, Conn; ***Other Facts:*** Court records at Massachusetts Historical Society in Boston show it was dissolved in 1827, but Boston directories show the business until 1830, and the Portsmouth, New Hampshire bell is dated 1828. Henry N. Hooper was an agent for this company.

# The Bowlden Bell

***Address:*** No Data; ***Year Established:*** No Data; ***Year Closed:*** No Data; ***Years Known In Operation:*** 1921 - 1922; ***Founder:*** No Data; ***Predecessor:*** No Data; ***Successor:*** No Data; ***Source:*** A page from the Teachers' Catalog No. 59 from J. R. Holcomb & Co of Cleveland, Ohio dated 1921 - 1922; ***Other Facts:*** The price of a 20" 108 lbs. school bell was $12.50, and the price of a 40" 820-lb. church bell was $106. A 7 1/2" school marm bell cost 80 cents.

# Bradley & Cochran

*Address:* New Haven, Connecticut; *Year Established:* No Data; *Year Closed:* No Data; *Years Known In Operation:* 1808; *Founder:* One was James Cochran; *Predecessor:* Fenton & Cochran; *Successor:* No Data; *Source:* Winthrop Warren of Fairfield, Connecticut; *Other Facts:* A bell dated 1808 is in the Staples Academy in Easton, Connecticut, with rosettes and spread eagle medallions, but in different locations on the bell than on the bells by Fenton and Cochran.

# Bradley & Hubbard Manufacturing Company

*Address:* 21 Barclay & 26 Park Pl., New York City, New York; *Year Established:* No Data; *Year Closed:* No Data; *Years Known In Operation:* 1881 - 1889; *Founder:* No Data; *Predecessor:* No Data; *Successor:* No Data; *Source:* Zell's United States Business Directory of 1881 and 1889; *Other Facts:* By 1888 the firm had moved to Meriden, Connecticut. Other New York address is 26 Park Place.

# Brass & Bell Foundry

*Address:* North side of 2nd Street between Lawrence and Ludlow, Cincinnati, Ohio; *Year Established:* 1841; *Year Closed:* No Data; *Years Known In Operation:* No Data; *Founder:* Levi Parker and Arthur Hanks; *Predecessor:* No Data; *Successor:* No Data; *Source:* Mrs. G. Lyle Ringland of Norwood, Ohio; *Other Facts:* Not to be confused with Bell & Brass Founder of the same city founded in the same year. They advertised "Bells of best materials and workmanship. Also brass castings."

# C. Brinkerhoff

*Address:* 164 Water Street, New York, New York; *Year Established:* No Data; *Year Closed:* No Data; *Years Known In Operation:* 1793; *Founder:* Cornelius Brinkerhoff; *Predecessor:* No Data; *Successor:* No Data; *Source:* Ryan Cooper of Yarmouthport, Mass; *Other Facts:* 25" ship bell from ship "Washington" found in a Caribbean scrap yard in 1990's is now at South Street Seaport Museum in N.Y.

# Edward M. Brown

*Address:* No Data; *Year Established:* No Data; *Year Closed:* No Data; *Years Known In Operation:* 1837; *Founder:* No Data; *Predecessor:* No Data; *Successor:* No Data; *Source:* Joe Duffy, Church Specialties Inc, Norwalk, Conn who does work for Verdin of Cincinnati; *Other Facts:* Mr. Duffy says a 32" diameter bell with a wooden yoke is in the Congregational Church of Seymour, Conn.

# Bucker - Gibbs

*Address:* Canton, Ohio; *Year Established:* No Data; *Year Closed:* No Data; *Years Known In Operation:* No Data; *Founder:* No Data; *Predecessor:* No Data; *Successor:* No Data; *Source:* Bell at Evergreen Farm, Eminence, Indiana, and bell purchased by Del Gilmore of Iowa City, Ia. in 2007; *Other Facts:* Iron dinner bell. Same basic shape as Eagle Bell Co of Lebanon, Pa. The Gilmore bell is made of steel or iron and is 20" in diameter with a small top.

# Buckeye Bell Foundry

***Address:*** 428 E. 2nd (in 1906), Cincinnati, Ohio; ***Year Established:*** No Data; ***Year Closed:*** No Data; ***Years Known In Operation:*** 1837 - 1950; ***Founder:*** No Data; ***Predecessor:*** No Data; ***Successor:*** No Data; ***Source:*** Thomas' Register 1905 - 1906; ***Other Facts:*** See "G. W. Coffin" and the "Vanduzen" foundries. Advertised chime, church and engine bells in 1906. The name "Buckeye Bell Foundry" appeared on all these firms' bells.

# William Buckley

***Address:*** 114 Cannon, New York, New York; ***Year Established:*** No Data; ***Year Closed:*** No Data; ***Years Known In Operation:*** 1829 - 1850; ***Founder:*** No Data; ***Predecessor:*** No Data; ***Successor:*** James Gregory; ***Source:*** New York Business Directory 1840/1841 (research papers of Lois Springer), bell owned by Ruth Bennington of N.Y, and article "James Gregory and the Dreamland Bell" by David Grider, architect, dated October 11, 2009 and posted on the Internet at davidgrider.com, and bell owned by Halifax United Methodist Church; ***Other Facts:*** 1838 Bell owned by Starchaser 1277 on 7/10/2013 ABA website post under Big Bells. The Bennington owned bell is nickel plated brass and appears to be a ship bell, inscribed "W. Buckley, N. York, Carrier Pidgeon". I believe "Carrier Pidgeon" was the name of the ship. Also, there is an undated bell by this firm which was installed in 1840 in Christ Church, Middle Haddam, Conn. The Halifax bell is a bronze church bell and dates to either 1829 or 1818, based on church records. They know it was in existence in 1829. The date is not on the bell.

# Burd & Tilden

***Address:*** 45 N. First, St Louis, Missouri; ***Year Established:*** No Data; ***Year Closed:*** No Data; ***Years Known In Operation:*** No Data; ***Founder:*** No Data; ***Predecessor:*** No Data; ***Successor:*** Burd, Tilden & Burd, Burd, Rucker & Co., John W. Burd; ***Source:*** Carl Scott Zimmerman research papers on St. Louis area large bells; ***Other Facts:*** No Data

# Burd, Tilden & Burd

***Address:*** 45 N. First, St Louis, Missouri; ***Year Established:*** No Data; ***Year Closed:*** No Data; ***Years Known In Operation:*** 1845; ***Founder:*** No Data; ***Predecessor:*** No Data; ***Successor:*** No Data; ***Source:*** Carl Scott Zimmerman research papers on St. Louis area large bells (1848 advertisement in St Louis Directory: "Bells weighing from 20 to 400 pounds"); ***Other Facts:*** No Data

# Burd, Rucker & Company

***Address:*** 45 N. First, St. Louis, Missouri; ***Year Established:*** No Data; ***Year Closed:*** No Data; ***Years Known In Operation:*** 1848; ***Founder:*** No Data; ***Predecessor:*** Burd, Tilden & Burd; ***Successor:*** John W. Burd; ***Source:*** Frank Redpath, I.T. Verdin Co Branch Manager, Prairie Village, Kansas (1984 address), and Carl Scott Zimmerman; ***Other Facts:*** Mr. Redpath saw a 28 1/4" diameter bronze church bell by this firm at the Christian Church in Independence, Missouri. The words "Burd" and "Rucker" are separated by a square on the bell.

# John W. Burd

***Address:*** 64 N. Second (later 3 N. Main), St Louis, Missouri; ***Year Established:*** No Data; ***Year Closed:*** No Data; ***Years Known In Operation:*** 1850 - 1871; ***Founder:*** No Data; ***Predecessor:*** Burd, Rucker & Co; ***Successor:*** No Data; ***Source:*** Carl Scott Zimmerman research papers on St. Louis area large bells (checked all city directories 1836 - 1873);

*Other Facts:* Carl Scott Zimmerman states: Primarily a store and tin ware dealer, but in 1850 was classified under "Bell and Brass Founders", also "Bell Hangers". Also included "Bell Founder" in an advertisement.

## John R. Calhoun & Co.

*Address:* 1024 - 1026 N., St Louis, Missouri; *Year Established:* No Data; *Year Closed:* No Data; *Years Known In Operation:* 1883 - 1888; *Founder:* No Data; *Predecessor:* No Data; *Successor:* No Data; *Source:* Carl Scott Zimmerman research in St Louis city directories for 1865 - 1900; *Other Facts:* This firm dealt primarily in agricultural implements, but in the 1883 and 1884 directories they were also classified under "Bells (Brass and Amalgam)".

## California Bell Company

*Address:* Los Angeles, California; *Year Established:* No Data; *Year Closed:* No Data; *Years Known In Operation:* 1906 - 1950's; *Founder:* Mrs. Armitage S. C. Forbes; *Predecessor:* No Data; *Successor:* No Data; *Source: That Vanishing Sound*, and *California's El Camino Real and Its Historic Bells* by Max Kurillo and Erline Tuttle; *Other Facts:* Made replicas of the old "El Camino Real" bells that had hung along the road of commerce from San Diego up to San Francisco. These were placed along the original highway, and by the 1950's most of them had been stolen. Only a few remained. They also cast some other bells, mostly replicas of old Spanish Mission Bells. Some were large. The firm was sold to Evangeline Aldrich in 1948 who carried on the work. They cast the first Camino Real bell in 1906, and by 1913 there were 450 of these bells along the road.

*Evangeline Aldrich who bought the California Bell Company*

*Mrs. A. S. C. Forbes*

# Gardiner Campbell & Sons

*Address:* 242 - 6 Oregon Street, Milwaukee, Wisconsin; *Year Established:* No Data; *Year Closed:* 1900 approx; *Years Known In Operation:* 1869 - 1890; *Founder:* No Data; *Predecessor:* No Data; *Successor:* No Data; *Source:* *That Vanishing Sound*, Milwaukee City Directory 1869 - 70 (research papers of Lois Springer). Bell described below, and Thomas' Register 1905 - 1906; *Other Facts:* There were other bell foundries in Milwaukee. This firm also operated under the name "The Centennial Bell Foundry, G. Campbell & Son" as cast into a 51 1/4" diameter bronze bell owned by Robert Brosamer of Brooklyn, Michigan dated 1890 and weighing 2,700 lbs. (bell only). The foundry was run by George Campbell in 1896. See "Centennial Bell Foundry" for more information on their largest bell cast.

# Carbon Bronze Company Limited

*Address:* 38 Water, Pittsburgh, Pennsylvania; *Year Established:* No Data; *Year Closed:* No Data; *Years Known In Operation:* 1888 - 1889; *Founder:* No Data; *Predecessor:* No Data; *Successor:* No Data; *Source:* Zell's U.S. Business Directories of 1888 and 1889. Listed as "Carbon Bronze Co lim't"; *Other Facts:* No Data

# Caughlan Bell & Brass Founders

*Address:* St Louis, Missouri; *Year Established:* No Data; *Year Closed:* No Data; *Years Known In Operation:* 1857; *Founder:* No Data; *Predecessor:* No Data; *Successor:* No Data; *Source:* Research by Carl Scott Zimmerman of St Louis, Missouri and posted on his website, towerbells.org; *Other Facts:* No Data

# Caughlan & Bro.

*Address:* St Louis, Missouri; *Year Established:* No Data; *Year Closed:* No Data; *Years Known In Operation:* 1856 - 1858; *Founder:* No Data; *Predecessor:* No Data; *Successor:* No Data; *Source:* Research by Carl Scott Zimmerman of St Louis, Missouri, and posted on his website, towerbells.org; *Other Facts:* No Data

# Caughlan & Dauernheim

*Address:* 261 Main Street, St. Louis, Missouri; *Year Established:* 1859; *Year Closed:* No Data; *Years Known In Operation:* 1859; *Founder:* Adam C. Caughlan and Louis Dauernheim; *Predecessor:* David Caughlan; *Successor:* Condry, Caughlan & Co; *Source:* David Caughlan of Bridgewater, N.J, great grandson of David Caughlan, and research of Carl Scott Zimmerman in St Louis directories; *Other Facts:* This was a separate business from that of David Caughlan, although they occupied premises formerly used by David Caughlan after he moved to the Locust Street address. Adam Caughlan was a brother of David Caughlan.

# David Caughlan

*Address:* Washington St (1853 - 1863), 29 Locust (1863 - 1866), St. Louis, Missouri; *Year Established:* No Data; *Year Closed:* No Data; *Years Known In Operation:* 1853 - 1866; *Founder:* David Caughlan; *Predecessor:* No Data; *Successor:* E. C. Mayer; *Source:* *That Vanishing Sound* and 1864 & 1866 City Directories for St. Louis, and David Caughlan, Bridgewater, New Jersey (great grandson), Carl Scott Zimmerman of St Louis, Mo., and Mary Caughlan Kelley of Virginia and Susan G. Caughlan of Pa., both descendants of David Caughlan the bell founder; *Other Facts:* In the 1840s David Caughlan ran a newspaper and wrote editorials against slavery in central Illinois. He was too far south and one night an angry mob burned his newspaper office including the printing equipment. He then started making church bells in St. Louis, but was still outspokenly for emancipation and made public speeches against slavery.

In 1858 another mob broke into his foundry and burned it. He took this to be a calling from God, entered the ministry, and eventually started the first Methodist Church in East St. Louis, Illinois. At one point he had a church in upstate Illinois and Abraham Lincoln came to his church and made a famous anti-slavery speech at his church. The speech was reprinted in a number of abolitionist's pamphlets. One of his bells is at McKendree College in Lebanon, Illinois. A 38" bell in the Metropolitan UMC of Alton, Illinois, a 31" belongs to Neil Goeppinger, a 39" dated 1866 with bah-relief medallion with head of Christ on one side of bell, and harp between 2 up facing horns of plenty on the other side, labeled "E. Mayer, maker" belongs to Robert Brosamer. A fire bell is at Jefferson Memorial in St. Louis, and an 8" riverboat bell exists. The firm's address was 33 Washington Av. in 1857, and 261 Main St. in 1859. They made bronze bells which were typically undated.

David and Edith Caughlan under
his Great Grandfather's Bell

David Caughlan Bell

# Caughlan & Piquette

*Address:* 144 N. 2nd, St Louis, Missouri; *Year Established:* No Data; *Year Closed:* No Data; *Years Known In Operation:* 1853 - 1854; *Founder:* David Caughlan and David Piquett; *Predecessor:* No Data; *Successor:* David Caughlan; *Source:* Carl Scott Zimmerman, St Louis, Mo; *Other Facts:* There is a bell by this firm in the Westport Methodist Church in Kansas City, Mo. Undoubtedly a partnership of David Caughlan. Zimmerman states "it is shaped very much like a couple of Kaye & Co bells from the 1880's, with a long waist and a heavy shoulder bead." The 1854 St Louis directory has "Cofland & Piquette" which obviously is wrong according to the above bell.

# C & D

*Address:* Frederick Town, Ohio; *Year Established:* No Data; *Year Closed:* No Data; *Years Known In Operation:* No Data; *Founder:* No Data; *Predecessor:* No Data; *Successor:* No Data; *Source:* Bell belonging to William Randolf, Belle Plaine, Iowa; *Other Facts:* This is probably a successor or predecessor of the Comings and Hosack bell firm of the same town.

# Centennial Bell Foundry

***Address:*** Milwaukee, Wisconsin; ***Year Established:*** No Data; ***Year Closed:*** No Data; ***Years Known In Operation:*** 1896; ***Founder:*** No Data; ***Predecessor:*** No Data; ***Successor:*** No Data; ***Source:*** Inscriptions on bells; ***Other Facts:*** See: "Gardiner Campell & Sons". The firm was run by George Campbell in 1896, the year they made an 8' 2" diameter bell weighing 20,505 lbs (22,555 lbs including the 500 lb clapper and the mountings) for the Milwaukee City Hall.

# Central Bell & Brass Foundry

***Address:*** 16 N. 3rd, St Louis, Missouri; ***Year Established:*** No Data; ***Year Closed:*** No Data; ***Years Known In Operation:*** 1865 - 1869; ***Founder:*** Wm Harpke; ***Predecessor:*** No Data; ***Successor:*** No Data; ***Source:*** Carl Scott Zimmerman research papers on St. Louis area large bells posted on his website "towerbells.org"; ***Other Facts:*** This was the name under which William Harpke did business in 1869. Carl Scott Zimmerman says "in 1870 it was used by Harpke & Dauernheim. Although the business can be traced from 1865 to 1891, the Central Bell & Brass Foundry name appears in St Louis directories only for these two years".

# Central Union Brass Co.

***Address:*** 811 N. 2nd, later 811 to 823 N. 2nd, St Louis, Missouri; ***Year Established:*** 1883; ***Year Closed:*** No Data; ***Years Known In Operation:*** 1883 - 1904; ***Founder:*** No Data; ***Predecessor:*** No Data; ***Successor:*** No Data; ***Source:*** Carl Scott Zimmerman research papers on St. Louis area large bells; ***Other Facts:*** Primarily a brass foundry with a wide range of products.

# Chaplin - Fulton Manufacturing Company

***Address:*** Pittsburgh, Pennsylvania; ***Year Established:*** 1885; ***Year Closed:*** No Data; ***Years Known In Operation:*** 1885 - 1913; ***Founder:*** Louis B Fulton, Pres., Melchior B. Chaplin, Treas., and William M. Ralston, Sect. Formed a partnership to take over old foundry. New name was Chaplin - Fulton; ***Predecessor:*** Andrew Fulton, and A. Fulton's Son & Co; ***Successor:*** No Data; ***Source:*** Bells belonging to Neil Goeppinger of Boone, Iowa, Iva May Long, Tarentum, Pennsylvania, Robert Cowie of Paris, Arkansas, and Chartiers Hill United Presbyterian Church, Canonsburg, Pa. (supplied by Carl Scott Zimmerman of St Louis, Mo.); ***Other Facts:*** Neil Goeppinger has one dated 1894 of 27 1/2" diameter in Boone, Iowa. Iva May Long had one dated 1892 which was 28" and weighed 475 lbs. from the Parnassus Public School. In the courtyard of the Pittsburgh Historical Landmarks Foundation in the Old Post Office Building in North Pittsburgh are 3 bells by this firm. One of them dated 1896 spelled the city as Pittsburg (no "H") as for a period that was the spelling of the city. Some of the bells by this firm use brackets which read "A. Fulton's Son & Co." verifying the predecessor. The Cowie bell is 48" in diameter and dated 1893. All their known bells have crowns.

*Chaplin - Fulton Manufacturing*
*Company Bell 1894*

# Chicago Bell Foundry

*Address:* Chicago, Illinois; *Year Established:* No Data; *Year Closed:* No Data; *Years Known In Operation:* No Data; *Founder:* No Data; *Predecessor:* No Data; *Successor:* No Data; *Source: That Vanishing Sound;* *Other Facts:* No Data

# Cincinnati Bell, Brass & Iron Foundry

*Address:* Richmond at Harriet, Cincinnati, Ohio; *Year Established:* 1814; *Year Closed:* No Data; *Years Known In Operation:* 1814 - 1889; *Founder:* No Data; *Predecessor:* No Data; *Successor:* No Data; *Source:* Mrs. G. Lyle Ringland of Norwood, Ohio and Zell's U.S. Business Directory of 1889; *Other Facts:* See "Cincinnati Bell Co" for possible connection.

# Cincinnati Bell Company

*Address:* Cincinnati, Ohio; *Year Established:* No Data; *Year Closed:* No Data; *Years Known In Operation:* 1897; *Founder:* No Data; *Predecessor:* Blymer Mfg Co., Cincinnati, Ohio; *Successor:* No Data; *Source:* 48" bell belonging to Neil Goeppinger, other bells, Carl Scott Zimmerman of St Louis, Mo., Mrs. G. Lyle Ringland, Zell's U.S. Business Directory, and Thomas' Register of 1905 - 1906, and ABAII website inquiry of Steve Allen of the Courtland Oakfield United Methodist Church on 10/17/2006, which quotes the Cincinnati Historical Society; *Other Facts:* 48" cast iron bell above purchased from Boyd Southard collection in Marshalltown, Iowa. That bell came originally out of the Methodist church in Casey, Iowa. This bell company may be the trade name used by the Cincinnati Bell Brass and Iron Foundry listed by Zell's U.S. Business Directory and by Mrs. G. Lyle Ringland. I have no certain way of knowing if it is only a trade name or if it is a separate firm. The name appears on the yoke of this large bell as "CIN BELL CO. A 30" with the same inscription was on a bell which belonged to Leonard Fleischer of Columbus, Nebraska. They advertised car, church, fire alarm, organ, school and steamboat bells in 1906. Carl Scott Zimmerman states that "the distinctive shapes of the bell, yoke, and wheel are all common to Blymer, Norton and Cin Bell Co in all variants that I have seen." Thus it appears there is either a tie between the two firms, or they operated one foundry but sold bells under different names. Carl Zimmerman has seen a large iron bell with a cast inscription by this firm. Todd Lower reported that a Blymer catalog cover states THOSE FAMOUS BLYMYER BELLS THE JOHN B MORRIS FUNDRY CO. PROPS CINCINNATI BELL FOUNDRY 1918. This brings up the question, are the Cincinnati Bell Foundry and the Cincinnati Bell Company the same firm? Since the shape of the bells is the same, I assume they are.

*Cincinnati Bell Company 48 Inch Diameter Bell*

# Cincinnati Bell Foundry Company

***Address:*** Cincinnati, Ohio; ***Year Established:*** No Data; ***Year Closed:*** No Data; ***Years Known In Operation:*** No Data; ***Founder:*** No Data; ***Predecessor:*** No Data; ***Successor:*** No Data; ***Source:*** A 42" diameter iron bell belonging to Robert Cowie of Paris, Ark; ***Other Facts:*** No Data

# Clampitt & Regester

***Address:*** 47 Holliday Street, Baltimore, Maryland; ***Year Established:*** No Data; ***Year Closed:*** No Data; ***Years Known In Operation:*** 1845 - 1848; ***Founder:*** Elias Clampitt and Joshua Regester; ***Predecessor:*** No Data; ***Successor:*** No Data; ***Source:*** Baltimore Business Directory of 1845, city diretory research of Carl Scott Zimmerman of St Louis, and an undated bell belonging to Neil Goeppinger; ***Other Facts:*** 47 Holliday Street was located near City Hall. Some city directories spell the second name Regester and others spell it Register. Because the author owns a bell with the "e" spelling, this book will use that one. In 1850 Henry McShane was 19 years old and living with Joseph Regester and working as a brass founder. In 1856 Henry McShane formed his own firm Henry McShane Brass and Bell Foundry on Concord St, between Lombard and Pratt in downtown Baltimore. This became a major bell foundry.

*Clampitt and Regester Bell*

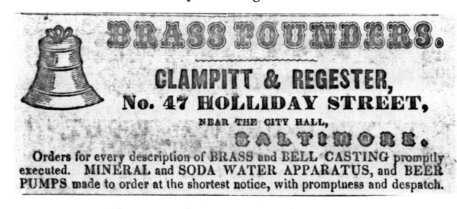

*Clampitt and Regester 1845 Advertisement*

# Clark & Elliot

*Address:* Newcomerstown, Ohio; *Year Established:* No Data; *Year Closed:* No Data; *Years Known In Operation:* 1888; *Founder:* No Data; *Predecessor:* No Data; *Successor:* No Data; *Source:* Zell's U.S. Business Directory of 1888; *Other Facts:* No Data

# J. C. Clark

*Address:* Middle Haddam, Connecticut; *Year Established:* No Data; *Year Closed:* No Data; *Years Known In Operation:* 1888, 1889; *Founder:* No Data; *Predecessor:* No Data; *Successor:* No Data; *Source:* Zell's U.S. Business Directory of 1888 and 1889; *Other Facts:* Advertised gongs in the above directories.

# R. S. Clark & Company

*Address:* Mount Carmel, Connecticut; *Year Established:* No Data; *Year Closed:* No Data; *Years Known In Operation:* 1889; *Founder:* No Data; *Predecessor:* No Data; *Successor:* No Data; *Source:* Zell's U.S. Business Directory of 1889; *Other Facts:* No Data

# The Cleveland Bell Mfg & Foundry Company

*Address:* Cleveland, Ohio; *Year Established:* No Data; *Year Closed:* No Data; *Years Known In Operation:* 1907; *Founder:* No Data; *Predecessor:* No Data; *Successor:* No Data; *Source:* 2 bells belonging to Robert Cowie of Paris, Ark; *Other Facts:* The two Cowie bells are 33" and 30" in diameter, made of bronze, and of the Germanic shape. One has a woman with a shield in heavy bah relief. The yokes have an unusual shape and taper vertically.

# Coast Guard Yard Foundry

*Address:* Curtis Bay, Maryland; *Year Established:* No Data; *Year Closed:* 1976; *Years Known In Operation:* No Data; *Founder:* No Data; *Predecessor:* No Data; *Successor:* No Data; *Source:* *That Vanishing Sound*; *Other Facts:* Made marker buoy bells in 3 sizes: 85 pounds, 225 pounds, and 1,000 pounds.

# James Cochran

*Address:* New Haven, Connecticut; *Year Established:* 1797; *Year Closed:* No Data; *Years Known In Operation:* 1797; *Founder:* James Cochran; *Predecessor:* Isaac Doolittle; *Successor:* Bradley & Cockran, Fenton & Cockran; *Source:* Winthrop Warren of Fairfield, Connecticut, and Carl Scott Zimmerman of St Louis, Mo; *Other Facts:* James Cochran bought the business from Isaac Doolittle's son, Isaac, who didn't make bells.

# Fenton & Cochran

*Address:* New Haven, Connecticut; *Year Established:* No Data; *Year Closed:* No Data; *Years Known In Operation:* 1803 - 1805; *Founder:* No Data; *Predecessor:* No Data; *Successor:* No Data; *Source:* Carl Scott Zimmerman of St Louis, Mo; *Other Facts:* No Data

# Bradley & Cochran

*Address:* New Haven, Connecticut; *Year Established:* 1808; *Year Closed:* 1808; *Years Known In Operation:* 1808; *Founder:* James Cochran; *Predecessor:* Fenton & Cochran, James Cochran, Isaac Doolittle; *Successor:* No Data; *Source:* Carl Scott Zimmerman of St Louis, Mo; *Other Facts:* No Data

# C. A. Coffin "Buckeye Bell Foundry"

*Address:* Cincinnati, Ohio; *Year Established:* No Data; *Year Closed:* No Data; *Years Known In Operation:* 1853 - 1860; *Founder:* No Data; *Predecessor:* G. W. Coffin & Co. "Buckeye Bell Foundry"; *Successor:* E.W. Vanduzen; *Source: That Vanishing Sound*, and Carl Scott Zimmerman of St Louis, Mo for dates; *Other Facts:* No Data

# G.W. Coffin & Company "Buckeye Bell Foundry"

*Address:* 194 Columbia Street or Second St. between Broadway & Ludlow Streets, Cincinnati, Ohio; *Year Established:* 1837; *Year Closed:* No Data; *Years Known In Operation:* 1837 - 1859; *Founder:* George Washington Coffin; *Predecessor:* Probably Mount Riga furnace in Salisbury, Conn founded by Holley and Coffin in 1810; *Successor:* C. A. Coffin Foundry "Buckeye Bell Foundry"; *Source:* That Vanishing Sound, History Cast in Metal, and Cin. In 1841 (latter copy supplied by Russell F. Frehse of Kendallville, Ind.), and many bells; *Other Facts:* Start of "Buckeye Bell Foundry" later run by Vanduzen's. They invented bell springs. Made bells at least up to 4,095 pounds. Some were very ornate with dancing veiled girls encircling the bell holding hands, etc. They advertised "Church, Academy, Steam-Boat and Tavern Bells, Composition & Brass Clocks, Hose & Salt-Well Joints, Brass Casting of any weight not exceeding 3,000 lbs. cast on a day's notice. Old Brass and Copper taken in exchange." Also, "Mathematical & Philosophical Instrument Makers" and "Philosophical Apparatus". G. W. Coffin was the guardian of W. A. Van Duzen who went to work in the Buckeye Bell Foundry at age 14. When Van Duzen was married at the age of 20 he owned a 1/5th interest in the foundry. Note that the spelling of their last name was changed later from Van Duzen to Vanduzen. In 1865 he and Mr. Tift bought the foundry and changed the name to Van Duzen and Tift, Buckeye Bell Foundry.

*G. W. Coffin Bell 1851*

# Joseph Collingridge

*Address:* Louisville, Kentucky; *Year Established:* No Data; *Year Closed:* No Data; *Years Known In Operation:* 1844; *Founder:* No Data; *Predecessor:* No Data; *Successor:* No Data; *Source:* Carl Scott Zimmerman of St Louis, Mo; *Other Facts:* Zimmerman found a bell by this firm dated 1844. He said "It has a long waist and heavy shoulder bead very like the Kaye & Co bell. It hangs from a rather ornate yoke which appears never to have had a wheel; it's rung by a rope and lever."

# Collingridge, Lawson & Co.

*Address:* Louisville,, Kentucky; *Year Established:* No Data; *Year Closed:* No Data; *Years Known In Operation:* 1844; *Founder:* No Data; *Predecessor:* No Data; *Successor:* No Data; *Source:* Research of city directories by Carl Scott Zimmerman of St Louis, Mo; *Other Facts:* No Data

# Commings & Hosack

*Address:* Fredricktown, Ohio; *Year Established:* No Data; *Year Closed:* No Data; *Years Known In Operation:* 1889; *Founder:* No Data; *Predecessor:* No Data; *Successor:* No Data; *Source:* Zell's U.S Business Directory of 1889; *Other Facts:* No Data

# Concordia

*Address:* No Data; *Year Established:* No Data; *Year Closed:* No Data; *Years Known In Operation:* No Data; *Founder:* No Data; *Predecessor:* No Data; *Successor:* No Data; *Source:* Photo of iron, or more likely steel, bell sent to Neil Goeppinger. Concordia is cast in the waist of the bell. There was no yoke for more inscription information; *Other Facts:* No Data

*Concordia Bell*

# J.P. Connell

***Address:*** Berlin, Connecticut; ***Year Established:*** No Data; ***Year Closed:*** No Data; ***Years Known In Operation:*** 1888 - 1889; ***Founder:*** No Data; ***Predecessor:*** No Data; ***Successor:*** No Data; ***Source:*** Zell's U.S. Business Directories of 1888 & 1889; ***Other Facts:*** No Data

# Melvin C. Corbett

***Address:*** No Data; ***Year Established:*** No Data; ***Year Closed:*** No Data; ***Years Known In Operation:*** 1923; ***Founder:*** Melvin C. Corbett; ***Predecessor:*** No Data; ***Successor:*** No Data; ***Source:*** GCNA Bulletin, Vol XLI 1992 "Carillons & Chimes in North America" article by Carl Scott Zimmerman; ***Other Facts:*** Bell which was part of chime in Trinity Episcopal Church, Williamsport, Pa. This "is the only bell Corbett ever made. It was removed from the chime, and now hangs on a dolly in the entryway in the base of the tower. A placard on the wall gives its full history." Quote of Carl Scott Zimmerman.

# Cordry Caughlin Co.

***Address:*** 261 N. Main, St Louis, Missouri; ***Year Established:*** No Data; ***Year Closed:*** No Data; ***Years Known In Operation:*** 1860; ***Founder:*** Adam C. Caughlin, Lewis Dauernheim, Lorenzo H. Cordry; ***Predecessor:*** Caughlan & Dauernheim; ***Successor:*** No Data; ***Source:*** Carl Scott Zimmerman of St Louis, Mo. reports this company was listed in the 1860 St Louis directory as "bell and brass founders"; ***Other Facts:*** No Data

# Charles Cory & Sons

***Address:*** Springfield, New York; ***Year Established:*** No Data; ***Year Closed:*** No Data; ***Years Known In Operation:*** No Data; ***Founder:*** No Data; ***Predecessor:*** No Data; ***Successor:*** No Data; ***Source:*** Thomas Smith of Mobile, Alabama; ***Other Facts:*** Mr. Smith owns a 20" brass fire bell from a Mobile, Alabama fire station which has two outside clappers with oak knobs on the ends instead of iron. The name of the firm, city and state are inscribed around the bottom of the bell.

# Cowing & Company

***Address:*** Seneca Falls, New York; ***Year Established:*** 1848; ***Year Closed:*** 1874 or 1875; ***Years Known In Operation:*** 1848 - 1874 or 1875; ***Founder:*** No Data; ***Predecessor:*** No Data; ***Successor:*** No Data; ***Source:*** Wayne E. Morrison, Sr. of Ovid, New York, and article in the Ithaca Journal titled "Bell Restoration and Replacement Proves To Be A Weighty Project", September 19, 2010; ***Other Facts:*** A cast iron bell hangs in the court house in Ovid, N.Y. which was erected in 1862. Cowing & Co. had a foundry and was mainly in the business of making fire equipment including suction hose, hand fire engines, etc. According to the newspaper article above, information taken from a company catalogue listed their No. 9 bell at 850 lbs, their No. 8 at 450 lbs, and their No. 7 at 300 lbs and 30" in diameter. The photo of the bell in the newspaper article is that of a pre civil war shaped cast iron or steel bell with an extremely small top. It starts to flare out toward the the waist immediately, with no vertical side above the waist.

# R.T. Crane Brass & Bell Foundry

*Address:* Chicago, Illinois; *Year Established:* 1855; *Year Closed:* No Data; *Years Known In Operation:* 1855; *Founder:* No Data; *Predecessor:* No Data; *Successor:* No Data; *Source:* List of Sydney J. Shep, Mississauga, Ontario, Canada, and photo of first building they operated out of with a sign on the top of the roof; *Other Facts:* This is the same firm which makes plumbing and bathroom fixtures today, along with many pipe products.

*R. T. Crane Foundry*

# Curtis

*Address:* Albany, New York; *Year Established:* No Data; *Year Closed:* No Data; *Years Known In Operation:* No Data; *Founder:* No Data; *Predecessor:* No Data; *Successor:* No Data; *Source:* Bell owned by Micky & Marie Varian of Maine; *Other Facts:* No Data

# S. Davis

*Address:* Detroit, Michigan; *Year Established:* No Data; *Year Closed:* No Data; *Years Known In Operation:* No Data; *Founder:* Solomon Davis; *Predecessor:* No Data; *Successor:* No Data; *Source:* Inquiry at ABAII website by lucky13 posted August 13, 2007, Bob Cowie of Paris, Arkansas; *Other Facts:* The above individual purchased a 16" diameter bronze bell, 18" tall with clapper and yoke. The inscription around the top read "S. Davis, Detroit, M.T. 1836". M.T. stood for Michigan Territory as Michigan didn't become a state until the following year, 1837.

# J. C. Deagan, Inc.

*Address:* Chicago, Illinois; *Year Established:* No Data; *Year Closed:* No Data; *Years Known In Operation:* 1917 - 1924; *Founder:* No Data; *Predecessor:* No Data; *Successor:* No Data; *Source:* List of Carl Scott Zimmerman of St Louis, and many sets of tubular chimes as part of church organs; *Other Facts:* All this firm's bells were tubular chimes as far as I know. I have seen many.

# Lewis Debozear

Address: Philadelphia, Pennsylvania (about 1857 moved to Chicago, Illinois); *Year Established:* No Data; *Year Closed:* No Data; *Years Known In Operation:* 1831 - 1860; *Founder:* No Data; *Predecessor:* No Data; *Successor:* No Data; *Source:* Bell Tower ad by Jack Keller of Consolidated Casting Corp. West, Herndon, Pennsylvania. (Lois Springer research papers), research of city directories by Carl Scott Zimmerman of St Louis, Missouri, and bronze bell at St. Patrick's Catholic Church on Village Drive in Fayetteville, North Carolina; *Other Facts:* Ad had photo of 22" bell. Inscription "Lewis Debozear Phila 184?". Made of yellow brass and turned on a lathe to tune it. His son, Joseph, worked as a bellfounder in his father's Philadelphia foundry, and did not move to Chicago with his father. The son continued to be listed in Philadelphia city directories from 1861 to 1881. After Lewis moved to Chicago, he was listed in directories there. On the Fayetteville bell it listed Lewis Debozear of Philadelphia St Patrick's Church Fayette Village 1831. There are two reports of the inscription, and they differ in an abbreviation and order of the information, but the information is the same.

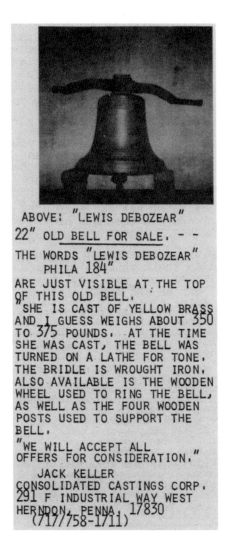

ABOVE: "LEWIS DEBOZEAR" 22" OLD BELL FOR SALE. -- THE WORDS "LEWIS DEBOZEAR" PHILA 184" ARE JUST VISIBLE AT THE TOP OF THIS OLD BELL. SHE IS CAST OF YELLOW BRASS AND I GUESS WEIGHS ABOUT 350 TO 375 POUNDS. AT THE TIME SHE WAS CAST, THE BELL WAS TURNED ON A LATHE FOR TONE. THE BRIDLE IS WROUGHT IRON. ALSO AVAILABLE IS THE WOODEN WHEEL USED TO RING THE BELL, AS WELL AS THE FOUR WOODEN POSTS USED TO SUPPORT THE BELL. "WE WILL ACCEPT ALL OFFERS FOR CONSIDERATION." JACK KELLER CONSOLIDATED CASTINGS CORP. 291 F INDUSTRIAL WAY WEST HERNDON, PENNA. 17830 (717/758-1711)

*Advertisement for Lewis Debozear Bell in The Bell Tower Magazine*

# Denver Brass Works

*Address:* 1421 17th Street, Denver, Colorado; *Year Established:* No Data; *Year Closed:* No Data; *Years Known In Operation:* 1884; *Founder:* No Data; *Predecessor:* No Data; *Successor:* No Data; *Source:* Winston Jones of Evergreen, Colorado; *Other Facts:* Winston Jones had a 20" bronze bell with a pear shaped clapper which came from Stumptown, Colorado, a few miles east of Leadville, Colorado. The only other bell known by this firm was on the original U.S. Navy cruiser "Denver" and has designs on it. That bell is larger than the one of Mr. Jones and is on display in the foyer of the City & County Building in Denver, Colorado.

# Derby

*Address:* No Data; *Year Established:* No Data; *Year Closed:* No Data; *Years Known In Operation:* 1784; *Founder:* No Data; *Predecessor:* No Data; *Successor:* No Data; *Source:* Bell belonging to Iva May Long in Pa; *Other Facts:* No Data

*Derby Bell*

# C. Dockray

*Address:* Zanesville, Ohio; *Year Established:* No Data; *Year Closed:* No Data; *Years Known In Operation:* 1881 - 1889; *Founder:* No Data; *Predecessor:* No Data; *Successor:* No Data; *Source:* Zell's United States Business Directory of 1881 and 1889; *Other Facts:* No Data

# William L. Dodd

*Address:* 101 Lewis Street (near Stanton Street), New York, New York; *Year Established:* No Data; *Year Closed:* No Data; *Years Known In Operation:* 1859; *Founder:* No Data; *Predecessor:* Lewis S. Dodd; *Successor:* No Data; *Source:* The Troy Directory for 1859 , Vol. 31 (advertisement) and Wilson's Business Directory of New York City for 1859 (listing); *Other Facts:* The above listed advertisement states that "The East Broadway Stages Pass and Repass Constantly".

# Enos Doolittle

*Address:* Hartford, Connecticut; *Year Established:* 1787; *Year Closed:* 1806; *Years Known In Operation:* 1787 - 1806; *Founder:* Enos Doolittle; *Predecessor:* No Data; *Successor:* James Doolittle (son); *Source:* Edward Stickney, Bedford, Massachusetts, Winthrop Warren of Fairfield, Connecticut, "The Historic Bell of Old First Church" by Stanley A. Ransom, Jr, Church Historian, January 31, 1972 available on the Internet at oldfirstchurchhuntington.org, and Carl Scott Zimmerman of St Louis, Mo; *Other Facts:* Dartmouth College had a bell of theirs in 1790. Enos Doolittle's uncle,

Isaac Doolittle, was also in the bell business (separate from this firm) because he bought the equipment for bell making from the estate of John Whitear Jr. Enos Doolittle did a large bell business and after his death in 1806 his son James Doolittle continued the business until 1811. The Old First Church article referenced above refers to the Old First Presbyterian Church of Huntington, N. Y. That bell is inscribed "Enos Doolittle, Hartford, 1793", and cast on the inside of the sound bow it reads "The Towne Endures". Enos Doolittle was the nephew of Isaac Doolittle who operated in New Haven, Connecticut.

# Doolittle & Goodyear

*Address:* Hartford, Connecticut; *Year Established:* 1788; *Year Closed:* 1791; *Years Known In Operation:* 1788 - 1791; *Founder:* Enos Doolittle and Jesse Goodyear of Hamden, Connecticut; *Predecessor:* No Data; *Successor:* No Data; *Source:* Eugene P. Burns of Troy, New York, and Winthrop Warren of Fairfield, Connecticut; *Other Facts:* Jesse Goodyear had learned bell making as an apprentice in the Isaac Doolittle foundry (uncle of Enos), and Enos Doolittle had learned clock making with his uncle in New Haven. 650 lb. bells went to Brookfield, Massachusetts and West Springfield, and an 1,100 lb. one went to Portland, Maine(?) in 1790. It was reported as Portland, Mass. but Carl Scott Zimmerman reports there is no Portland, in Mass., so I assume it is in Maine due to proximity.

# Isaac Doolittle

*Address:* New Haven, Connecticut; *Year Established:* 1774; *Year Closed:* 1797; *Years Known In Operation:* 1774 - 1797; *Founder:* Isaac Doolittle; *Predecessor:* John Whitear; *Successor:* James Cochran; *Source:* Winthrop Warren of Fairfield, Connecticut; *Other Facts:* A 600 lb. Bell went to the 1st Congregational Church, Bristol, Connecticut. Isaac Doolittle was an uncle of Enos Doolittle. He bought the equipment from John Whitear Jr's estate and added bells to his line of clocks. Later, James Cochran bought the bell business from Isaac Doolittle's son.

# James Doolittle

*Address:* Hartford, Connecticut; *Year Established:* No Data; *Year Closed:* No Data; *Years Known In Operation:* 1802 - 1839; *Founder:* James Doolittle; *Predecessor:* Enos Doolittle; *Successor:* No Data; *Source:* Winthrop Warren of Fairfield, Connecticut, and Edward Stickney, Bedford, Mass., and 1822 bell belonging to North Canaan Congregational meeting house, displayed at the North Canaan Green in North Canaan, Conn; *Other Facts:* Enos Doolittle was the father of James Doolittle. A bell dated 1802 by this firm is in the Historical Society building, formerly a church, in Haverhill, New Hampshire. A 28" diameter bell dated 1815 was offered for sale by Brosamers Bells in 2016.

# William C. Downey & Company

*Address:* Springfield, Ohio; *Year Established:* No Data; *Year Closed:* No Data; *Years Known In Operation:* 1905 - 1906; *Founder:* No Data; *Predecessor:* No Data; *Successor:* No Data; *Source:* Minutes of May 17, 1992 Bell Study Group of Northern Ohio, Origin of Bells List of Carl Scott Zimmerman of St Louis, Mo., and Thomas' Register 1905 - 1906; *Other Facts:* Steel alloy bell of James H. Baker of Walbridge, Ohio (ABAII member). This was reported as being made by "W. C. Donney", but since another firm, William. C. Downey, existed in the same town, it is very likely a typo with n instead of w. They advertised farm bells. There was also a bell by this firm in a post of October 7, 2009 on the ABAII website by Elaine of Arizona regarding a family owned bell from a farm in SE Ohio.

# Downs & Company

*Address:* Seneca Falls, New York; *Year Established:* No Data; *Year Closed:* No Data; *Years Known In Operation:* 1862 - 1869; *Founder:* No Data; *Predecessor:* No Data; *Successor:* No Data; *Source:* Old advertisement for their bells; *Other Facts:* They made steel amalgam bells, which is a fancy way of saying steel bells. They sold on price and shipped to both the U.S. and Canada. They advertised their bells for use on farms, plantations, school houses and factories. Their size #1, 15 1/2" diameter bell cost $6 and their #7, 30" diameter bell cost $30.

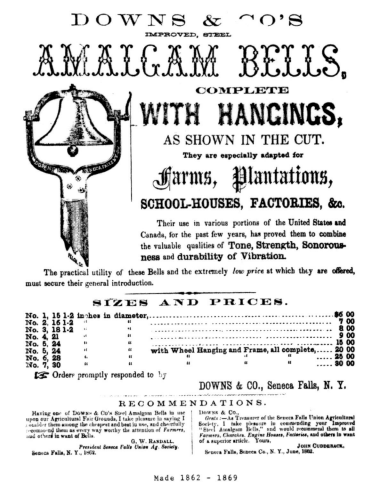

*Downs and Company Advertisement*

# Durand & Thiac

*Address:* New Orleans, Louisiana; *Year Established:* No Data; *Year Closed:* No Data; *Years Known In Operation:* 1827; *Founder:* No Data; *Predecessor:* No Data; *Successor:* No Data; *Source:* *That Vanishing Sound*, Louise Springer letter of 3/4/1985, her source: Paxton's Directory and Registry for New Orleans, 1827; *Other Facts:* The above directory listed "bells of all sizes" so presumably they made church bells.

# T. I. Dyre Jr

*Address:* Philadelphia, Pennsylvania; *Year Established:* No Data; *Year Closed:* No Data; *Years Known In Operation:* 1849; *Founder:* No Data; *Predecessor:* No Data; *Successor:* No Data; *Source:* Bell belonging to Robert Traines, Mt Pleasant, MI; *Other Facts:* Above bell weighs approx 300 lbs. Cast into bell: T.I. Dyre, Jr Philadelphia, Pa For Bradley Chapel Flint River Indian Mission Michigan Conference found 1846 Presented by Wharton St Methodist Church Sunday School 1849.

# Eagle Bell & Brass Foundry

*Address:* 192 N. 2nd in 1866 and 809 N. 2nd in 1869 - 1900, St. Louis, Missouri; *Year Established:* No Data; *Year Closed:* No Data; *Years Known In Operation:* 1866 - 1869; *Founder:* John Kupferle & G. E. Boisselier, proprietors; *Predecessor:* John Kupferle who had his own firm in 1860 in St. Louis; *Successor:* No Data; *Source:* Gould's 1900 Directory for St. Louis (thru Missouri Historical Society), and City Directories for 1848 - 1899 (thru Carl Scott Zimmerman of St Louis, Mo.); *Other Facts:* The following information was furnished by Carl Scott Zimmerman. Kupferle and Boisselier proprietors (1866 - 1867), then Kupferle, Boisselier & Company (1868 - 1869). The name Eagle Bell & Brass Foundry was used by the partnership of Kupferle and Boisselier for only four years, although the foundry was operated by the partners from 1858 to 1886. There were two men named John Kupferle who operated brass foundries in St Louis which was very confusing.

# Eagle Bell Co

*Address:* Lebanon, Pennsylvania; *Year Established:* No Data; *Year Closed:* No Data; *Years Known In Operation:* 1867; *Founder:* P. L. Weimer; *Predecessor:* No Data; *Successor:* No Data; *Source:* 28" diameter bell and dinner bell at Evergreen Farm, Eminence, Indiana, a bell inquiry of March 6, 2002 to the ABAII regarding an iron farm bell of approx. 60 - 70 lbs, and three bells in the Ben Tuck collection in Lebanon, Pa; *Other Facts:* Iron bells. On back of yoke on 28" bell "P.L. Weimer Pat July 23, 1867". Also, Kathy on the ABAII website said on July 9, 2007 that she had a 22" diameter bell by Eagle Bell Co. with the clapper on the exterior of the bell so it ratcheted around the bell so it never hit the bell in the same spot. Another person, "Morrison Works" posted on the ABAII website on Dec. 18, 2012 that they had an Eagle Bell and that it said "E. Whitman and Sons" "Baltimore" on the other side of the yoke. Their research showed E. Whitman and Sons to be a southern agricultural warehouse and they gathered that it was made for them by Eagle Bell Co. Their bell had a counter weight on the top as part of a ratcheting mechanism. The Tuck bells were as follows (#4 20", #5 15", and #3 22").

# Eagle Pitcher Bearing

*Address:* San Francisco or San Jose, California; *Year Established:* No Data; *Year Closed:* No Data; *Years Known In Operation:* No Data; *Founder:* No Data; *Predecessor:* Kingwell Brothers Ltd., and before that Weed & Kingwell; *Successor:* South Bay Bronze/Aluminum Foundry Inc; *Source:* Letter from Gil Hernandy, owner of South Bay Bronze/Aluminum Foundry; *Other Facts:* These must have been bronze bells as bearings are made of bronze, not iron, and Weed and Kingwell made bronze bells.

# East Hampton Bell Company

*Address:* East Hampton, Connecticut; *Year Established:* No Data; *Year Closed:* No Data; *Years Known In Operation:* No Data; *Founder:* Louis & Eugene Goff, Amiel Chapman & Lyman Thomas; *Predecessor:* No Data; *Successor:* No Data; *Source:* Material supplied by Marion Bradley of Connecticut; *Other Facts:* No Data

# Everhardt & Company

*Address:* Chicago, Illinois; *Year Established:* No Data; *Year Closed:* No Data; *Years Known In Operation:* No Data; *Founder:* No Data; *Predecessor:* No Data; *Successor:* No Data; *Source: That Vanishing Sound*; *Other Facts:* No Data

# Over Ewald

*Address:* 240 South Penna, Indianapolis, Indiana; *Year Established:* No Data; *Year Closed:* No Data; *Years Known In Operation:* 1881; *Founder:* No Data; *Predecessor:* No Data; *Successor:* No Data; *Source:* Zell's United States Business Directory of 1881; *Other Facts:* No Data

# B.W. Felthousen Company

*Address:* 187 E. Water Street, Milwaukee, Wisconsin; *Year Established:* No Data; *Year Closed:* No Data; *Years Known In Operation:* 1869 - 1870; *Founder:* No Data; *Predecessor:* No Data; *Successor:* No Data; *Source:* Milwaukee City Directory 1869 and 1870 (research papers of Lois Springer); *Other Facts:* No Data

# Fenton & Cochran

*Address:* New Haven, Connecticut; *Year Established:* No Data; *Year Closed:* No Data; *Years Known In Operation:* 1803 - 1805; *Founder:* Gamaliel Fenton, James Cochran; *Predecessor:* Gamaliel Fenton, James Cochran; *Successor:* No Data; *Source:* Winthrop Warren of Fairfield, Connecticut, and Edward Stickney, Bedford, Mass; *Other Facts:* Bell dated 1804 is in Old Academy in Fairfield, Connecticut and is decorated with rosettes and spread eagle medallions. In 1803 a bell was shipped to the armory in Richmond, Virginia on the schooner Pearl (588 lbs.). Another bell by this firm went to Trinity Church, Newport, R.I. on October 5, 1805.

# Gamaliel Fenton

*Address:* Walpole, New Hampshire; *Year Established:* No Data; *Year Closed:* No Data; *Years Known In Operation:* 1798; *Founder:* No Data; *Predecessor:* No Data; *Successor:* No Data; *Source:* Winthrop Warren of Fairfield, Connecticut; *Other Facts:* Ran an advertisement for bell casting in the Farmers Weekly Museum of 2/24/1798. According to Mr. Warren, he may or may not have actually made bells. He may have only been looking for business prior to making bells. His advertisement did say, however, "Gamaliel Fenton respectfully informs the public that he is now carrying on the bell foundry in Walpole: where bells of any weight may be had, on as reasonable terms, and on as short a notice as at any foundry in the United States."

# E. Field

*Address:* Nantucket, Massachusetts; *Year Established:* No Data; *Year Closed:* No Data; *Years Known In Operation:* 1800's; *Founder:* No Data; *Predecessor:* No Data; *Successor:* No Data; *Source:* Ryan Cooper, Limerick, Maine; *Other Facts:* Above individual quotes the curator of the Nantucket Whaling Museum as saying this firm, which made bells for whaling boats, also made church bells and that a church in Nantucket still had a bell by this firm in 1989. See "Field & Macy" entry for more information.

# Field & Macy

*Address:* Nantucket, Massachusetts; *Year Established:* 1821; *Year Closed:* 1875; *Years Known In Operation:* 1821 - 1875; *Founder:* Benjamin Field from Providence, RI; *Predecessor:* No Data; *Successor:* No Data; *Source:* Ryan Cooper of Yarmouthport, Mass; *Other Facts:* Mr. Cooper has a bell labeled E. Field and Nantucket Historical Society in Nantucket has at least 3 bells by Field & Macy. The firm was offered for sale in 1875 but no one bought it so it went out of business. They also made andirons and door hardware. A school bell by them was decorated with rococo flourishes and swag, stars and hearts. Mr. Cooper's bell is from the whaling ship "Ohio" dated 1833. They also cast church bells. All bells were sold around Nantucket as far as known.

# Foote Foundry

*Address:* Fredericktown, Ohio; *Year Established:* No Data; *Year Closed:* No Data; *Years Known In Operation:* 1851 - 1900; *Founder:* No Data; *Predecessor:* No Data; *Successor:* No Data; *Source:* Post on ABAII website forum by jackbell on November 13, 2010 regarding Fredericktown Bells; *Other Facts:* The above post included a photo of the foundry with many church bells stacked outdoors for storage. They were iron, and a man and woman were with them which allowed for size comparison. Jackbell stated that a former employee of the Foote Foundry had told him their largest bell was 50" in diameter, and at least one of the bells in the photo looked to be that large. Although no longer making bells, the Foote Foundry was still in business in 2006

*Evangeline Aldrich who bought*
*the California Bell Company*

*Mrs. A. S. C. Forbes*

## Mrs. A. S. C. Forbes Manufacturer

*Address:* 335 West 31st Street, Los Angeles, California; *Year Established:* No Data; *Year Closed:* No Data; *Years Known In Operation:* 1908 - 1948; *Founder:* No Data; *Predecessor:* No Data; *Successor:* No Data; *Source:* Lois Springer's research papers, letters from Mrs. A. S. C Forbes, and *California's El Camino Real and Its Historic Bells* by Max Kurillo and Erline Tuttle; *Other Facts:* Her husband made bells and she carried on and expanded after his death in 1928. At some point they called the firm the California Bell Company, and in 1948 she sold the firm to Evangeline Aldrich. They made church bells as well as small bells and El Camino Real Marker Bells. The latter weighed a little over 100 pounds, and the church bells were up to at least 24" in diameter based on photos.

## C. B. Force & Company

*Address:* 265 Water, New York, New York; *Year Established:* No Data; *Year Closed:* No Data; *Years Known In Operation:* 1840, 1841; *Founder:* No Data; *Predecessor:* No Data; *Successor:* No Data; *Source:* New York Business Directory 1840 - 1841 (research papers of Lois Springer); *Other Facts:* No Data

## Ephraim Force

*Address:* Various Eastside addresses, New York City, New York; *Year Established:* No Data; *Year Closed:* No Data; *Years Known In Operation:* 1807 - 1848; *Founder:* Ephraim Force; *Predecessor:* No Data; *Successor:* No Data; *Source:* Louise Springer letter of 3/4/1985, her sources: several directories, several bells, Del Gilmore of Iowa City, Ia, Ron Kramer of Ca., Micky & Marie Varian of Maine, and Robert Cowie of Paris, Ark; *Other Facts:* Letter quote: "Listed in several directories as a brass founder at various Eastside addresses 1807 - 1848, but only as a maker of ornamental brasses and plumbing equipment. Nonetheless, the old Georgia Statehouse at Milledgeville has an E. Force bell... in its belfry." A 16 1/2" bell belongs to Holly Tolston of North Carolina. A 22" E. Force bell is in the Old Capitol Building on the University of Iowa campus dated 1844 (reported by Del Gilmore of Iowa City, location of the University of Iowa), an 1834 E. Force bell is in the clock tower of Mission Viejo Country Club in Mission Viejo, CA., and a 28" belongs to Robert Cowie of Paris, Ark.

## Frank and Johnston

*Address:* Dayton, Ohio; *Year Established:* No Data; *Year Closed:* No Data; *Years Known In Operation:* No Data; *Founder:* No Data; *Predecessor:* No Data; *Successor:* No Data; *Source:* Emails between Carl Scott Zimmerman of St Louis, Mo. and Nina Jones of December 29, 2003 regarding a bell; *Other Facts:* Above referenced bell was cast iron and 16" in diameter. On the pole mount it read Buckeye Foundry Dayton, Oh.

## Frederick Town Bell Company

*Address:* Frederick Town, Ohio; *Year Established:* 1851; *Year Closed:* No Data; *Years Known In Operation:* 1851; *Founder:* No Data; *Predecessor:* No Data; *Successor:* No Data; *Source:* 40" diameter bell located in town square of Panora Iowa and 16" bell belonging to Neil Goeppinger of Boone Iowa and 2 pre-Civil War dinner bells at Evergreen Farm Eminence Indiana, (farm belongs to John Slaven of Lafayette, Indiana), 8 - 16 - 07 discussion on ABA web site in big bells discussion section for year established; *Other Facts:* The 40" bell listed above was examined on 4/15/1984. Both bells are cast iron. Note this firm is spelled differently than the Fredricktown Bell Co Cory Pa. According to a comment posted to the ABAII website there was no connection between this firm and the Fredericktown Pa. firm. The Pa. firm is older than this firm.

# Fredricktown

***Address:*** Corry, Pennsylvania; ***Year Established:*** 1851; ***Year Closed:*** No Data; ***Years Known In Operation:*** 1851; ***Founder:*** No Data; ***Predecessor:*** No Data; ***Successor:*** No Data; ***Source:*** Wayne E. Morrison Sr. of Ovid, New York, and ABAII website comment, and bell belonging to Robert Cowie of Paris, Ark. ; ***Other Facts:*** Bells were listed in the Barlow Hardware Catalogue. Note Fredricktown is spelled differently from the Frederick Town Bell Company. According to a comment posted to the ABAII website there was no connection between the two firms, and this firm is older than the Ohio firm. The Cowie bell is 48" in diameter.

# Free & Company

***Address:*** Cincinnati, Ohio; ***Year Established:*** No Data; ***Year Closed:*** No Data; ***Years Known In Operation:*** No Data; ***Founder:*** No Data; ***Predecessor:*** No Data; ***Successor:*** No Data; ***Source:*** Bell at Evergreen Farm, Eminence, Indiana; ***Other Facts:*** Unusual shaped iron dinner bell. It has heavy ridges, but not like reeds. They protrude as if the bell was squashed from the top while the metal was hot, but it is smooth. It has a heavy squat look.

# F. Fuller

***Address:*** 438 N. Main, Providence, Rhode Island; ***Year Established:*** No Data; ***Year Closed:*** No Data; ***Years Known In Operation:*** 1860 - 1890; ***Founder:*** Frederick Fuller; ***Predecessor:*** No Data; ***Successor:*** No Data; ***Source:*** Zell's United State Business Directories of 1881, 1888, 1889, a 21" bell of R.E. Dewart, Edward Stickney, Bedford, Massachusetts, an email from Martin Hanoian of YMCA Camp Fuller in Wakefield, Rhode Island, a bell at the Parish Hall of St Michael's Episcopal Church in Bristol, R.I. (supplied by Carl Scott Zimmerman of St Louis, Mo. in 2002); ***Other Facts:*** In Zell's U.S. Business Directory of 1888 the address was shown as 438 S. Main, but this was probably a printing error as the address was 438 N. Main in the other two years of the directory. A large bell of about 1200 lbs is outside the original Slater Mill in Pawtucket, Rhode Island, inscribed "F. Fuller 1871 Providence R I." A 25 1/2" bell dated 1886 belongs to Neil

*F. Fuller Bell 1886*

Goeppinger of Boone, Iowa. Mr Hanoian has a copy of "Fuller's Catalog of Bells" and did research on remaining existing bells. The catalog says between 1860 and 1890 they listed 256 bells ranging in weight from 100 pound school bells to 4,000 pound fire alarm bells. This firm was run by a father then his son, both named Frederic Fuller, but the son used a "c" on the end of his first name and the father sometimes used a "c" and sometimes a "ck".

# Fuller Iron Works

***Address:*** 40 Tockwolton, Providence, Rhode Island; ***Year Established:*** No Data; ***Year Closed:*** No Data; ***Years Known In Operation:*** 1905 - 1906; ***Founder:*** No Data; ***Predecessor:*** No Data; ***Successor:*** No Data; ***Source:*** Thomas' Register 1905 - 1906. ***Other Facts:*** Advertised church bells.

# Fulton Brass & Bell Foundry

*Address:* Pittsburgh, Pennsylvania; *Year Established:* 1832; *Year Closed:* 1845; *Years Known In Operation:* 1832 - 1845; *Founder:* Andrew Fulton Sr; *Predecessor:* Andrew Fulton; *Successor:* No Data; *Source:* That Vanishing Sound; *Other Facts:* Cast a 4,000 pound fire bell for the city of Pittsburgh. The foundry burned out in the Great Pittsburgh Fire of 1845 (1/4 of Pittsburgh burned in 5 hours on April 10, 1845)

*Andrew Fulton Advertisement*

# A. Fulton & M. McDonald Brass Foundry

*Address:* 1st St. and Market Street, Pittsburgh, Pennsylvania; *Year Established:* 1847; *Year Closed:* 1847; *Years Known In Operation:* 1847; *Founder:* No Data; *Predecessor:* No Data; *Successor:* No Data; *Source:* Research papers of Lois Springer; *Other Facts:* No Data

# A. Fulton's Son & Company

*Address:* 91 1st Avenue (2nd Ave. between West and Short Streets), Pittsburgh, Pennsylvania; *Year Established:* No Data; *Year Closed:* No Data; *Years Known In Operation:* 1864 - 1892; *Founder:* Andrew Fulton Jr., the son, lived from 1850 to 1935 and was the 33rd Mayor of Pittsburgh, Pennsylvania in 1888. He started in the foundry at 16; *Predecessor:* Andrew Fulton; *Successor:* No Data; *Source:* Zell's U.S. Business Directories of 1888 and 1889, and Iva May Long of Tarentum, Pennsylvania, bell belonging to Neil Goeppinger of Boone, Iowa, and photo of 18" diameter bell dated 1890 on ABA web site post under big bells by Bonnie; *Other Facts:* The West Pennsylvania Historical Society has a bell in Oakland, Pittsburgh which is 4' high, and 5'2" in diameter, weighs 2 tons, and is dated 1866. Some of this firms bells have scallops and drapes on them, and some have a crown type top cast into them. A 33" diam one at the Corning, Iowa, Presbyterian Church is 23" tall to top of bell, plus it has a 4" crown and weighs 600 lbs. This bell is much shorter than wide, has a smoothly round top and a fast flaring, "fat" lip at the bottom. It is unlike any other bronze bell I've seen in shape (dated 1872). Their bells were bronze.

# Fulton & Reno Company

*Address:* Allegheny, Pennsylvania; *Year Established:* 1883; *Year Closed:* 1921 approximately; *Years Known In Operation:* 1883 - 1921 approx.; *Founder:* No Data; *Predecessor:* A. Fulton's Son & Company, Andrew Fulton; *Successor:* No Data; *Source:* Research papers of Lois Springer, and Iva May Long of Tarentum, Pa; *Other Facts:* Iva May Long's brother in law has a 19" diameter bell by this firm dated 1883. Allegheny, Pa. is now the north side of Pittsburgh, Pa. At one point the firm moved to Nevelle Island and operated until about 1921.

# Andrew Fulton

*Address:* Between Market and Ferry Streets, Pittsburgh, Pennsylvania; *Year Established:* 1827; *Year Closed:* 1865; *Years Known In Operation:* 1827 - 1865; *Founder:* Andrew F. Fulton; *Predecessor:* No Data; *Successor:* A. Fulton's Son & Company; *Source:* *That Vanishing Sound* and Iva May Long of Tarentum, Pennsylvania; *Other Facts:* Also cast some of their smaller undated bells under the name A. Fulton. This firm cast the first bell on the west side of the Allegheny Mountains, and also cast boat whistles and boat bells. In 2016 Brosamers Bells offered a 21" diameter river boat bell dated 1848 by this firm for sale.

# Fulton Iron & Engine Works

*Address:* Detroit, Michigan; *Year Established:* No Data; *Year Closed:* No Data; *Years Known In Operation:* 1889; *Founder:* No Data; *Predecessor:* No Data; *Successor:* No Data; *Source:* 25" bronze bell belonging to Bob Brosamer of Michigan; *Other Facts:* Inscription is oval in center of the bell's waist.

# J. Gallagher

*Address:* Pittsburgh, Pennsylvania; *Year Established:* No Data; *Year Closed:* No Data; *Years Known In Operation:* 1828; *Founder:* No Data; *Predecessor:* No Data; *Successor:* James Gallagher?; *Source:* Bell belonging to Cain Callon of Natchez, Mississippi; *Other Facts:* Above bell is inscribed "J. Gallagher Pittsb'g 1828." It is 22 3/4" in diameter and came from the Court House in Jefferson County, Mississippi. It had a wood yoke, one clapper and no stands. Because this bell was made 61 years before the only date we know the James Gallagher foundry in N.Y. was in business, I assume this is a different foundry.

# James Gallagher

*Address:* 87 Centre Street, New York City, New York; *Year Established:* No Data; *Year Closed:* No Data; *Years Known In Operation:* 1889; *Founder:* No Data; *Predecessor:* No Data; *Successor:* No Data; *Source:* Zell's U.S. Business Directory of 1889, and list submitted by Roger Plaquet to ABAII website and posted November 14, 2008 from Sid Gelman's bell papers listing bells made by New York City firms. ; *Other Facts:* No Data

# Gallagher, Long & Miller

*Address:* No Data; *Year Established:* No Data; *Year Closed:* No Data; *Years Known In Operation:* No Data; *Founder:* No Data; *Predecessor:* No Data; *Successor:* No Data; *Source:* Walter Lamb of Ohio, and bell belonging to Robert Brosamer of Michigan in July 2000; *Other Facts:* 21" bronze bell by this firm has a very unique shape, rather like early Christian bells from Eastern Europe with tall straight sides, small top, and a fast flair near the bottom, then a 45-degree straight line down to the lip. The top is approximately 6" in diameter. The iron yoke is a forged 6- or 7-sided bar, somewhat like a train bell yoke. Very heavy duty. Mr. Lamb says the yoke reminds him of the horns of an African water buffalo. No date. It may be from New York if this was a partnership of James Gallagher.

# Joseph Garratt & Son

*Address:* Mill Street, Madison, Indiana; *Year Established:* No Data; *Year Closed:* No Data; *Years Known In Operation:* 1851; *Founder:* No Data; *Predecessor:* No Data; *Successor:* No Data; *Source:* Russell F. Frehse of Kendallville, Indiana, the September 18, 1851 issue of the Daily Madison paper, and bell at Evergreen Farm, Eminence, Indiana; *Other Facts:* Mr. Frehse reports (and supplied photos of) an ornate bronze bell located at ground level at the corner of Thrid and West Streets in Madison, Indiana. The photos show the bell to be nickel plated bronze with an ornate ring of flowers below which is a scalloped ring. Above this is the ring of lettering which also is very flowery. All ornamentation is in deep relief. Another bell is at Evergreen Farm, Eminence, Indiana. It also is ornamented and reads Madison, IA (old abbreviation for Indiana?) and is dated 1851. I postulate the "nickel plate" is actually the tin patina.

*Joseph Garratt and Son Advertisement*

# J. W. Garratt Brass Foundry Co.

*Address:* St Louis, Missouri; *Year Established:* No Data; *Year Closed:* No Data; *Years Known In Operation:* 1900 - 1906; *Founder:* No Data; *Predecessor:* J. W. Garratt & Co; *Successor:* Hewitt Mfg. Co; *Source:* Research of Carl Scott Zimmerman of St Louis, Mo. Posted on his website, towerbells.org; *Other Facts:* No Data

# J. W. Garratt & Co

*Address:* St Louis, Missouri; *Year Established:* No Data; *Year Closed:* No Data; *Years Known In Operation:* 1880 - 1899; *Founder:* No Data; *Predecessor:* No Data; *Successor:* J. W. Garratt Brass Foundry Co; *Source:* Research of Carl Scott Zimmerman of St Louis, Mo. Posted on his website, towerbells.org; *Other Facts:* No Data

# Garratt & Company

*Address:* Folsom St. at Fremont St. (about 3 blocks from the Embarcadero) in downtown San Francisco, California; *Year Established:* No Data; *Year Closed:* No Data; *Years Known In Operation:* 1885; *Founder:* William Thompson Garratt (1829 - 1890); *Predecessor:* No Data; *Successor:* No Data; *Source:* Ryan Cooper of Yarmouthport, Mass., an ABAII website post dated May 25, 2006 by Jeff Garratt, descendant of W. T. Garrett, and ABAII website inquiry by Chuck Schoppe of Los Gatos, Ca. who has a 21 1/4" diameter bell by W. T. Garratt dated 1885; *Other Facts:* Mr. Cooper used to have a 16" ship bell by this firm. Jeff Garratt states "There are many bells in the area, but none for sale." referring to W. T. Garratt bells.

*Garratt and Son Madison Ia (early abbreviation for Indiana)*

# J. Garrett

*Address:* Cincinnati, Ohio; *Year Established:* No Data; *Year Closed:* No Data; *Years Known In Operation:* 1849; *Founder:* No Data; *Predecessor:* No Data; *Successor:* No Data; *Source:* Russell Frehse of Kendallville, Indiana; *Other Facts:* Mr. Frehse reports a 36" bronze bell which was a station bell and is presently near the James F.D. Lanier House on the State Museums and Memorials property in Madison, Indiana. It hung at the old station of the Madison and Indianapolis Railroad on the riverfront about 1850. Mr Frehse states that "it is a beautiful, ornate bell...".

# W. T. Garratt & Son

*Address:* 140 Fremont street, San Francisco, California; *Year Established:* No Data; *Year Closed:* No Data; *Years Known In Operation:* 1881 - 1910; *Founder:* No Data; *Predecessor:* No Data; *Successor:* No Data; *Source:* *That Vanishing Sound*, and Zell's U.S. Business Directories of 1881 & 1889, and Thomas' Register 1905 - 1906; *Other Facts:* No Data

# John A. Gifford & Sons

*Address:* New York City, New York; *Year Established:* No Data; *Year Closed:* No Data; *Years Known In Operation:* No Data; *Founder:* No Data; *Predecessor:* No Data; *Successor:* No Data; *Source:* List submitted by Roger Plaquet to ABAII website and posted November 14, 2008 from Sid Gelman's bell papers listing bells made by New York City firms. ; *Other Facts:* No Data

# Gilbert & Meredith

*Address:* No Data; *Year Established:* No Data; *Year Closed:* No Data; *Years Known In Operation:* No Data; *Founder:* No Data; *Predecessor:* No Data; *Successor:* No Data; *Source:* Martha Tatum inquiry with photos of bell on June 18, 2003; *Other Facts:* This is an 18" diameter dinner bell with a ridge above the lip and a small top (pre Civil War shape). It has a long tang attached to the top for ringing, with a counter weight extending on the other side of the tang.

# Giron

*Address:* San Antonio, Texas; *Year Established:* No Data; *Year Closed:* No Data; *Years Known In Operation:* 1870 - 1871; *Founder:* Giron; *Predecessor:* No Data; *Successor:* No Data; *Source:* *Bells Over Texas* by Bessie Lee Fitzhugh (Carl Hertzog El Paso, Texas, Texas Western Press, 1955); *Other Facts:* Giron was a bell founder operating out of Juarez, Mexico. He came to and cast a bell for The Presidio of San Elizario in 1870 - 1871 in what is now San Antonio, Texas. "Excavations in the church yard have unearthed bits of metal and revealed traces of a furnace." "In the early days a migratory bell founder often set up temporary foundries in the yards of those churches for which he worked."

# Globe Bell & Brass Foundry

*Address:* 137 Beale in 1889 (292 Howard in 1888), (128 Main in 1906), San Francisco, California; *Year Established:* No Data; *Year Closed:* No Data; *Years Known In Operation:* 1888 - 1906; *Founder:* No Data; *Predecessor:* No Data; *Successor:* No Data; *Source:* *That Vanishing Sound*, and Zell's U.S. Business Directories of 1888 and 1889, and Thomas' Register 1905 - 1906; *Other Facts:* No Data

# Globe Furniture Company

*Address:* Northville, Michigan; *Year Established:* No Data; *Year Closed:* No Data; *Years Known In Operation:* No Data; *Founder:* No Data; *Predecessor:* No Data; *Successor:* American Bell Foundry Company; *Source:* Bell located in private wildlife park just N.W. of Peoria, Illinois (outside of old restored school), and June 1982 Mill Race Quarterly of Northville Historical Society; *Other Facts:* Did business as American Bell Foundry, burned in 1899 and buildings and patterns were purchased by new owners who changed the name to American Bell Foundry Company.

# Godfrey & Meyer

*Address:* Baltimore, Maryland; *Year Established:* No Data; *Year Closed:* No Data; *Years Known In Operation:* 1828; *Founder:* No Data; *Predecessor:* No Data; *Successor:* No Data; *Source:* Bell owned by John Hash of Hillsville, Virginia; *Other Facts:* Above bell is 13" in diameter, has letters 1" tall, an iron yoke and arm for a rope.

# Gong Bell Manufacturing Company

*Address:* East Hampton, Connecticut; *Year Established:* No Data; *Year Closed:* No Data; *Years Known In Operation:* 1866 - 1906; *Founder:* No Data; *Predecessor:* No Data; *Successor:* No Data; *Source:* Zell's U.S. Business Directories of 1888 and 1889, Thomas' Register of 1905 - 1906, and East Hampton Connecticut Bicentennial Celebration 1966 pamphlet; *Other Facts:* Advertised Engine and Steamboat bells in 1906.

# Good & Moores

*Address:* 21 Ohio Street, Buffalo, New York; *Year Established:* No Data; *Year Closed:* No Data; *Years Known In Operation:* 1855 (and likely in the 1870's according to Morrison); *Founder:* A. Good and William P. Moores; *Predecessor:* No Data; *Successor:* No Data; *Source:* Wayne E. Morrison of Ovid, N.Y. in his letter of 4/3/1984. The Buffalo Business Directory, Volume 1, 1855 (thru New York State Historical Association); *Other Facts:* Wayne Morrison sent me a photo of a bell made by this firm which he took in Seneca Falls, New York. It was a 24" diameter bell with a 36" diameter cast wheel with 6 curved spokes. The bell was bronze and the cast iron stands say Good & Moores on them. In the 1855 advertisement they list "Brass & Bell Founders and Manufacturers. A. Good, Wm P. Moores." In 1855 one of their sales outlets was Pratt & Co of Buffalo, New York which also sold the Lafayette Bell Foundry line of bells.

# Jesse Goodyear

*Address:* Hamden, Connecticut; *Year Established:* 1791; *Year Closed:* No Data; *Years Known In Operation:* 1791; *Founder:* Jesse Goodyear; *Predecessor:* Doolittle & Goodyear of Hartford, Conn; *Successor:* No Data; *Source:* Winthrop Warren of Fairfield, Connecticut; *Other Facts:* No Data

# Goulds Manufacturing Company

*Address:* 60 Barclay, Seneca Falls (New York City), New York; *Year Established:* No Data; *Year Closed:* No Data; *Years Known In Operation:* 1830 - 1905; *Founder:* No Data; *Predecessor:* No Data; *Successor:* No Data; *Source:* Zell's U.S. Business Directory of 1888, Thomas' Register 1905 - 1906, and letter from Goulds Pumps, Inc of 4 - 5-1982, many bells, and Carl Scott Zimmerman of St Louis, Mo.; *Other Facts:* Bells in Tiffin, Iowa, and belonging to Neil Goeppinger of Boone, Iowa read "The Goulds Mfg Co, Seneca Falls, N.Y." so the firm was located in that city at some time in its existence. The bells were undated and made of cast iron. There also is a 30" bell in front of the Lancaster Christian Church just southeast of Sigourney, Iowa, near the airport. Another bell owned by Leonard Fleischer of Columbus, Nebraksa, reads "Seneca Falls, N.Y." Another 24" on the state capitol grounds of Augusta, Maine, reads "Seneca Falls, New York". Carl Scott Zimmerman postulates that the New York City address may have only been a sales office address for the firm. Their 33" steel bell weighed 414 pounds and cost $75 sometime prior to 1848.

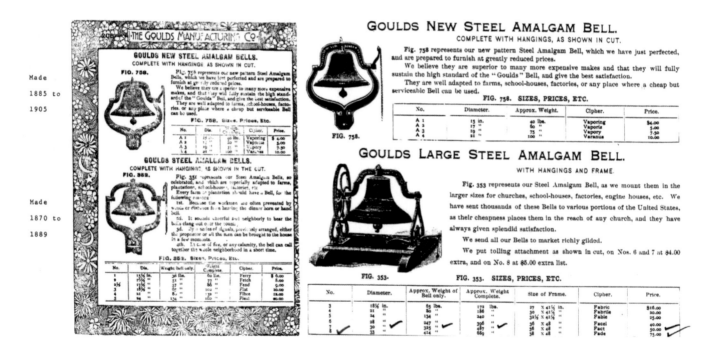

*Goulds Manufacturing Company Advertisements*

# Goulds and Ostrander

*Address:* 8th and South East Corner of St. Charles Street, St. Louis, Missouri; *Year Established:* No Data; *Year Closed:* No Data; *Years Known In Operation:* 1880 - 1881; *Founder:* No Data; *Predecessor:* Bignall & Ostrander, and M. C. Bignall & Co; *Successor:* N. O. Nelson Mfg. Co; *Source:* 1873 - 1899 City Directories (thru Carl Scott Zimmerman of St Louis, Mo., and L. Elsinore Springer); *Other Facts:* Two of the partners in this firm were J. H. Gould and S. S. Gould Jr. both of Seneca Falls, N.Y., so they were likely related to the Goulds Mfg. Co. of Seneca Falls, N.Y.

# Greenberg & Company

*Address:* 205 Fremont in 1881, 205 Front in 1888, San Francisco, California; *Year Established:* No Data; *Year Closed:* No Data; *Years Known In Operation:* 1881 - 1888; *Founder:* No Data; *Predecessor:* No Data; *Successor:* No Data; *Source:* Zell's United States Business Directory of 1881 and 1888; *Other Facts:* No Data

# George W. Gregg

*Address:* 10 Spruce (1888 - 1898), 1629 Clark Ave (1899 - 1901), 219 South 20th (1902), St. Louis, Missouri; *Year Established:* No Data; *Year Closed:* No Data; *Years Known In Operation:* 1888 - 1902; *Founder:* George W. Gregg; *Predecessor:* No Data; *Successor:* No Data; *Source:* 1890 Gould's City Directory & 1898 1899 City Directory and 1898 - 1899 Missouri Gazetteer and Business Directory (thru Missouri Historical Society), and research of Carl Scott Zimmerman of St Louis, Mo. ; *Other Facts:* Also known as G. W. Gregg in 1898 and 1899 when advertised "Bell Metal Castings". In 1890 - 1891, 1893 - 1894, and 1898 he was classified under the heading "Bell, Gong (Mfrs)."

# James Gregory

*Address:* Cannon at Stanton, New York City, New York; *Year Established:* No Data; *Year Closed:* No Data; *Years Known In Operation:* 1850 - 1889; *Founder:* No Data; *Predecessor:* William Buckley; *Successor:* No Data; *Source:* Zell's U.S. Business Directories of 1888 and 1889, an article "James Gregory and the Dreamland Bell" dated October 11, 2009 by David Grider, architect and posted on the Internet at davidgrider.com, and emails between Carl Scott Zimmerman of St Louis, Mo. and Fred Dahlinger regarding circus bells; *Other Facts:* James Gregory was an apprentice of William Buckley and took over his business in 1850 upon Buckley's death. In 1880 he cast the "Mechanic's Bell" which, according to Mr. Grider, was "rung by the workers of Manhattan's 19th century shipyards to mark the 10-hour day they had won from owners accustomed to working them much longer". This firm also made a set of show bells for the Barnum Circus.

# Hall & Allen

*Address:* Mansfield, Ohio; *Year Established:* No Data; *Year Closed:* No Data; *Years Known In Operation:* No Data; *Founder:* No Data; *Predecessor:* No Data; *Successor:* No Data; *Source:* Bell belonging to Ed Young of Riverside (Kansas City) Missouri; *Other Facts:* Cast iron bell.

# Hall & Whittermore

*Address:* Havana, New York; *Year Established:* 1866; *Year Closed:* 1880; *Years Known In Operation:* 1866 - 1880; *Founder:* No Data; *Predecessor:* No Data; *Successor:* No Data; *Source:* Wayne E. Morrison, Sr. of Ovid, New York; *Other Facts:* This firm made at least two iron bells. An 800 lb. one for the Methodist Church in Havana made in 1868 and one for a school in that city. There are records referring to both bells but both are missing in 1986. The main business of the firm was pottery, agricultural equipment and boilers. The name of Havana was changed to Montoure Falls, New York in 1895.

# Benjamin Hanks Foundry

*Address:* Gibbonsville (later town name changed to West Troy, then to Watervliet), New York; *Year Established:* 1785; *Year Closed:* 1826; *Years Known In Operation:* 1785 - 1826; *Founder:* Benjamin Hanks; *Predecessor:* No Data; *Successor:* Hanks & Meneely; *Source:* Mrs. G. Lyle Ringland, *That Vanishing Sound*, Winthrop Warren of

Fairfield, Connecticut, a Hanks family history The Trojan Bell Founders (thru Rensselaer County Historical Society), and genealogical research by Carl Scott Zimmerman of St Louis, Mo; *Other Facts:* According to Mrs. Ringland the firm was started in Duxburry, Massachusetts, in 1785, then moved to Storrs, Conn (in Mansfield County), then moved to West Troy in 1808. An apprentice, Andrew Meneely, married Benjamin Hank's niece, Phelina, and started the Hanks and Meneely firm in 1826. The name was later changed to Meneely & Co and continued in operation until 1950. Other sources say it started out in either Litchfield or Duxburry, Connecticut, in 1785 and moved to Mansfield, Connecticut in 1790. In any case they were in a close geographic area. A 932 lb Bell in Hadley, Massachusetts has "Mansfield" on it. A 932 lb bell in Hadley, Mass has "Mansfield" on it. He first operated on Hanks Hill, which became part of Mansfield, Conn. Mansfield later became part of what is now Storrs, Conn. Later, Benjamine and his son Julius (George L. Hank's cousin) moved their bell making to Gibbonsville, N. Y. (later called West Troy).

# Julius Hanks

*Address:* Gibbonsville, New York; *Year Established:* 1808; *Year Closed:* No Data; *Years Known In Operation:* 1808 - 1830; *Founder:* Benjamin Hanks (Father) and Julius Hanks; *Predecessor:* Benjamin Hanks Foundry; *Successor:* Meneely & Company; *Source: That Vanishing Sound,* Winthrop Warren of Fairfield, Connecticut, a Hanks family history The Trojan Bellfounders (thru Rensselaer County Historical Society), and an article in The Daily Star of Oneonta, N. Y. on May 29, 1999; *Other Facts:* The town name was changed from Gibbonsville to West Troy, and then in 1896 its name was changed to its present name of Watervliet, New York. A bell dated 1815 was at Hartwick College in Oneonta, N.Y. in April 2002.

*Julius Hanks Bell 1829*

# Hanks & Meneely Company

*Address:* West Troy, New York; *Year Established:* 1826; *Year Closed:* 1850 approx; *Years Known In Operation:* 1826 - 1850; *Founder:* Julius Hanks and Andrew Meneely; *Predecessor:* Julius Hanks; *Successor:* No Data; *Source: That Vanishing Sound,* and Hanks family history The Trojan Bell Founders (thru Rensselaer County Historical Society); *Other Facts:* No Data

# A & T Hanks

*Address:* Troy, New York; *Year Established:* 1830; *Year Closed:* 1834; *Years Known In Operation:* 1830 - 1834; *Founder:* Alpheus Hanks (uncle of Julius) and Truman Hanks (brother of Julius); *Predecessor:* Julius Hanks; *Successor:* No Data; *Source:* Winthrop Warren of Fairfield, Connecticut; *Other Facts:* 32" A & T Hanks bell dated 1831 in Rensselaer County Historical Society, Troy, N.Y. They made bronze bells.

# O. Hanks

*Address:* Troy, New York; *Year Established:* 1834; *Year Closed:* 1855; *Years Known In Operation:* 1834 - 1855; *Founder:* Oscar Hanks; *Predecessor:* A & T Hanks; *Successor:* No Data; *Source:* Winthrop Warren of Fairfield, Connecticut; *Other Facts:* Bell in Milton, Connecticut, Church.

## Hanks & McGraw

*Address:* Cincinnati, Ohio; *Year Established:* No Data; *Year Closed:* No Data; *Years Known In Operation:* No Data; *Founder:* No Data; *Predecessor:* No Data; *Successor:* No Data; *Source:* Photos of 19 inch diameter bell belonging to Todd Lower of Lowerbells.com in 2016, and a bell belonging to Robert Cowie of Paris, Ark; *Other Facts:* The Lower bell is bronze, 17" to 18" in diameter, has a flat tang on top with a round hole for a cross bolt and is simply inscribed with "HANKS & McGRAW." in large block letters with no city or date. It appears to be well finished. The Cowie bell is 26" in diameter and has the city inscribed. It has a large tang on top for mounting.

## George L. Hanks

*Address:* Columbus Street (also 120 & 122 E. 2nd St.), Cincinnati, Ohio; *Year Established:* No Data; *Year Closed:* No Data; *Years Known In Operation:* 1847 - 1859; *Founder:* George Lucius Hanks; *Predecessor:* No Data; *Successor:* No Data; *Source:* That Vanishing Sound, and genealogical research of Carl Scott Zimmerman of St Louis, Mo; *Other Facts:* Made bells up to 5,000 lbs. One weighing 3,400 lbs. was located in St Peter in Chains Cathedral in Cincinnati which was very ornate and dated 1851. In 1955 this bell was transferred to St. Teresa Church in Cincinnati. He was a nephew of Col. Benjamin Hanks who operated a bell foundry at Hanks Hill in what is now Storrs, Connecticut. George Hanks' cousins were Nancy Hanks, the mother of President Abraham Lincoln, and another bell founder, Julius Hanks, son of Col. Benjamin Hanks.

BELLS! BELLS! BELLS!

The subscriber is extensively engaged in manufacturing

**BELLS OF EVERY SIZE**

USED BY

Churches, Colleges, Public Buildings, Steam-boats, Plantations, etc.

His Bells are constructed upon true and correct principles in their form and thickness, and in the proportion and combination of metals ; thus attaining

The Greatest Degree of Sonorousness,

The most melodious tone, and the requisite strength and durability.

An assortment of medium sizes are kept on hand, enabling purchasers to hear and judge of their quality for themselves.

Larger sizes, and, if desired, of a particular tone and key, and

*Chimes of any Number or Size of Bells,*

cast at a short notice.

Bells cast at this foundery are furnished with springs, to prevent the unpleasant sound produced by the clapper jarring on the Bell, and the most approved plan of iron yokes, wheels and frames.

A warrantee against breakage of Bell or hangings—if properly rung—is given for one year. Communications will receive prompt attention by addressing

GEORGE L. HANKS,
*Nos. 120 and 122 East Second Street, Cincinnati.*

1859.

*George L. Hanks Advertisement*

# Hardy & Newsom

*Address:* La Grange, North Carolina; *Year Established:* No Data; *Year Closed:* No Data; *Years Known In Operation:* No Data; *Founder:* No Data; *Predecessor:* No Data; *Successor:* No Data; *Source:* Milford Turner; *Other Facts:* Made dinner bells in the 1990's in 11", 14" and 18" diameters.

# William Harpke

*Address:* 9 N. 3rd (1865 - 1866), St. Louis, Missouri; *Year Established:* No Data; *Year Closed:* No Data; *Years Known In Operation:* 1865 - 1873; *Founder:* William Harpke; *Predecessor:* David Caughlan (William Harpke was a moulder in this foundry before starting his own firm); *Successor:* No Data; *Source:* Gould's 1900 Directory for St. Louis & 1867 - 1868 City Directories (thru Missouri Historical Society) and research papers of Carl Scott Zimmerman of St Louis, Mo; *Other Facts:* Zimmerman says they did business as Central Bell & Brass Foundry (1865 - 1869). Other addresses for the foundry were 16 N. 3rd (1867 - 1872), 317 N. 3rd (1873 - 1884), 313 N. 3rd (1885), 216 Locust (1886 - 1887). (Do you suppose they didn't pay their rent on time?)

# Harpke & Dauernheim

*Address:* St Louis, Missouri; *Year Established:* No Data; *Year Closed:* No Data; *Years Known In Operation:* 1870 - 1873; *Founder:* William Harpke, Louis/Lewis(?) Dauernheim; *Predecessor:* No Data; *Successor:* No Data; *Source:* Carl Scott Zimmerman of St Louis, Mo. Review of business directories for St Louis 1860 - 1900; *Other Facts:* Primarily a brass foundry; bells are mentioned in business listings only until 1873, but could well have been made later.

# Harpke Manufacturing Company

*Address:* 307 Cedar, St Louis, Missouri; *Year Established:* No Data; *Year Closed:* No Data; *Years Known In Operation:* 1888 - 1891; *Founder:* William Harpke; *Predecessor:* Harpke & Dauernheim (1865 - 1869), William Harpke (1867 - 1873); *Successor:* No Data; *Source:* Research papers of Carl Scott Zimmerman of St Louis, Mo; *Other Facts:* No Data

# J. C. Harrington

*Address:* West Main Street, near Central depot, Oskaloosa, Iowa; *Year Established:* No Data; *Year Closed:* No Data; *Years Known In Operation:* 1885; *Founder:* John C. Harrington; *Predecessor:* No Data; *Successor:* No Data; *Source:* Old advertising card and 16 1/2" bell belonging to Neil Goeppinger of Boone, Iowa and interview with Dennis Liebus, grandson of August Gottslich who worked in the foundry. Liebus later bought original Harrington casting forms and cast both bells and parts in the late 1960s and early 1970s; *Other Facts:* Above bell has the name of the firm cast in the bell, not the yoke. On old advertising card it states "Iron Founder and manufacturer of FARM BELLS! Iron Fences, Iron Stairways, Stoves, Mill Gearing and General Casting." Mary Noe researched and could find no connection between this firm and the W. S. Harrington firm of Belleville, Ohio.

*J. C. Harrington Advertisement*

# W. S. Harrington

*Address:* Belleville (Mansfield), Ohio; *Year Established:* No Data; *Year Closed:* No Data; *Years Known In Operation:* 1864 - 1888; *Founder:* Wilson Shannon Harrington; *Predecessor:* No Data; *Successor:* No Data; *Source:* Zell's U.S. Business Directory of 1888, a 16 3/4" bell belonging to Mary Noe of Kellogg, Iowa, an email dated 12/27/2006 from Peggy Mershon of Bellville, Ohio, and a letter from Robert Jeffrey of Clio, Michigan; *Other Facts:* Mary Noe researched and could find no connection between this firm and the J. C. Harrington firm of Oskaloosa, Iowa. The Jeffrey bell reads Mansfield, Ohio instead of Belleville, Ohio.

*W. S. Harrington Bell*

# Harrison and Davis

*Address:* No Data; *Year Established:* No Data; *Year Closed:* No Data; *Years Known In Operation:* No Data; *Founder:* No Data; *Predecessor:* No Data; *Successor:* Veazey and White Co; *Source:* ABAII website inquiry by Jeff Bell dated July 6, 2007; *Other Facts:* Mr. Bell believes this firm was not from the New England area. It was making large bells, was purchased by Hiram Veazey of Veazey and White Co., and then they started making large bells in East Hampton, Conn. Prior to the purchase, Veazey and White had been making small bells.

# James L. Haven Company

*Address:* Cincinnati, Ohio; *Year Established:* 1845; *Year Closed:* 1954; *Years Known In Operation:* 1845-1954; *Founder:* James L. Haven; *Predecessor:* No Data; *Successor:* No Data; *Source:* Jim Haven, great grandson of above bell founder, and bells owned by Neil Goeppinger of Boone, Iowa and Ben Tuck of Lebanon, Pa; *Other Facts:* Firm made bells and agricultural related products (cane, cider mills, sausage grinders, etc). Likely quit making bells around 1897 when they discontinued agricultural products and concentrated on industrial items. See "Haven Malleable Castings Company" entry for more information. See Hedges, Free & Company of Cincinnati, Ohio for a possible connection. The Tuck bell is 18" in diameter and is their #3 size bell, and the Goeppinger bell is 27" in diameter and says "Jas L. Haven Steel Composition Bell" around the bell just above the sound bow.

*J. L. Haven and Company Composition Steel Church Bell*

## Haven Malleable Castings Company

*Address:* Cincinnati, Ohio; *Year Established:* 1846; *Year Closed:* No Data; *Years Known In Operation:* 1846; *Founder:* Jos. L. Haven; *Predecessor:* No Data; *Successor:* No Data; *Source:* Mrs. G. Lyle Ringland of Norwood, Ohio. Bell owned by Neil Goeppinger, Boone, Iowa; *Other Facts:* Also did business as Jos. L. Haven Co. Made steel composition bells similar to those of the C. S. Bell Co. of Hillsboro, Ohio. Unique to this firm, at least some of their bells had the company name and city cast into the bell about 2" above the bottom lip in approximately 1 1/2" tall letters circling the bell, along with the words "STEEL COMPOSITION BELL". Also made dinner bells, some with the name on the bell, and some with it on the yoke. See "James L. Haven Company" entry for more information.

## William Hedderly

*Address:* 38 Nassau Street, near John Street, New York City, New York; *Year Established:* No Data; *Year Closed:* No Data; *Years Known In Operation:* No Data; *Founder:* William Hedderly; *Predecessor:* No Data; *Successor:* No Data; *Source:* Louis Springer letter of 3 - 3 - 1985, her source: Dictionary of Colonial Craftsmen, and The Arts and Crafts of New York 1777 - 1799; *Other Facts:* Church, ship and house bell founder. May have been brother of George Hedderly.

## Bailey & Hedderly

*Address:* Little Dock Street, New York, New York; *Year Established:* 1794; *Year Closed:* 1795; *Years Known In Operation:* 1794 - 1795; *Founder:* John Bailey and George Hedderly; *Predecessor:* No Data; *Successor:* No Data; *Source:* "George Hedderly, Bellfounder on Two Continents," available at georgedawson. homestead.com (author could be George Dawson), New York Daily Advertiser, April 21, 1794, and research material supplied by Gary A. Trudgen of Endwell, N.Y in 1994; *Other Facts:* 4 bells known by this firm. One at Museum of City of New York, one at Reformed Church, New Platz, New York, one in private ownership, and one at Dyrham Park, The Garden House,. Gloucestershire, UK. The N.Y. Daily Advertiser stated "Geo. Hedderly from England, and John Bailey No. 20 Little Dock street, New-York begs leave to inform the citizens of United States, that they have established a bell foundry, in the Bowery, where they intend casting Bells, or peals of church bells set to music. Also plantation, turret, ship and hand bells, church turret, or house bells, hung on the most modern construction..."

*Bailey and Hedderly 1794 Advertisement*

# George Hedderly

*Address:* 63 South 5th Street, Philadelphia, Pennsylvania; *Year Established:* 1800; *Year Closed:* No Data; *Years Known In Operation:* 1800 - 1813; *Founder:* George Hedderly; *Predecessor:* William Hedderly foundry in N.Y., Daniel Hedderly foundry in Nottingham, England which closed in 1794; *Successor:* Edwin Hedderly, eldest son of George Hedderly, and Thomas Washigton Levering; *Source:* Phone conversation with Carl Scott Zimmerman of St Louis, Mo. on 3 - 10 - 1997, and paper titled "George Hedderly, Bellfounder on Two Continents" by George Dawson(?), and article "The Courthouse Bell Rings Once Again..." by Joan Blank available at the ABAII website and at historicwilliamsport.com/joanblank. html, and bell belonging to Todd Lowrer when he was in Toledo, Ohio; *Other Facts:* Old family foundry in Nottingham England closed in 1794 and George

*George Hedderly Advertisement*

Hedderly emigrated to New York City where he made bells with John Bailey. In 1800 George went to Philadelphia, Pa. Both set up new bell foundries. Bells by this foundry are in the Orange Co Courthouse in Hillsborough, North Carolina dated 1805 and in Wake County (which includes Raleigh), North Carolina, dated 1804. Both are marked Philadelphia. Large bells by this firm have been found with dates 1805 - 1813 with the exception of 1810. I am sure he cast bells in1810 also, they just haven't been found. The Joan Blank article lists the location of 6 of his bells. The Lowrer bell was 22" in diameter, bronze and dated 1812. It had crude reeds and was shaped rather like a Meneely bell.

# Edwin Hedderly

*Address:* Philadelphia, Pennsylvania; *Year Established:* 1813; *Year Closed:* 1821; *Years Known In Operation:* 1813 - 1821; *Founder:* Edwin Hedderly; *Predecessor:* No Data; *Successor:* No Data; *Source:* George Hedderly Bellfounder On Two Continents by George Dawson(?), and bell belonging to the Bucks County Historical Society of Pennsylvania from the Bucks County Academy dated 1821 (via an ABAII website inquiry of Lynette Greenwald of Doylestown, Pa on 8/10/2005); *Other Facts:* Edwin was the son of George Hedderly and cast bells from his father's death in 1813 until his own death in 1821 at age 27. Known bells by Edwin are in the Doylestown, Pa. Courthouse dated 1813, in St Peters Lutheran Church, Middletown, Pa., dated 1815, in the Lynchberg, Virginia Methodist Church (undated) and in Bucks County Academy, Doylestown, Pa., dated 1821.

# Hedges, Free & Company

*Address:* Cincinnati, Ohio; *Year Established:* No Data; *Year Closed:* No Data; *Years Known In Operation:* No Data; *Founder:* No Data; *Predecessor:* No Data; *Successor:* No Data; *Source:* Bell owned by Vic Sinderman who inquired about it on ABAII website on 7 - 11 - 2009; *Other Facts:* The Sinderman bell is 27" in diameter and 22" tall. At the top it says No 55, and around the bottom it says "Iron Amalgam Bells By Hedges, Free & Co. Cinn. O." There is another firm which made a similar inscription around the bottom of their ferris bells. Their inscription read "J. L. Haven & Co Cincinnati O. Steel Composition Bell". This was on a 30" bell. Because few makers of iron or steel bells put inscriptions on their bells (usually just on the mountings), and fewer still did it on bells larger than dinner bells, and because both these firms were in Cincinnati, I suspect there was a connection between the firms.

# Henry-Bonnard Company

***Address:*** Cleveland, Ohio; ***Year Established:*** No Data; ***Year Closed:*** No Data; ***Years Known In Operation:*** prior to 1925; ***Founder:*** No Data; ***Predecessor:*** No Data; ***Successor:*** No Data; ***Source:*** *Bells, Their History, Legends, Making, and Uses* by Satis N. Coleman, Rand McNally & Co., 1928; ***Other Facts:*** This firm cast a very ornate, large ship's bell prior to 1925 for the U.S. Cleveland navy ship. Part of the wording around the rim read "Citizens of Cleveland" and it had a man in bah relief around the waist of the bell. The fact that the Henry-Bonnard Co. was located in Cleveland is not certain. To have cast a bell this ornate (it's pictured in the above book on page 393) the firm must have had prior bell casting experience to gain the ability to cast such a bell,

# Hewitt Mfg. Co.

***Address:*** St Louis, Missouri; ***Year Established:*** No Data; ***Year Closed:*** No Data; ***Years Known In Operation:*** 1904 - 1912; ***Founder:*** No Data; ***Predecessor:*** J. W. Garratt & Co; ***Successor:*** No Data; ***Source:*** Research of Carl Scott Zimmerman of St Louis, Mo. Posted on his website, towerbells.org; ***Other Facts:*** No Data

# Hibbard, Spencer, Bartlett & Company

***Address:*** Next to the State Street Bridge in downtown., Chicago, Illinois; ***Year Established:*** No Data; ***Year Closed:*** No Data; ***Years Known In Operation:*** 1886; ***Founder:*** No Data; ***Predecessor:*** No Data; ***Successor:*** No Data; ***Source:*** Bell owned by Clarence Kline of Prescott, Iowa (died in October, 1985), bell post of 4 - 8 - 2010 by Holly on the ABAII website regarding a 13 1/2" dinner bell, and research of Carl Scott Zimmerman of St Louis, Mo; ***Other Facts:*** This was a large wholesale hardware firm with sales of $1 million in 1867 and $30 million in 1948. They developed the "True Value" hardware line. The owners were William G. Hibbard, Franklin F. Spencer and A. C. Bartlett. I believe they had some foundry or foundries make bells for them with their name on the yokes. They were iron or steel bells.

# N. N. Hill Brass Company

***Address:*** East Hampton, Connecticut; ***Year Established:*** 1889; ***Year Closed:*** No Data; ***Years Known In Operation:*** 1889 - 1906; ***Founder:*** No Data; ***Predecessor:*** No Data; ***Successor:*** No Data; ***Source:*** Thomas' Register 1905 - 1906, and East Hampton Connecticut Bicentennial Celebration 1967 pamphlet; ***Other Facts:*** Advertised school and church bells.

# Hillsboro Ohio Bell Company

***Address:*** Hillsboro, Ohio; ***Year Established:*** No Data; ***Year Closed:*** No Data; ***Years Known In Operation:*** No Data; ***Founder:*** No Data; ***Predecessor:*** No Data; ***Successor:*** No Data; ***Source:*** Eugene P. Burns, Troy, N.Y; ***Other Facts:*** No Data

# Hish Brothers

***Address:*** No Data; ***Year Established:*** No Data; ***Year Closed:*** No Data; ***Years Known In Operation:*** No Data; ***Founder:*** No Data; ***Predecessor:*** No Data; ***Successor:*** No Data; ***Source:*** 28" diameter iron bell in Ben Tuck collection in Lebanon, Pa; ***Other Facts:*** No Data

# A. Hissler

*Address:* 192 Dumaine, New Orleans, Louisiana; *Year Established:* No Data; *Year Closed:* No Data; *Years Known In Operation:* 1888 - 1889; *Founder:* No Data; *Predecessor:* No Data; *Successor:* No Data; *Source:* Zell's U.S. Business Directories of 1888 and 1889; *Other Facts:* No Data

# Colonel Aaron Hobart

*Address:* Abington, Massachusetts; *Year Established:* 1761; *Year Closed:* No Data; *Years Known In Operation:* 1761 - 1791; *Founder:* No Data; *Predecessor:* No Data; *Successor:* No Data; *Source:* *That Vanishing Sound*, Edward Stickney, Bedford, Massachusetts; *Other Facts:* The first major bell foundry in the U.S. A bell at the Salisbury, New Hampshire, Community Church is inscribed "A.H. 1791." He learned bell casting from an Englishman named Gillimore who deserted the British Navy. Gillimore had worked in a bell foundry in England before joining the military. After the Revolutionary War, Paul Revere was owed money by the new government for casting cannon during the war. The government gave Revere some of the cannon as part payment but Rever needed to convert the bronze to something he could sell. Hobart sent his son Benjamine and Gillimore to Boston to teach Revere how to cast bells. Col. Hobart also cast cannon for the Revolutionary War. See J. Webb entry, page 164.

# Major George Holbrook

*Address:* East Medway (later Millis), Massachusetts; *Year Established:* 1798; *Year Closed:* 1880; *Years Known In Operation:* 1798 - 1880; *Founder:* George Handel Holbrook; *Predecessor:* Paul Revere 3rd; *Successor:* Holbrook & Son; *Source:* Winthrop Warren of Fairfield, Connecticut, *That Vanishing Sound*, Edward Stickney of Bedford, Massachusetts, Milford Daily News, Sat Aug 7, 1933, and Old Colony Historical Society, Taunton, Massachusetts 1806; *Other Facts:* Holbrook originally was an apprentice of Paul Revere. He left in 1798 to start his own foundry in Brookfield, Massachusetts that same year. He had financial problems in 1811 and closed the business. He then started up again in 1816 in East Medway. His successor was still in business in 1889 listed in Zells United States Business Directory. This firm also made undated bells inscribed G.H.H. which stood for George H. Holbrook. Bells with this inscription were owned by Winston Jones of Evergreen, Colorado and Neil Goeppinger, Boone, Iowa. All bells are bronze. The Unitarian Church

*George Holbrook Bell 1837*

bell in Taunton Massachusetts reads "FOR TAUNTON I TO THE CHURCH THE LIVING CALL. AND TO THE GRAVE I SUMMONS ALL. GEORGE HOLBROOK BROOKFIELD MASSACHUSETTS 1804" Major George Holbrook was succeeded by his son Colonel George H. Holbrook, a musician, then by the Colonel's son E. L. Holbrook, Esq., then by the Colonel's grandson, Edwin H. Holbrook. This firm cast over 11,000 bells.

# Edwin H. Holbrook

*Address:* Medway, Massachusetts; *Year Established:* 1871; *Year Closed:* 1880; *Years Known In Operation:* 1871 - 1880; *Founder:* Edwin H. Holbrook, grandson of Colonel George Holbrook; *Predecessor:* Holbrook & Son; *Successor:* No Data; *Source:* Winthrop Warren of Fairfield, Connecticut; *Other Facts:* Edwin H. Holbrook joined his grandfather's firm in 1867 and carried on the business after his grandfather retired in 1871. In 1880 he sold the business to a Western firm.

# Holbrook & Son

*Address:* East M Street, Medway, Massachusetts; *Year Established:* No Data; *Year Closed:* No Data; *Years Known In Operation:* 1888, 1889; *Founder:* Major George Holbrook and his son Colonel George Handel Holbrook; *Predecessor:* Major George Holbrook; *Successor:* No Data; *Source:* Zell's United States Business Directory (1888 & 1889); *Other Facts:* No Data

# Holly Manufacturing Company

*Address:* Lockport, New York; *Year Established:* No Data; *Year Closed:* No Data; *Years Known In Operation:* No Data; *Founder:* No Data; *Predecessor:* No Data; *Successor:* No Data; *Source:* Bell at Evergreen Farm, Eminence, Indiana, and bell inquired about on ABAII website on May 31, 2008 by bpennington; *Other Facts:* The Evergreen Farm bell is an iron dinner bell, approximately 14" diameter.

# Holmes, Booth & Haydens

*Address:* Waterbury, Connecticut; *Year Established:* No Data; *Year Closed:* No Data; *Years Known In Operation:* 1888; *Founder:* No Data; *Predecessor:* No Data; *Successor:* No Data; *Source:* Zell's U.S. Business Directory of 1888; *Other Facts:* No Data

# James Homan Foundry

*Address:* Cincinnati, Ohio; *Year Established:* 1954; *Year Closed:* mid 1950's; *Years Known In Operation:* 1954 - mid-1950's; *Founder:* No Data; *Predecessor:* E.W. Vanduzen (Buckeye Bell Foundry); *Successor:* No Data; *Source:* Mrs. G. Lyle Ringland of Norwood, Ohio; *Other Facts:* This man bought out the Vanduzen family. He ran the firm for a short time and scraped it out selling much of it to the I.T. Verdin firm of Cincinnati. Verdin got many of the Vanduzen records according to Mrs. Ringland. This was verified by Bob Verdin of the I. T. Verdin firm.

# Hooper, Blake & Richardson

*Address:* Boston, Massachusetts; *Year Established:* 1830; *Year Closed:* No Data; *Years Known In Operation:* 1830 - 1871; *Founder:* William Blake; *Predecessor:* William Blake; *Successor:* W. Blake & Company; *Source:* *That Vanishing Sound*, Edward Stickney, Bedford, Massachusetts; *Other Facts:* Another partnership of William Blake which sold bells under this and the Hooper & Co names. Hooper was the owner. See Henry N. Hooper file for Winthrop Warren's information which appears as if it applies to this firm. Names were Henry N. Hooper, William Blake, & Thomas Richardson. Winthrop Warren says they made bell chimes of 13 and 16 bells in the mid 1800's. In 2012 Todd Lower of Lower Bells had a 40" diameter Hooper bell dated 1834, likely the oldest one known.

# Henry N. Hooper & Company

*Address:* Boston, Massachusetts; *Year Established:* 1830; *Year Closed:* 1890; *Years Known In Operation:* 1830 - 1890; *Founder:* William Blake; *Predecessor:* Hooper, Blake & Richardson; *Successor:* Blake Bell Company; *Source:* That Vanishing Sound, Edward Stickney, Bedford, Massachusetts, Winthrop Warren of Fairfield, Connecticut, Carl Scott Zimmerman of St Louis, Mo., and Robert Cowie of Paris, Ark; *Other Facts:* Bells were sold and advertised under the "Hooper & Co." name by this and several other firms and partnerships formed by William Blake over the course of his bell founding career (1820-mid 1890's). Robert Cowie of Paris, Ark. has a 38" bell with a crown dated 1834. A bell with this name dated 1859 is in St. Paul's Methodist in Lynn, Massachusetts, and one is in Old Round Church, Richmond, Vermont, also one in Congregational Church in Bluehill, Maine dated 1841. The un-recast part of the 16 bell chime in Grace Church, Providence, R.I. Bears "Henry N. Hooper & Co. Boston 1861". Hooper died in

*Henry N. Hooper Bell 1852*

1865, and Blake evidently had full control by then. Warren says this was a partnership of Henry N. Hooper, William Blake & Thomas Richardson. Hooper's full name was Henry Northey Hooper.

*Henry N. Hooper Foundry and Chime*

# G.M. Hotchkiss & Company

*Address:* West Haven, Connecticut; *Year Established:* No Data; *Year Closed:* No Data; *Years Known In Operation:* 1888 - 1889; *Founder:* No Data; *Predecessor:* No Data; *Successor:* No Data; *Source:* Zell's U.S. Business Directories of 1888 and 1889; *Other Facts:* No Data

# Howell Works Company

*Address:* Allaire Village, New Jersey; *Year Established:* No Data; *Year Closed:* No Data; *Years Known In Operation:* No Data; *Founder:* No Data; *Predecessor:* No Data; *Successor:* No Data; *Source:* allairevillage.org website; *Other Facts:* The above website lists a 3 ton iron bell made by the Howell Works Company in their chapel. This village was founded by James P. Allaire (a bell maker) who also owned the Howell Works Company. It is likely this firm did make bells, but unlikely they made one so heavy out of iron. Someone at the Allaire Village perhaps thought it weighed that much. If it does weigh 3 tons, it would be more than twice the weight of the largest iron bell I have ever discovered. See James P. Allaire bell foundry for more information.

# A. J. Hunt

*Address:* St Louis, Missouri; *Year Established:* No Data; *Year Closed:* No Data; *Years Known In Operation:* 1883; *Founder:* No Data; *Predecessor:* No Data; *Successor:* No Data; *Source:* Carl Scott Zimmerman research of St Louis bell foundries; *Other Facts:* The Missouri State directory for 1883 shows this firm as classified under "Bell and Brass Foundries"

# George S. Hunt

*Address:* St Louis, Missouri; *Year Established:* No Data; *Year Closed:* No Data; *Years Known In Operation:* No Data; *Founder:* No Data; *Predecessor:* No Data; *Successor:* No Data; *Source:* Carl Scott Zimmerman research papers re: large bells in St Louis area; *Other Facts:* Did business as Diamond Anti-Friction Metal Company. Carl is not certain if this firm actually made bells.

# Alfred Ivers & Company

*Address:* 409 Cherry, New York, New York; *Year Established:* No Data; *Year Closed:* No Data; *Years Known In Operation:* 1840 - 1841; *Founder:* No Data; *Predecessor:* No Data; *Successor:* No Data; *Source:* New York Business Directory 1840/1841 (research papers of Lois Springer); *Other Facts:* No Data

# R. Ives

*Address:* Plymouth, Connecticut; *Year Established:* No Data; *Year Closed:* No Data; *Years Known In Operation:* 1889; *Founder:* No Data; *Predecessor:* No Data; *Successor:* No Data; *Source:* Zell's U.S. Business Directory of 1889; *Other Facts:* Possibly related to Samuel Ives, the bell maker in New Orleans, Louisiana.

# Samuel Ives

*Address:* New Orleans, Louisiana; *Year Established:* No Data; *Year Closed:* No Data; *Years Known In Operation:* 1827; *Founder:* No Data; *Predecessor:* No Data; *Successor:* No Data; *Source:* *That Vanishing Sound*, & for the year, Sydney J. Shep, Mississauga, Ontario, Canada; *Other Facts:* No Data

# Jackson Bell and Brass Foundry

*Address:* 203 N. Main (also 804 N. Main) (& Convent between Main & 2nd in 1869), St. Louis, Missouri; *Year Established:* 1866; *Year Closed:* 1869; *Years Known In Operation:* 1866 - 1869; *Founder:* Emil C. Mayer & Jacob Ruppenthal, proprietors; *Predecessor:* No Data; *Successor:* Emil C. Mayer, Jacob Ruppenthal; *Source:* Gould's 1900 Directory for St. Louis & 1866, 1867, 1868, & 1869 City Directories (thru Missouri Historical Society). Research of Carl Scott Zimmerman re: St Louis bell foundries; *Other Facts:* Emil C. Mayer was probably a descendant of Francis Mayer. Carl Scott Zimmerman reports that neither the 1868 or 1869 St Louis city directories he checked list Mayer and Rupenthal together with the Jackson Bell and Brass Foundry, which would indicate they may not have been connected with the firm.

# S. & J. T. Jackson

*Address:* Providence, Rhode Island; *Year Established:* No Data; *Year Closed:* No Data; *Years Known In Operation:* 1810; *Founder:* No Data; *Predecessor:* No Data; *Successor:* No Data; *Source:* Bell bought by Dusty and Joanne Lussman of Storm Lake, Iowa in July 1999; *Other Facts:* The above bell was bronze, 14" in diameter and dated 1810.

# Jenny & Manning

*Address:* Washington Court House, Ohio; *Year Established:* No Data; *Year Closed:* No Data; *Years Known In Operation:* 1888, 1889; *Founder:* No Data; *Predecessor:* No Data; *Successor:* No Data; *Source:* Zell's U.S. Business Directories of 1888 & 1889, and Carl Scott Zimmerman letter of 4 - 30 - 1997; *Other Facts:* In South St Louis Carl Scott Zimmerman saw a 20" diameter iron bell with the following inscription on the yoke "Jenny & Manning Washington C. H. O" which Carl took to mean Washington Court House, Ohio, which is a town about 25 miles north of Hillsboro, between Cincinnati and Columbus. The shape was similar to a C. S. Bell Co bell.

# Frederick A. Jensch

*Address:* Chicago, Illinois; *Year Established:* 1857; *Year Closed:* No Data; *Years Known In Operation:* 1857 - 1870 (approximately); *Founder:* No Data; *Predecessor:* No Data; *Successor:* No Data; *Source:* *That Vanishing Sound*, research of city directories by Carl Scott Zimmerman of St Louis, Missouri, an ABAII bell inquiry of April 14, 1999, and bells; *Other Facts:* "Bells up to 50,000 pounds." E. Elsinore Springer lists the firm as E. A. Jensch, and the city directories for Chicago researched by Carl Zimmerman show the firm as Frederick A. Jensch. They may have been father and son, but more likely an inscription from a bell of F. A. Jensch was misread as E. A. Jensch. A 22" diameter bell with a 24" diameter rope wheel inscribed F. A. Jensch's Bell Foundry Chicago, Ill., 1868, was listed for sale on ebay on Nov. 22, 2003. It was bronze from a plantation north of Vicksburg, Miss. An F. A. Jensch Bell Foundry, Chicago bell dated 1868 is in Raymond, Ms.

# John Deere Plow Company

*Address:* Moline, Illinois; *Year Established:* No Data; *Year Closed:* No Data; *Years Known In Operation:* No Data; *Founder:* No Data; *Predecessor:* No Data; *Successor:* No Data; *Source:* Advertisement by Kraft Auction Services for auction at Lake County Fairgrounds, Crown Point, Indiana. Advertisement was in Antiques Week newspaper, Eastern Edition, December 21, 2015, page 13, as reported by Micky Varian of Maine; *Other Facts:* Advertisement listed a #4 cast iron bell with 2 A frame stands and yoke.

# Cyril Johnston

*Address:* No Data; *Year Established:* No Data; *Year Closed:* No Data; *Years Known In Operation:* No Data; *Founder:* No Data; *Predecessor:* No Data; *Successor:* No Data; *Source:* GCNA Carillon News, Nov. 2003; *Other Facts:* No Data

# Jones & Company Troy Bell Foundry

*Address:* Corner of Adams & First Streets, Troy, New York; *Year Established:* 1852; *Year Closed:* 1887; *Years Known In Operation:* 1852 - 1887; *Founder:* Eber Jones; *Predecessor:* Jones & Hitchcock Troy Bell Foundry; *Successor:* No Data; *Source:* Jones & Co reprinted catalogue of 1870 by W. E. Morrison & Co of Ovid, New York / The Troy Directory of 1876 / The Buffalo Bus Dir Vol 1, 1855; *Other Facts:* Made church bells up to 5,000 lbs. 62" diameter. One of their bells dated 1874 went to the Methodist Church of Monona, Iowa, another large one is in front of the United Church of Christ in Shenandoah, Iowa dated 1878. The 1855 advertisement states that they made the first chime in the U.S. for St. Stephens Church in Philadelphia, Pa in 1853 and that they made church bells in 25 different diameters from 27" (400 lbs) to 62" (5,000 lbs), and that they supplied other bells from 15 to 20,000 lbs. In 1857 Harvey J. King, a prominent attorney, joined the firm for one year. Eber Jones was born in Dorset, VT. and died in 1867 at the age of 59. His son, Octavous Jones, then ran the firm for another 20 years, closing it in 1887. Through the partnership of Eber Jones and James Harvey Hitchcock from 1852 to 1857, this firm traces it's roots back to Paul Revere. James H. Hitchcock learned bell making over several years at the Meneely foundry in Troy, N.Y. prior to partnering with Eber Jones. Andrew Meneely and James H. Hitchcock married sisters, so were brothers in law. The two Meneely foundries of Troy and West Troy, N.Y. originated in the Hanks foundry, and Benjamine Hanks had learned bell making as an apprentice in the Paul Revere bell foundry. For more information, see each of those foundry entries.

*Octavous Jones*

*Jones and Company Troy Bell Foundry Bell 1871*

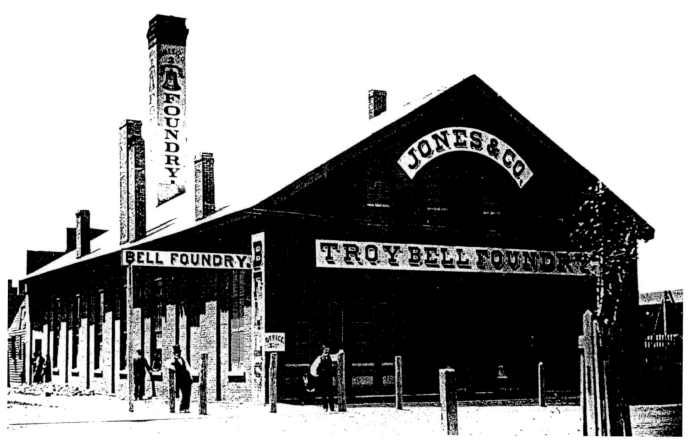

*Jones and Company Troy Bell Foundry*

*Jones and Company 1870 Catalogue Church Bell*

*Jones and Company
Troy Bell Foundry Advertisement*

# Jones & Hitchcock Troy Bell Foundry

*Address:* Peck Building, N.W. Corner of First and Adams, Troy, New York; *Year Established:* 1852; *Year Closed:* 1857; *Years Known In Operation:* 1852 - 1857; *Founder:* Eber Jones & James Harvey Hitchcock; *Predecessor:* Andrew Meneely & Company; *Successor:* Jones & Company; *Source:* 1870 Jones & Co Catalogue reprinted in 1984, including company history addendum, by W.E. Morrison & Co., Ovid, New York, and Mr. Wayne E. Morrison, Sr. of Ovid, New York; *Other Facts:* James H. Hitchcock had learned bell making in the Andrew Meneely foundry and left when Andrew died, probably because he knew the sons didn't get along. He and Andrew Meneely were brothers in law, having married sisters, Philena and Juliaette Hanks. Juliaette was Hitchcock's wife. Juliaette and Philena were related to President Abraham Lincoln's mother, Nancy Hanks. Through Hitchcock, Meneely and Hanks, this firm traced it's lineage back to the Paul Revere Foundry. A 12 1/2" diameter bronze bell dated 1856 belongs to Neil Goeppinger of Boone, Iowa. Eki Vaisenan of Michigan reported Robert Brosamer had a 29" bell by this firm.

*Octavous Jones*

**JONES & HITCHCOCK, Proprietors**

CORNER OF ADAMS AND FIRST STREETS,

**BELLS**

FOR CHURCHES, FACTORIES, STEAMBOATS, SCHOOL HOUSES, PLANTATIONS, Locomotives and Hose Carriages.

Hangings furnished complete.

*Jones and Hitchcock Bell 1856*

*Jones and Hitchcock Troy Bell Foundry Advertisement*

# Tho's Kane & Company

*Address:* Chicago, Illinois; *Year Established:* No Data; *Year Closed:* No Data; *Years Known In Operation:* No Data; *Founder:* No Data; *Predecessor:* No Data; *Successor:* No Data; *Source:* Bell owned by Neil Goeppinger of Boone, Iowa; *Other Facts:* The above bell is a 36" diameter cast iron bell with an iron wheel containing 4 curved spokes.

# Kaye & Company

*Address:* 132 Water Street, Louisville, Kentucky; *Year Established:* No Data; *Year Closed:* 1895; *Years Known In Operation:* 1840 - 1895; *Founder:* William Kaye; *Predecessor:* No Data; *Successor:* No Data; *Source:* Zell's U.S. Business Directories of 1888 & 1889, a bronze 27" bell belonging to Neil Goeppinger of Boone, Iowa, and a 25 1/2" diameter bell reported in the ABA big bells forum belonging to a church (4 - 29 - 2013 post); *Other Facts:* Advertised their church bells in the above directory in 1888 as well as being listed as a manufacturer. William Kaye served Louisville as Chief of Police, City Council member, and as Mayor. He was born in Yorkshire, England Feb 13, 1813, and emigrated to Pittsburgh, Pa in 1819 with his family. He moved to Louisville in 1836 as an engine builder and started a bell and scales foundry in 1841. He died in Louisville at the age of 76. The bell belonging to Neil Goeppinger is inscribed "W. Kaye Louisville Ky." and has 2 1/2" high angels or cherubs around the top. A 35" bell was

*William Kaye Advertisement*

in the 1st Presbyterian Chruch, Belleview, Illinois, in 1992. The art work on these bells was identical to that on some G. W. Coffin bells and was likely purchased from a supplier of art molds. The Kaye bells were not finished as well as the Coffin bells, but the tone was better. The 25 1/2" bell reported above is dated 1840, which shows the firm actually started earlier than the 1841 date reported.

*W. Kaye Bell*

# William Kaye

***Address:*** Louisville, Kentucky; ***Year Established:*** No Data; ***Year Closed:*** No Data; ***Years Known In Operation:*** No Data; ***Founder:*** No Data; ***Predecessor:*** No Data; ***Successor:*** No Data; ***Source:*** Carl Scott Zimmerman of St Louis, Mo. List; ***Other Facts:*** A bell with this name is at the First Presbyterian Church, Belleville, Illinois.

# Peter & Benjamine Keith

***Address:*** Noble County, Ohio; ***Year Established:*** No Data; ***Year Closed:*** No Data; ***Years Known In Operation:*** 1817; ***Founder:*** Peter Keith and brother Benjamine Keith; ***Predecessor:*** No Data; ***Successor:*** No Data; ***Source:*** Dr. Frederick D. Thurston, Auburndale, Florida, a descendant of the two brothers; ***Other Facts:*** The brothers were active in the Revolutionary War effort and later moved to Ohio where they were blacksmiths and bell makers. Being blacksmiths, they probably made iron bells.

# Kentucky Bell Company

***Address:*** 1509 Jackson, Louisville, Kentucky; ***Year Established:*** No Data; ***Year Closed:*** No Data; ***Years Known In Operation:*** 1888 - 1889; ***Founder:*** No Data; ***Predecessor:*** No Data; ***Successor:*** No Data; ***Source:*** Zell's U.S. Business Directories of 1888 and 1889; ***Other Facts:*** No Data

# Kentucky Brass & Bell Foundry

***Address:*** Louisville, Kentucky; ***Year Established:*** No Data; ***Year Closed:*** No Data; ***Years Known In Operation:*** 1838 - 1844; ***Founder:*** William Collingridge; ***Predecessor:*** No Data; ***Successor:*** No Data; ***Source:*** Research of city directories by Carl Scott Zimmerman of St Louis, Mo; ***Other Facts:*** No Data

# George H. Kimberly

***Address:*** Troy, New York; ***Year Established:*** No Data; ***Year Closed:*** No Data; ***Years Known In Operation:*** No Data; ***Founder:*** No Data; ***Predecessor:*** No Data; ***Successor:*** No Data; ***Source:*** Sydney J. Shep, Mississauga, Ontario, Canada; ***Other Facts:*** I'm not sure of the connection to Meneely & Kimberly. This is the only reference I've ever seen to Kimberly having a separate foundry, and I have never come across a bell with this name standing alone. George H. Kimberly is the same name as the partner in Meneely & Kimberely.

# Daniel King

***Address:*** Corner Norris' Alley, on Front Street, Philadelphia, Pennsylvania; ***Year Established:*** No Data; ***Year Closed:*** No Data; ***Years Known In Operation:*** 1767; ***Founder:*** Daniel King, Jr.; ***Predecessor:*** No Data; ***Successor:*** Daniel King, Jr; ***Source:*** L. Elsinore Springer letter of 1/22/1985; ***Other Facts:*** Advertised in all local papers, including 4/20/1767 Pennsylvania Gazette which lists church bells and many other fine brass objects. His work is considered superior and is illustrated in books on American metal arts.

# Daniel King, Jr.

*Address:* Corner Norris' Alley, on Front Street, Philadelphia, Pennsylvania; *Year Established:* No Data; *Year Closed:* No Data; *Years Known In Operation:* 1811; *Founder:* Daniel King, Jr. *Predecessor:* Daniel King; *Successor:* No Data; *Source:* L. Elsinore Springer letter of 1/22/1985; *Other Facts:* Continued his father's foundry business.

# Kingwell Brothers Ltd.

*Address:* San Francisco or San Jose, California; *Year Established:* No Data; *Year Closed:* No Data; *Years Known In Operation:* No Data; *Founder:* No Data; *Predecessor:* Weed & Kingwell; *Successor:* Eagle Pitcher Bearing, South Bay Bronze/Aluminum Foundry Inc; *Source:* Letter from Gil Hernandy, owner of South Bay Bronze/Aluminum Foundry Inc; *Other Facts:* No Data

# Vincent Kingwell

*Address:* 228 Freemont, San Francisco, California; *Year Established:* No Data; *Year Closed:* No Data; *Years Known In Operation:* 1905 - 1906; *Founder:* No Data; *Predecessor:* No Data; *Successor:* No Data; *Source:* Thomas' Register 1905 - 1906; *Other Facts:* No Data

# Wm. Kirkup & Son Foundry

*Address:* 250 East Front St., Cincinnati, Ohio; *Year Established:* 1859; *Year Closed:* No Data; *Years Known In Operation:* 1859; *Founder:* No Data; *Predecessor:* No Data; *Successor:* No Data; *Source:* Mrs. G. Lyle Ringland, Norwood, Ohio; *Other Facts:* No Data

# William Koennker

*Address:* 15 or 19 Jackson; 367 S. 3rd, St. Louis, Mo.; *Year Established:* No Data; *Year Closed:* 1866; *Years Known In Operation:* 1848 - 1866; *Founder:* William Koennker; *Predecessor:* No Data; *Successor:* No Data; *Source:* Carl Scott Zimmerman research papers re: large bells in the St Louis area including business directories for 1848 - 1870; *Other Facts:* Carl Scott Zimmerman reports he was listed in city directories under locksmith, scales and lock factory, brass foundry. He was listed under "brass and bell founder" in 1864 and 1866 directories. Carl reports he died in either 1866 or 1867.

# Justin Kramer

*Address:* Los Angles, California; *Year Established:* No Data; *Year Closed:* No Data; *Years Known In Operation:* 1963 - 1975; *Founder:* No Data; *Predecessor:* California Bell Co; *Successor:* No Data; *Source:* Adeline Keehan Hill of California, Wikipedia, and California Dept. of Transportation website; *Other Facts:* In 1963 Justin Kramer took on the reproduction of the El Camino Royal bells (King's Highway bells) stretching over 700 miles from San Diego Mission to Sonoma Mission, California. These were originally placed by Friar Serra when Spain ruled California, and were first replaced by Mrs. A. S. C. Forbes starting in 1906.

## The Ktown Bell Company

*Address:* Frederick, Ohio; *Year Established:* No Data; *Year Closed:* No Data; *Years Known In Operation:* No Data; *Founder:* No Data; *Predecessor:* No Data; *Successor:* No Data; *Source:* 40" to 42" cast iron bell in tower in front of the Evangelical Covenant Church of Aurora, Nebraska; *Other Facts:* No Data

## Kupferle, Boisselier & Company

*Address:* St. Louis, Mo.; *Year Established:* 1868; *Year Closed:* 1870; *Years Known In Operation:* 1868 - 1870; *Founder:* John C. Kupferle and G. E. Boisselier; *Predecessor:* Kupferle & Boisselier; *Successor:* St Louis Brass & Hardware Mnfg Co. (1871 - 1873), Kupferle Boisselier (1873 - 1886), John C. Kuipferle (1887 - 1905+); *Source:* Carl Scott Zimmerman research papers on St Louis large bell foundries including St Louis city directories for 1847 - 1905; *Other Facts:* Also did business as Eagle Bell & Brass Foundry in 1868 - 1869.

## Kupferle & Boisselier

*Address:* 5th Street between Green and Morgan, St. Louis, Missouri; *Year Established:* No Data; *Year Closed:* No Data; *Years Known In Operation:* 1859 - 1867; *Founder:* John C. Kupferle and G. E. Boisselier; *Predecessor:* No Data; *Successor:* Kupferle, Boisselier & Co. (1868 - 1870), St. Louis Brass & Hardware Mnfg Co (1871 - 1873), John C. Kupferle (1887 - 1905+); *Source:* St. Louis Business Directory of 1859, Carl Scott Zimmerman research papers re: large bells in the St Louis area including St Louis city directories 1847 - 1905; *Other Facts:* The names of the partners appear on the top of a bell in St. John's UCC Church, Bellville, Illinois. This firm also did business as Eagle Bell and Brass Company in 1866 - 1867.

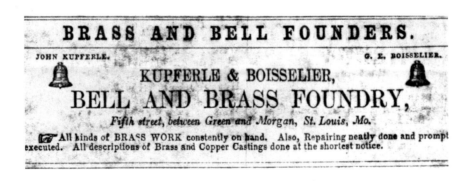

*Kupferle and Boisselier Advertisement*

## John Kupferle

*Address:* 159 N. 2nd St., St Louis, Missouri; *Year Established:* 1851; *Year Closed:* 1863; *Years Known In Operation:* 1851 - 1863; *Founder:* John Kupferle; *Predecessor:* No Data; *Successor:* John Kupferle & Bro, Missouri Bell and Brass Foundry; *Source:* Carl Scott Zimmerman research papers of large bell foundries in St Louis including city directories for 1847 - 1905, also Kennedy's 1860 St. Louis Directory through Missouri Historical Society; *Other Facts:* This man is different from John C. Kupferle who also made bells in St Louis. Carl Scott Zimmerman reports they both made bells but had different wives, widows and children. Very confusing.

# John Kupferle & Bro.

*Address:* 159 N. 2nd St, St Louis, Missouri; *Year Established:* No Data; *Year Closed:* No Data; *Years Known In Operation:* 1852 - 1864; *Founder:* John Kupferle and brother Charles Kupferle; *Predecessor:* John Kupferle (1852 - 1863); *Successor:* No Data; *Source:* Carl Scott Zimmerman research papers regarding large bell foundries of St Louis including city directories for 1847 - 1905; *Other Facts:* Carl Scott Zimmerman reports this John Kupferle was not the same man as John C. Kupferle. They had different wives, widows and children, but both made large bells in St Louis. Very confusing. This firm also did business as Missouri Bell and Brass Foundry in 1864 only.

# John C. Kupferle

*Address:* 159 N. 2nd Street, St. Louis, Missouri; *Year Established:* No Data; *Year Closed:* No Data; *Years Known In Operation:* 1860; *Founder:* No Data; *Predecessor:* No Data; *Successor:* Eagle Bell & Brass Foundry (probably) (1900); *Source:* Kennedy's 1860 St. Louis Directory (Information from the Missouri Historical Society), and Carl Scott Zimmerman of St Louis, Mo.; *Other Facts:* Different from the other John Kupferle. Carl Scott Zimmerman says they had different wives, different addresses, etc. Very confusing.

# John C. Kupferle

*Address:* St Louis, Missouri; *Year Established:* 1887; *Year Closed:* No Data; *Years Known In Operation:* 1887 - 1905; *Founder:* John C. Kupferle; *Predecessor:* Kupferle, Boisselier & Co (1868 - 1870), Kupferle & Boisselier (1873 - 1886), St Louis Brass & Hardware Mnfg Co (1871 - 1873); *Successor:* No Data; *Source:* Research papers of Carl Scott Zimmerman regarding large bell foundries of the St Louis area, including city directories of 1847 - 1905; *Other Facts:* There were two men with the same name of John C. Kupferle making bells in St Louis, which is very confusing. Carl Scott Zimmerman reports that they had different wives, different widows and different children, so they were in fact different men making bells in St Louis. The other had a brother Charles and the firm was located at 159 N. 2nd.

# Lafayette Foundry

*Address:* 800, 802, and 804 N. Main (office 1867 - 1885) (2nd St. & N.E. Corner of Carr in 1875), St. Louis, Missouri; *Year Established:* No Data; *Year Closed:* No Data; *Years Known In Operation:* 1866 - 1878; *Founder:* No Data; *Predecessor:* No Data; *Successor:* No Data; *Source:* 1868 - 1875 City Directories (thru Missouri Historical Society) and The Buffalo Business Directory - Volume 1, 1855 (thru New York State Historical Association), Research of Carl Scott Zimmerman of St Louis business directories for 1847 - 1905; *Other Facts:* In 1855 it was listed as "Lafayette Bell Foundry" and its bells were sold by Pratt & Co. of Buffalo, New York, along with those of Good & Moores Bells of Buffalo, New York. They listed the following: Church Bells 400 to 4,000 lbs, Factory and School Bells 100 to 500 lbs, Steamboat & Propellers 100 to 700 lbs, Plantation & Locomotive 40 to 150 lbs, Engine, Hose Cart & Hotel 5 to 40 lbs. Carl Scott Zimmerman reports the earliest date the firm was in business was 1866, the Buffalo Business Directory reports it as being in business in 1855.

# Laird & Company

*Address:* Canton, Ohio; *Year Established:* No Data; *Year Closed:* No Data; *Years Known In Operation:* No Data; *Founder:* No Data; *Predecessor:* No Data; *Successor:* No Data; *Source:* Yoke and clapper belonging to Neil Goeppinger of Boone, Iowa, and dinner bell belonging to Bob Richards, Longmeadow, Massachusetts; *Other Facts:* No Data

# Lakeside Foundry Company

*Address:* Chicago, Illinois; *Year Established:* No Data; *Year Closed:* No Data; *Years Known In Operation:* No Data; *Founder:* No Data; *Predecessor:* No Data; *Successor:* No Data; *Source:* # 3 iron or steel dinner bell belonging to M. Smith of Tavares, Fl; *Other Facts:* Many bells by other firms have cradles made by this firm, but this bell proves the firm made bells as well as the cradles.

# Lawson & Frank

*Address:* Louisville, Kentucky; *Year Established:* No Data; *Year Closed:* No Data; *Years Known In Operation:* 1848 - 1852; *Founder:* No Data; *Predecessor:* No Data; *Successor:* No Data; *Source:* Research of city directories by Carl Scott Zimmerman of St Louis, Mo; *Other Facts:* No Data

*Lakeside Foundry Company Bell*

# Lebanon Manufacturing Company

*Address:* Lebanan, Pennsylvania; *Year Established:* No Data; *Year Closed:* No Data; *Years Known In Operation:* 1876; *Founder:* No Data; *Predecessor:* No Data; *Successor:* No Data; *Source:* Bell in collection of Ben Tuck of Lebanon, Pa; *Other Facts:* Above bell is inscribed Centennial 1876 as well as Leb Mfg Co.Pa. It is a 24" diameter bell.

# LEB Mfg Company

*Address:* No Data; *Year Established:* No Data; *Year Closed:* No Data; *Years Known In Operation:* 1876; *Founder:* No Data; *Predecessor:* No Data; *Successor:* No Data; *Source:* Carolyn L. Forbes, Jeffersonville, Indiana; *Other Facts:* Carolyn Forbes owns a 23 1/2" diameter school bell, 15 1/2" tall with the following inscription in the iron bell "Centennial 1876 L.E.B. Mfg. Co." It has a smooth curved iron yoke with no inscription.

*L.E.B. Manufacturing Company Bell*

# John S. Lee & Company

*Address:* Philadelphia, Pennsylvania; *Year Established:* No Data; *Year Closed:* No Data; *Years Known In Operation:* No Data; *Founder:* No Data; *Predecessor:* No Data; *Successor:* No Data; *Source:* Ryan Cooper of Yarmouthport, Mass; *Other Facts:* Mr. Cooper owns a 10 1/2" diameter bronze ship bell by this firm with fluting at the shoulder, under that the name of the foundry and abbreviated city Philad'a, below that some decorative beading. He thinks it is from the 1800's.

# Lehr Agricul. Company

*Address:* Fremont, Ohio; *Year Established:* No Data; *Year Closed:* No Data; *Years Known In Operation:* 1905 - 1906; *Founder:* No Data; *Predecessor:* No Data; *Successor:* No Data; *Source:* Thomas' Register 1905 - 1906; *Other Facts:* Advertised farm and school bells.

# T.W. Levering

*Address:* Philadelphia, Pennsylvania; *Year Established:* No Data; *Year Closed:* No Data; *Years Known In Operation:* 1815 - 1816; *Founder:* Thomas Washington Levering; *Predecessor:* George Hedderly; *Successor:* No Data; *Source:* 16" high, 14 1/2" diameter bronze bell in collection of the late Arthur J. Sussel, research papers of Lois Springer; *Other Facts:* Above bell is dedicated to Robert Fulton. Inscription: "T. W. LEVERING facit Philadelphia A.D. 1816 NOW FULTON IS GONE. HE IS NO MORE BUT HE LEFT HIS GENIUS TO CARRY US FROM SHORE TO SHORE. UNION STEAMBOAT." Thomas Washington Levering learned bellfounding in George Hedderly's bell foundry

```
Memorial bell dedicated to Robert Fulton with an embossed
inscription: T. W. LEVERING fecit Philadelphia A. D. 1816.
NOW FULTON IS GONE.  HE IS NO MORE BUT HE LEFT HIS GENIUS
TO CARRY US FROM SHORE TO SHORE.  UNION STEAMBOAT."  The
bell is 16 in. high and 14½ in. in diameter.

formerly in the late Arthur J. Sussel Collection
```

*T. W. Levering Bell Inscription*

*T. W. Levering Bell*

# Dennis Liebus

*Address:* 115 - 8th Ave East, Oscaloosa, Iowa; *Year Established:* 1973; *Year Closed:* 1974 or 1975; *Years Known In Operation:* 1973 - 1974 or 1975; *Founder:* Dennis Liebus; *Predecessor:* J. C. Harrington Iron Founder; *Successor:* No Data; *Source:* Interview with Dennis Liebus, and Mary Noe of Colefax, Ia; *Other Facts:* Mr. Liebus' grandfather, August Gottslich, worked for the J. C. Harrington foundry which made bells in Oscaloosa in the late 1800's and had an ownership interest in the firm. Gottslich later started his own iron foundry. Dennis Liebus bought the original Harrington bell and parts molds and made both bells and parts for a short time. Neil Goeppinger bought parts from him in the mid 1990's. Liebus made 600 to 700 bells and paid his way through Central College by selling them. He now runs Liebus Concrete Products in Oscaloosa, Iowa.

# Loudoun Manufacturing Company

*Address:* Purcellville, Virginia; *Year Established:* No Data; *Year Closed:* No Data; *Years Known In Operation:* No Data; *Founder:* No Data; *Predecessor:* No Data; *Successor:* No Data; *Source:* Bell at Buckskin Manor B & B, 13452 Harpers Ferry Rd, in Hillsboro, VA. in December 1999; *Other Facts:* Bell is an 18" iron dinner bell and had the number "2" on the yoke between "Loudoun Mfg Co" and "Purcellville Va"

# Louisville Foundry

*Address:* Louisville, Kentucky; *Year Established:* No Data; *Year Closed:* No Data; *Years Known In Operation:* 1836 - 1846; *Founder:* No Data; *Predecessor:* No Data; *Successor:* No Data; *Source:* Research of city directories by Carl Scott Zimmerman of St Louis, Mo; *Other Facts:* Run by L. M. Rickets, et al.

# Lusk & Company

*Address:* Jackson, ; *Year Established:* No Data; *Year Closed:* No Data; *Years Known In Operation:* 1854 - 1878; *Founder:* T. E. Lusk and Henry Vandercook; *Predecessor:* No Data; *Successor:* No Data; *Source:* Robert Thompson of Movers, N. Y., and ABAII website inquiry by Rosemary from Michigan dated Aug 28, 2007; *Other Facts:* Robert Thompson has a 17 1/2" diameter bell with "Lusk & Co" on the yoke. It has fancy side frames.

# A. Major & Brother

*Address:* Lebanon (Sommerset in 1868), Pennsylvania; *Year Established:* No Data; *Year Closed:* No Data; *Years Known In Operation:* 1860 - 1868; *Founder:* No Data; *Predecessor:* No Data; *Successor:* No Data; *Source:* 10/14/1992 letter from Dick Hains of Crimora, Virginia, a bell purchased by Del Gilmore of Iowa City, Ia in 2008, a 20" diameter school bell belonging to Jim Wood of Riverside, Ca. in Feb 2000, and three 21" bells and a 20" bell in the Ben Tuck collection in Lebanon, Pa; *Other Facts:* Mr. Hains has a 20" diameter iron bell by this firm. The Gilmore bell is 20" diameter and dated 1860. It reads A. Major & Brother., Summerset, Pa. It has a small top and is either steel or iron. The name of the firm is cast into the bell. The town and state are cast into a ringing arm attached to the top at the center bolt with a counter weight. The Wood bell was inscribed "A. Major & Brother 1868." All the Tuck bells have the inscription in the iron bells, and the 20" one also has the inscription on the yoke (A. Major & Brother Lebanaon, Pa).

# A. H. Manchester

*Address:* Providence, Rhode Island; *Year Established:* No Data; *Year Closed:* No Data; *Years Known In Operation:* No Data; *Founder:* No Data; *Predecessor:* No Data; *Successor:* No Data; *Source:* Bell belonging to Robert Brosamer of Michigan on July 13, 2000; *Other Facts:* The above bell is 16 1/2" in diameter, bronze, and has no clapper or stands.

# P. P. Manion Blacksmith & Wrecking Company

*Address:* St Louis, Missouri; *Year Established:* No Data; *Year Closed:* No Data; *Years Known In Operation:* 1878 - 1898; *Founder:* No Data; *Predecessor:* No Data; *Successor:* No Data; *Source:* Carl Scott Zimmerman city directory research; *Other Facts:* Mr. Zimmerman has not found any bells by this firm, so it is possible they advertised for bell business, but never received any orders.

# Manny & Company

*Address:* 1248 Broadway, 19 & 22 S. 2nd, 14 N. Main, 20 N. Main, 819 - 823 S. 3rd, St. Louis, Missouri; *Year Established:* No Data; *Year Closed:* No Data; *Years Known In Operation:* 1867 - 1880; *Founder:* No Data; *Predecessor:* No Data; *Successor:* Manny & Baver Mnfg Co (1881 - 1883), Manny Mfg. Co (1884 - 1887); *Source:* 1875 City Directory (thru Missouri Historical Society), and research of Carl Scott Zimmerman of St Louis on large bell foundries in St Louis; *Other Facts:* This firm's advertising in the city directory didn't list bells, but was listed under the "bells" heading in that publication. They did, however, advertise farm equipment, and many manufactures of farm equipment also made farm bells. Carl Scott Zimmerman reports they were listed under "Bells (Brass and Amalgam)" from 1872 - 1878, but he further states he has not found any evidence they actually made any.

# Emil C. Mayer

*Address:* 147 Covent between Main & 2nd (see Other Facts below), St. Louis, Missouri; *Year Established:* 1870; *Year Closed:* 1871; *Years Known In Operation:* 1870 - 1871; *Founder:* Emil C. Mayer; *Predecessor:* Mayer & Ruppenthal, dba Jackson Bell & Brass Foundry, also David Caughlan; *Successor:* No Data; *Source:* 1875 Gould's City Directory, 1876 - 1877 Missouri Gazetteer & Business Directory (thru Missouri Historical Society), and "Inventory of bells in the St. Louis Area" of 6 - 4 - 1996 by Carl Scott Zimmerman of St Louis, Mo.; *Other Facts:* Other addresses used: 111 S. 2nd St. in 1875, 1114 S. 2nd St. in 1874 - 1877, and in 1890, although not listed under bell manufacturers, the firm was still listed under foundries at 1214 S. 7th. Thus, although still in business in 1900 (listed in Gould's) it isnt known if they still manufactured bells. A fancy 39 inch D. Caughlan bell belonging to Robert Brosamer dated 1866 says "E. Mayer maker" thus E. Mayer worked for David Cauglan in 1866. That bell has a harp sided by 2 up facing horns of plenty on it, and this appears in 1870 ad for E. C. Mayer.

# Francis Mayer & Company

*Address:* South Covent St. between 3rd and 4th Streets, St. Louis, Missouri; *Year Established:* 1852; *Year Closed:* 1866; *Years Known In Operation:* 1852 - 1866; *Founder:* Francis Mayer; *Predecessor:* No Data; *Successor:* Emil C. Mayer; *Source:* City Directory of 1854 and Kennedy's 1860 Directory & City Directories for 1860, 1864, & 1865 (thru Missouri Historical Society), and Inventory of bells in the St. Louis Area" dated 6 - 4 - 1996 by Carl Scott Zimmerman of St Louis, Mo; *Other Facts:* Bells have been found with the following inscriptions "Fr. Mayer & Co.", "Fr. Mayer, Agt." and "F. Mayer". Zimmerman reports an 1852 bell by F. Mayer is currently the oldest known St. Louis made bell.

# Mayer & Ruppenthal

*Address:* 203 N. Main (1866), 804 N. Main (1867 - 1869), St Louis, Missouri; *Year Established:* 1866; *Year Closed:* 1869; *Years Known In Operation:* 1866 - 1869; *Founder:* No Data; *Predecessor:* Francis Mayer & Company; *Successor:* No Data; *Source:* Inventory of bells in the St. Louis Area dated 6 - 4 - 1996 by Carl Scott Zimmerman of St Louis, Mo; *Other Facts:* A bell is located in the Emmanuel Episcopal Church, Webster Groves, Missouri dated 1867. The firm also did business under the name Jackson Bell & Brass Foundry.

# M. M'Donald

*Address:* Philadelphia, Pennsylvania; *Year Established:* 1841; *Year Closed:* No Data; *Years Known In Operation:* 1841; *Founder:* No Data; *Predecessor:* No Data; *Successor:* No Data; *Source:* Wayne E. Morrison, Sr., Ovid, New York; *Other Facts:* No Data

## Wm. McKenna & Son

*Address:* No 396 Broome Street, New York, New York; *Year Established:* No Data; *Year Closed:* No Data; *Years Known In Operation:* 1877; *Founder:* No Data; *Predecessor:* No Data; *Successor:* Emil C. Mayer; *Source:* Trow's New York City Directory for 1877 (thru New York State Historical Association); *Other Facts:* Advertised "Gongs for Railroad Cars, Horse Bells, General Brass Foundry. Railroad and Machinist's Work of All Kinds." Later known as Wm McKenna & Sons.

## Duncan McKiernan

*Address:* P. O. Box 2022, Port Angeles, Washington; *Year Established:* No Data; *Year Closed:* No Data; *Years Known In Operation:* 1993; *Founder:* Duncan McKiernan; *Predecessor:* No Data; *Successor:* No Data; *Source:* David Mahler, Washington State Bell Museum, Seattle, Washington; *Other Facts:* Founder and sculptor-does bronzes. He did a church bell for a church in Port Angeles and in the fall of 1993 was doing a new railroad bell for the State of Washington bell museum. Bells are a small part of his work.

## Henry McShane & Company

*Address:* Concord Street, between Lombard and Pratt in downtown Baltimore in 1856, Baltimore, Maryland; *Year Established:* 1856; *Year Closed:* No Data; *Years Known In Operation:* 1856 - 1887; *Founder:* Henry McShane; *Predecessor:* Register & Webb; *Successor:* McShane Bell Foundry Company; *Source:* Mrs. C. Parker of the McShane Bell Foundry, That Vanishing Sound, a conversation with Iva May Long of Pa., and the Winter/Spring 2000 issue of the Timepiece Journal of the American Clock and Watch Museum, Inc; *Other Facts:* In a conversation with Iva May Long, she quoted Russell McShane as saying the owners of Regester & Webb were related to the McShanes and were likely the forerunners of the McShane foundry. Other information shows Henry McShane at age 19 working as a brass founder for Clampitt & Regester foundry in 1850 and living with Joseph McShane (who may have been a cousin). Henry McShane emigrated from Ireland at age 16 in 1847 during the Irish Potato Famine.

*Henry McShane*

*Henry McShane and Company Bell 1878*

# McShane Bell Foundry Company

*Address:* 161 North Street (1881) , 441 North Street (1888 &1889), Baltimore, Maryland; *Year Established:* 1856; *Year Closed:* Still in operation in 2016 but not casting bells in the U.S; *Years Known In Operation:* 1856 - still operating 2016; *Founder:* Henry McShane; *Predecessor:* Henry McShane & Co; *Successor:* No Data; *Source: That Vanishing Sound* and Mrs. C. Parker of the McShane Bell Foundry, Thomas' Register 1905 - 1906, Carl Scott Zimmerman of St Louis, Mo., and the Timepiece Journal of the American Clock & Watch Museum, Inc, Winter/ Spring 2000; *Other Facts:* The address in 1984 of this firm was 400 Arundel Corporation Road, Building C, Glen Burnie, Maryland, 21061, which is about 20 miles outside of Baltimore. They are a thick walled, highly finished bell with a deep voice in any given size. As far as I know , this was the only church bell foundry still in existence in the United States as of 1984. Since then others have started up. They made a beautiful bell.. All bells were bronze. As of 1950 they had made 130,000 bells.

FIGURE 1

## CHURCH BELLS

RANGING IN WEIGHT FROM 1400 TO 7000 POUNDS

Fully warranted as to excellence of tone, composition and workmanship, mounted with McShane's Rotary Yoke, which permits the bell to be turned at pleasure, so as to prevent the liability of fracture; steel spring which holds the clapper from the bell after it has been struck, to improve and prolong the sound; frame, standards, wheel, tolling attachment, and our patented anti-friction journal rollers, all constituting the most complete, perfect, and convenient fixtures yet devised for using the bell under all circumstances.

## SHIP BELLS

The accompanying illustration shows the watch bell made at this foundry for the United States ship *New Orleans.* This is said to be not only the most beautiful bell on any ship in our Navy, but the finest cast in this country.

We have also supplied bells of this class for the United States ships *Maryland, Virginia, West Virginia, Charleston, Chattanooga, Georgia, Louisiana, Missouri, Minnesota, Washington,* and many others.

*McShane 1915 Catalogue Church Bell*

*McShane 1915 Catalogue Ship Bell*

*McShane Centennial Chime in 1888 Catalogue*

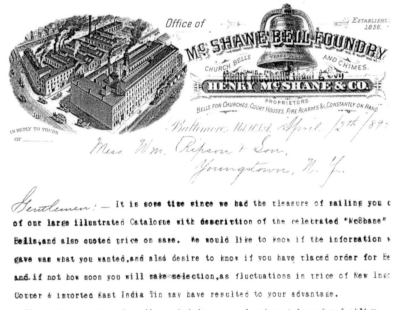

*McShane Letterhead and Foundry*

# McShane and Bailey

*Address:* 157 North Street, Baltimore, Maryland; *Year Established:* 1857; *Year Closed:* No Data; *Years Known In Operation:* 1857; *Founder:* Henry McShane of Baltimore and Edwin Bailey of Philadelphia; *Predecessor:* No Data; *Successor:* No Data; *Source:* Timepiece Journal of the American Clock & Watch Museum, Inc, Winter/Spring 2000 article by Mollie McShane Fenger; *Other Facts:* By 1863 Edwin Bailey was no longer part of the name (it had changed to Henry McShane and Company), but Edwin Bailey remained associated with the business until 1864. By 1863, Henry McShane's older brother John was also associated with the firm.

# Meeks & Watson

*Address:* Georgetown, Ohio; *Year Established:* 1995; *Year Closed:* No Data; *Years Known In Operation:* 1995 - 2001; *Founder:* William Meeks and Richard Watson; *Predecessor:* Arthur Lynds Bigelow (sort of); *Successor:* No Data; *Source:* Bulletin of GCNA, Vol. XLIV 1995; *Other Facts:* Watson worked with Bigelow who did experimental bell patterns. Meeks & Watson started casting bells for carillons in 1995, and also did tuning of old American-made bells.

# Andrew Meneely

*Address:* 205 Broadway, West Troy, New York; *Year Established:* 1826; *Year Closed:* 1849; *Years Known In Operation:* 1826 - 1849; *Founder:* Andrew Meneely; *Predecessor:* Julius Hanks; *Successor:* Andrew Meneely & Son, Andrew Meneely & Sons, E.A. & G.R. Meneely, Meneely & Company; *Source:* Bell poster dated 1846, Meneely & Co pamphlets, and a 32 inch diameter bell dated 1834 for sale by Brosamers Bells in 2016; *Other Facts:* They sometimes put A. Meneely on their bells. One of thier advertised references in 1846 was Rev. Hummer of Iowa City. Also made surveyor's compasses, levels, theodolites, and transit instruments. They also made town clocks and church and parlor organs. All their bells were bronze. Andrew Meneely was apprenticed to Julius Hanks and then married his niece, Philena Hanks, and took over the foundry. He had a musical ear, improved the shape of the bells and thus the tone, and made both chimes and carillons. This became one of the seven major bronze bell foundries in the U.S. and made thousands of bells. This firm traced it's lineage back to Paul Revere through Julius Hanks and his father Benjamine Hanks (who learned bell founding in the Revere foundry).

*Andrew Meneely*

# Meneely & Oothout

*Address:* 205 Broadway, West Troy, New York; *Year Established:* 1836; *Year Closed:* 1841; *Years Known In Operation:* 1836 - 1841; *Founder:* Andrew Meneely; *Predecessor:* Andrew Meneely; *Successor:* Andrew Meneely; *Source:* Bell Casting in Troy - A Family Affair by Charles Skinner from the Internet in April 2002, and a bell as part of a tower clock dated 1840 reported by Joe Connors, and a 14 1/2" diameter bell dated 1836 offered for sale on e-bay, Feb 11,2003; *Other Facts:* Mr. Skinner states that due to poor health, Andrew Meneely took his foreman, Jonas Volkert Oothout as a partner for five years, after which the partnership was dissolved and reverted to "Andrew Meneely."

# Andrew Meneely & Son

*Address:* 205 Broadway, West Troy, New York; *Year Established:* 1850; *Year Closed:* 1850; *Years Known In Operation:* 1850; *Founder:* Andrew Meneely, Edwin A. Meneely was the son; *Predecessor:* Andrew Meneely, the Hanks family (Andrew Meneely married Phelina Hanks and learned bell making under Julius Hanks); *Successor:* Andrew Meneely's Sons, E. A. & G. R. Meneely, Meneely & Co; *Source:* Meneely & Co pamphlets; *Other Facts:* All bronze bells. Andrew Meneely married Philena Hanks, niece of Julius Hanks, and a relative of Nancy Hanks, Abraham Lincoln's mother.

# Andrew Meneely's Sons

*Address:* 205 Broadway, West Troy, New York; *Year Established:* 1851; *Year Closed:* 1862; *Years Known In Operation:* 1851 - 1862; *Founder:* Andrew Meneely, his sons were Edwin A. and George R. Meneely; *Predecessor:* Andrew Meneely, Andrew Meneely & Son, The Hanks family; *Successor:* E. A. & G. R. Meneely (1863 - 1873), Meneely & Co. 1874 - 1950; *Source:* Meneely & Co pamphlets which tell history of the firm; *Other Facts:* Made all bronze bells. Andrew Meneely died in 1851

# E.A. & G.R. Meneely

*Address:* 205 Broadway, West Troy, New York; *Year Established:* 1863; *Year Closed:* 1873; *Years Known In Operation:* 1863 - 1873; *Founder:* Edwin Andrew Meneely and George Rodney Meneely (brothers); *Predecessor:* Andrew Meneely, Andrew Meneely & Son, Andrew Meneely & Sons, and the Hanks family; *Successor:* Meneely & Company; *Source:* Meneely & Co. pamphlets which give company history, and Bell Casting in Troy - A Family Affair by Charles Skinner which was on the Internet in April 2002; *Other Facts:* Made all bronze bells. Andrew Meneely married Philena Hanks, niece of Julius Hanks. In 1868 the firm advertised 27" diameter (400 lb) bells to 64" diameter (5,000 lb) bells, and that the firm, going back to Andrew Meneely, had made more bells than all other U.S. foundries combined

# Meneely & Company

*Address:* 205 Broadway (in 1855 the corner of Broad St. & Rochester St.) also 1531 - 1541 Broadway, West Troy (Watervliet), New York; *Year Established:* 1874; *Year Closed:* 1950; *Years Known In Operation:* 1874 - 1950; *Founder:* Edwin A. & George R. Meneely (Andrew H. in 1874); *Predecessor:* Andrew Meneely, Andrew Meneely & Son, Andrew Meneely's Sons, E.A. & G.R. Meneely, the Hanks family; *Successor:* No Data; *Source:* *That Vanishing Sound*, Eugene Burns, Ballou's Pictorial Drawing Room Companion of 10/20/1855, Troy Directory of 1876, Company Pamphlets, New York State Directory 1870, 1936 letter from Andrew E. Meneely, President of Meneely & Co. to Miss Hazel A. Hicks, and an article "Meneely Bells an American Heritage" by William De Turk published April 1978 in the Bulletin of the Guild of Carillonneurs in North America; *Other Facts:* Including the prior used names listed above under "Predecessor" this firm made the first complete chime in the U.S. in 1850 and the first carillon in the U.S. in 1829 for the Worlds Fair in New York. West Troy changed its name to Watervliet in 1896 but the firm still used the West Troy name until the 1920's out of fear their brother's firm in Troy, New York, would benefit if they didn't. In 1874 they made 33 sizes of church bells (27" & 400 lbs to 72" and 7,500 lbs). From 1826 to 1855 they made over 10,00 church bells plus smaller bells for boats, railroads, etc. This firm made 5 carillons, all located in the U.S.

*Meneely and Company Bell Foundry*

*Meneely and Company West Troy Bell 1882*

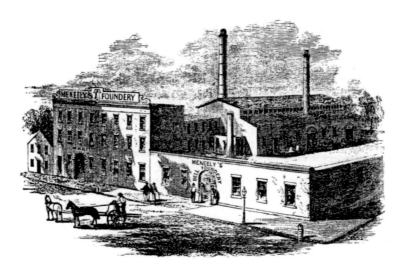

*Meneely Bell Foundry West Troy, N.Y.*

# Meneely & Kimberly, Founders

*Address:* 24 & 26 River (in 1876), 22 & 24 River (in 1878), Troy, New York; *Year Established:* 1869; *Year Closed:* 1878; *Years Known In Operation:* 1869 - 1878; *Founder:* Col. Clinton H. Meneely and George Kimberly (cousins); *Predecessor:* No Data; *Successor:* No Data; *Source:* Wayne Morrison, Ovid, New York. The Troy Directory - Volume XLVII (1876). Company Catalogue dated 1878 (7 pages), 28" diameter bell of Neil Goeppinger, Boone, Iowa, and The Troy Bell Founders by Clinton Meneely, grandson of original Clinton Meneely and great grandson of Andrew Meneely; *Other Facts:* The first bells by this firm were cast in 1871. Above bell is from the Methodist church at Bostwick, Nebraska. This was a partnership of Col. Clinton H. Meneely and his cousin. There is an undated 17" fire gong from Allerton, Iowa, now at the Wayne County Historical Museum in Corydon and there are several bells by this firm in upstate New York. In 1878 they advertised 28 sizes of church bells from 27" (400 lbs) to 67" (6,000 lbs) all in bronze, and stated bells had been shipped to South America, China, and India.

*Meneely & Kimberly 1878*

# Meneely Bell Company

*Address:* 22 River (22 - 28 River in 1937), Troy, New York; *Year Established:* 1869; *Year Closed:* 1950; *Years Known In Operation:* 1869 - 1950; *Founder:* Colonel Clinton Hanks Meneely; *Predecessor:* Meneely & Kimberly, Clinton H. Meneely Bell Co (1888 - 1889),; *Successor:* No Data; *Source:* *That Vanishing Sound*, Eugene Burns, Wayne Morrison of Ovid, New York, 1937 Company Catalogue; *Other Facts:* This firm made a 13,000 pound replica of the Liberty Bell in 1876, and cast approximately 25,000 bells in all. In Meneely Bell Company's 1937 catalogue they advertised chimes with electric console, auto paper roll player, clock works, and baton console. Inscription was free on bells made to order. That catalogue had a photo of a bell "pour" with one worker wearing a necktie. Colonel Clinton H. Meneely's mother's maiden name was Philena Hanks, and Col. Meneely's middle name was Hanks. His mother was related to President Abraham Lincoln's mother, Nancy Hanks. During the Civil War Col. Clinton H. Meneely served on the personal staffs of Major General McClellan and Brig. General J.J. Wadsworth and was in many battles, including Gettysburg. When he returned from the war his two brothers, Edwin A. and George R. Meneely, who were running the West Troy foundry, told him there wasn't enough business to support another family member. He then sold army surplus for a time, then went across the river and started his own bell foundry in Troy in partnership with his cousin, George H. Kimberly (Meneely and Kimberly). The brothers sued him for using the Meneely name in his bell firm. The court found that a man has the right to use his own name in his business, even if it is the same as some one elses. With two foundries using the Meneely name located in Troy and West Troy, confusion in bell ordering was unavoidable. The competition drove a split in the family, and the two sides of the family didn't speak to each other from the 1870's to the 1950's. Both firms went out of business in the same year, 1950.

*Meneely Bell Company 20 Bell Chime, Grace Church, N.Y.*

CHIME AND PEAL BELLS

CHURCH BELLS

There is no limit to the number of bells necessary to constitute a chime or peal, except that which is suggested by the necessarily constant decrease of weight and the consequent shrillness of tone ; but in this country a *chime* is generally said to consist of eight bells, attuned to the eight tones of the octave, or diatonic scale. In nearly every case a bell, attuned to the flat seventh tone of the scale, is added, thus rendering the chime capable of producing music in two keys. The finest chimes in this country were manufactured in our foundry, and we can furnish them of any weight and number, with or without mountings, and adapted to any position.

*Meneely Bell Company Troy, N.Y. Chime*

Church Bells, fully warranted as to excellence of tone, purity of composition, and strength of casting ; mounted in the most approved manner ; of weight, dimension, and tone, noted in the accompanying table. The mountings consist of our "Conical Rotary Yoke", described on page 19, and for which Letters Patent have been granted, so arranged as to firmly sustain the bell, greatly

*Meneely Bell Company Troy, N.Y. Church Bell*

*Meneely Bell Company Troy, N.Y. Foundry*

# Clinton H. Meneely Bell Company

***Address:*** Troy, New York; ***Year Established:*** No Data; ***Year Closed:*** No Data; ***Years Known In Operation:*** 1885 - 1886; ***Founder:*** Clinton H. Meneely; ***Predecessor:*** Meneely Bell Company; ***Successor:*** No Data; ***Source:*** Eugene P. Burns of Troy, New York, Sydney J. Shepp, Mississauga, Ontario, Canada, and list of bells in the St Louis area compiled by Carl Scott Zimmerman of St Louis, Mo; ***Other Facts:*** H in his middle name stood for Hanks. A 17" bronze bell made by this company in 1886 was located at the Episcopal Center of Camps and Conferences, Boone, Iowa. It specifically lists the city as Troy, N. York. Another, larger bell is in the Iowa State University Stadium dated 1860 which reads "Iowa Agricultural College/Science with Practice". His middle name was Hanks, and his mother's maiden name was Phelina Hanks. Thru her Clinton H. Meneely was related to President Abraham Lincoln as President Lincoln's mother was Nancy Hanks. Clinton Meneely was a colonel in the Union Army during the Civil War and served on the staffs of two generals and was in many battles including Gettysburg.

*Clinton H. Meneely Bell 1883*

# G. R. Meneely & Company

***Address:*** Atlanta, Georgia; ***Year Established:*** No Data; ***Year Closed:*** No Data; ***Years Known In Operation:*** 1889; ***Founder:*** No Data; ***Predecessor:*** No Data; ***Successor:*** No Data; ***Source:*** Zell's U.S. Business Directory of 1889; ***Other Facts:*** Listed in above directory under Brass Foundries-its not a certainty that this firm made bells, but likely did as they were probably a descendant or relative of the Meneely families of Troy and West Troy, New York, which made thousands of bells.

# John Meneely

***Address:*** 32 Wilelinor Dr., Edgewater, Maryland; ***Year Established:*** No Data; ***Year Closed:*** No Data; ***Years Known In Operation:*** 1993 - 2001; ***Founder:*** John Meneely; ***Predecessor:*** No Data; ***Successor:*** No Data; ***Source:*** Joe Connors, Albany, N.Y., and Eugene Burns, Troy, N.Y.; ***Other Facts:*** As of February 12, 1994 John Meneely had made several bells. He is either the grandson or great grandson of Colonel Clinton H. Meneely. He ran a marine business and made new bells for navy ships Annapolis and U. S. Maryland as well as other bells.

## Messinger Mfg Company

*Address:* Tatamy, Pennsylvania; *Year Established:* No Data; *Year Closed:* No Data; *Years Known In Operation:* 1905 - 1906; *Founder:* No Data; *Predecessor:* No Data; *Successor:* No Data; *Source:* Thomas' Register 1905 - 1906; *Other Facts:* Advertised farm bells.

## Millbank Foundry Company

*Address:* Germantown, Pennsylvania; *Year Established:* No Data; *Year Closed:* No Data; *Years Known In Operation:* No Data; *Founder:* No Data; *Predecessor:* No Data; *Successor:* No Data; *Source:* Iva May Long of Tarentum, Pennsylvania; *Other Facts:* Mrs. Long had a Susquehanna River Bell by this firm. Germantown is an old section of Philadelphia, Pennsylvania. This firm once owned the Liberty Bell as it was given a scrap value of $400 and this firm was to make a bell twice the size of the Liberty Bell, but they couldn't get it down from its mounting. The City sued him and he left it for posterity, and thus today it's still the Liberty Bell. When the Liberty bell cracked it was not yet a famous bell. Iva May Long may have had her spelling mixed up. See Wilbank Foundry, page 167.

## Aaron Miller

*Address:* Elizabeth Town, New Jersey; *Year Established:* No Data; *Year Closed:* No Data; *Years Known In Operation:* 1747 - 1759; *Founder:* Aaron Miller; *Predecessor:* No Data; *Successor:* No Data; *Source:* Louise Springer letter of 3/4/1985, her source: Sunday Newark News, August 9th, 1964. Weekly Post-Boy January 4, 1748, The Arts and Crafts of New York 1726 - 1776; *Other Facts:* Letter quote: "That state's first bell maker of record, and a noted clockmaker as well. His notice in the New Jersey Journal of Nov. 23, 1747, lists everything from surveyor chains to bells of any size. In 1759 Miller installed a public clock in the belfry of the town's First Presbyterian Church, where one of his bells already hung." Jan 4, 1748 Post Boy quote, " Church Bells of any size, he having a Foundry for that Purpose, and has cast several which have been approved to be good"

## The Miller Company

*Address:* Canton, Ohio; *Year Established:* No Data; *Year Closed:* No Data; *Years Known In Operation:* No Data; *Founder:* No Data; *Predecessor:* No Data; *Successor:* No Data; *Source:* 24" diameter bell belonging to Eve Brown of Pa in 1993; *Other Facts:* This is an iron bell with a small top pre-Civil War style. The firm made both pre and post civil war shaped bells, so we know they worked in that era.

*Miller Foundry Bell - Pre Civil War Shape*      *Miller Foundry Bell - Post Civil War Shape*

# John Millers Foundry

*Address:* Miamisburg, Ohio; *Year Established:* No Data; *Year Closed:* No Data; *Years Known In Operation:* 1839; *Founder:* No Data; *Predecessor:* No Data; *Successor:* No Data; *Source:* Eugene Burns of Troy, N. Y. March 16, 2001; *Other Facts:* Mr. Burns reports a bell is at St Jacob's Luthern Church, Miamisburg, Ohio.

# Milwaukee Foundry

*Address:* Milwaukee, Wisconsin; *Year Established:* No Data; *Year Closed:* No Data; *Years Known In Operation:* 1892; *Founder:* No Data; *Predecessor:* No Data; *Successor:* No Data; *Source:* Bell at First Congregational U.C.C, South Milwaukee, Wi.; *Other Facts:* Photo shows bell has 3 single reed lines equally spaced from the shoulder to the center of the waist, three close together just above the sound bow, and one just below it. It is the Germanic shape with a ridge on the outside of the soundbow. It is an unusual spacing of the reeds. The bell appears to be quite smooth.

# Mish Brothers

*Address:* Lebanon, Pennsylvania; *Year Established:* No Data; *Year Closed:* No Data; *Years Known In Operation:* 1888, 1889; *Founder:* No Data; *Predecessor:* No Data; *Successor:* No Data; *Source:* Zell's U.S. Business Directories of 1888 and 1889; *Other Facts:* No Data

# Montgomery Ward

*Address:* Chicago, Illinois; *Year Established:* No Data; *Year Closed:* No Data; *Years Known In Operation:* No Data; *Founder:* No Data; *Predecessor:* No Data; *Successor:* No Data; *Source:* Many bells; *Other Facts:* Although not a bell founder, so many U.S. made bells bore this name that I am including it for people who are trying to trace the origin of their bell. Montgomery Ward started in 1872 and by 1883 issued an annual large general merchandise catalogue with 10,000 items for sale including dinner bells. These bells had their name cast on them. They hired other firms to cast their bells, and they may have been made by the American Bell Foundry of Northville, Michigan, the C. S. Bell Company of Hillsboro, Ohio, or any of many foundries which made cast iron or steel dinner bells. Sears Robuck also issued an annual large catalogue of general merchandise and listed bells, but I don't believe they had their name put on the bells as I have never seen or heard of one. They even sold church bells. Both the Montgomery Ward and Sears Robuck bells were of cast iron or steel, not of bronze.

# More, Jones & Company

*Address:* 1608 N. 8th, St Louis, Missouri; *Year Established:* No Data; *Year Closed:* No Data; *Years Known In Operation:* 1877 - 1899; *Founder:* No Data; *Predecessor:* No Data; *Successor:* More-Jones Brass and Metal Co (1900 - 1915+); *Source:* Missouri business directories of 1874 - 1915 examined by Carl Scott Zimmerman of St Louis; *Other Facts:* In the 1883 state directory they were classified under "Bell and Brass Founders" but not under "Brass Founders". Carl Scott Zimmerman has not found any bells by this firm.

# Morgan Iron Works

*Address:* New York, New York; *Year Established:* No Data; *Year Closed:* No Data; *Years Known In Operation:* 1853; *Founder:* No Data; *Predecessor:* No Data; *Successor:* No Data; *Source:* Book *America's Lost Treasure*, by Tommy Thompson pages 94 - 95, and the book, *Ship of Gold in the Deep Blue Sea* by Gary Kinder referred to by Carl Scott Zimmerman of St Louis, Mo; *Other Facts:* The above book tells about the 275 lb bell from the ship Central

America which sank in 1857 and was recovered in 1988. The bell may have been the only one made by this firm. This firm made the two large single cylinder steam engines for the ship as well. The bell was bronze and two feet in diameter.

# Thornton N. Motley

*Address:* New York, New York; *Year Established:* No Data; *Year Closed:* No Data; *Years Known In Operation:* 1891; *Founder:* No Data; *Predecessor:* No Data; *Successor:* No Data; *Source:* The firm's 1891 catalogue pages supplied by Marion Bradley; *Other Facts:* They listed bronze bells from 15 lbs to 6,000 lbs, and Steel Amalgam bells of 13" to 42".

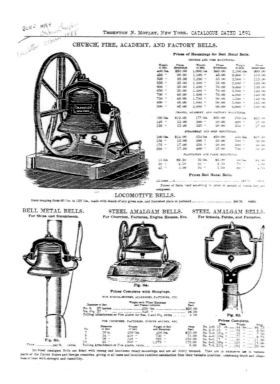

*Thornton N. Motley Advertisement for Bronze and Steel Bells*

# Charles Mousley

*Address:* 7241 Howard, Philadelphia, Pennsylvania; *Year Established:* No Data; *Year Closed:* No Data; *Years Known In Operation:* 1905 - 1906; *Founder:* No Data; *Predecessor:* No Data; *Successor:* No Data; *Source:* Thomas' Register 1905 - 1906; *Other Facts:* No Data

# National Bell Foundry

*Address:* Cincinnati, Ohio; *Year Established:* No Data; *Year Closed:* No Data; *Years Known In Operation:* No Data; *Founder:* No Data; *Predecessor:* No Data; *Successor:* No Data; *Source:* Bell owned by Clarence Kline (94 in 1985) of RR Prescott, Iowa, and by Neil Goeppinger of Boone, Iowa, and by Gladwater Middle School, and bells in Calhoon County, Missouri examined by Carl Scott Zimmerman of St Louis; *Other Facts:* The above bells are cast steel and the Kline bell and the Gladwater Middle School Bell of Gladwater Texas, both have cast iron weels. A 44" bell is in Buck Grove, Iowa, a 35" is in the Presbyterian church of Bellevue, Ill in 1992, also two churches in Calhoon County Missouri have bells.

## N. O. Nelson Mfg Copmpany

*Address:* 8th St, SE corner of Saint Charles, Saint Louis, Missouri; *Year Established:* 1884; *Year Closed:* 1917; *Years Known In Operation:* 1884 - 1917; *Founder:* Nelson O. Nelson; *Predecessor:* Goulds & Ostraander; *Successor:* No Data; *Source:* Carl Scott Zimmerman of St Louis, and bell in Marine, Illinois; *Other Facts:* Zimmerman found a 24 1/4" diameter bronze bell dated 1896 with this name at the fire department of Marine, Ill, which weighs approximately 400 lbs, hung on a 6x6 with an eye on the clapper, 2 pulleys, and leather hand loops for ends of the ropes. Nelson O. Nelson worked for Bignall & Co, which later became Bignall & Ostrander and still later Goulds & Ostrander. Eventually Nelson bought Goulds & Ostrander and moved to their location. He did plumbing supplies, etc. They paid 16 1/4 cents/lb for bronze. Carl Scott Zimmerman says the finish and shape of the bell and lettering look like that of Stuckstede & Bros. bells, so he believes that firm made the bell for the N. O. Nelson Mfg Company.

## N. O. Nelson & Company

*Address:* St Louis, Missouri; *Year Established:* No Data; *Year Closed:* No Data; *Years Known In Operation:* 1877 - 1883; *Founder:* No Data; *Predecessor:* No Data; *Successor:* No Data; *Source:* Research of city directories by Carl Scott Zimmerman of St Louis, Mo; *Other Facts:* This firm advertised that they made bells in city directories, but no bells have been found.

## New Departure Bell Company

*Address:* Bristol, Connecticut; *Year Established:* No Data; *Year Closed:* No Data; *Years Known In Operation:* 1905 - 1906; *Founder:* No Data; *Predecessor:* No Data; *Successor:* No Data; *Source:* Thomas' Register 1905 - 1906; *Other Facts:* Although this firm is known for their small bells, at one time they advertised larger bells as well.

## New York Bell Foundry

*Address:* located in the Bowery, just north of the city limits, New York, New York; *Year Established:* 1794; *Year Closed:* 1795; *Years Known In Operation:* 1794 - 1795; *Founder:* John Bailey and George Hedderly; *Predecessor:* No Data; *Successor:* No Data; *Source:* Lois Springer letter of 3/11/1985, The Arts & Crafts in New York 1726 - 1776 (research papers of Lois Springer), Gary Trudgen article in the January 1993 Bell Tower of the American Bell Association International, Inc., and the New York Daily Advertiser, April 21, 1794; *Other Facts:* Museum of City of New York has brass bell cast in 1794 which was possibly an alarm bell for the Watch House at Wall and Broad Streets. Also an ABAII Minnesota Chapter member found another similarly dated bell, presumable church type, at the Reformed Church in New Paltz, N.Y. These bells were either inscribed John Bailey or I. Bailey. Hedderly emigrated from England shortly before 1794 and had worked in England in bell foundries as had his ancestors. Bailey was a cutler and made swords for the Revolutionary War, including General George Washington's sword.

## Niles Bell Foundry

*Address:* 223 East Front Street (between Butler and the old Miami Canal, next to the Deer-creek Bridge), Cincinnati, Ohio; *Year Established:* 1845; *Year Closed:* 1869; *Years Known In Operation:* 1845 - 1869; *Founder:* James Niles and Jonathan Niles, brothers; *Predecessor:* Cincinnati Bell Foundry; *Successor:* No Data; *Source:* Mrs. G. Lyle Ringland, Norwood, Ohio, Carl Scott Zimmerman of St Louis, Mo., and The Cincinnati Times-Star newspaper of April 25, 1940; *Other Facts:* Also did business as Niles Works and as Niles & Company. Carl Scott Zimmerman reports a chime of eight bells in the First English Lutheran Church (ELCT) in Dayton, Ohio, marked "Niles Works,

Cincinnati". It has three bass bells dated 1869, two mid bells dated 1868, one mid and two trebles that are undated. The largest bell is about two tons. On January 1, 1870 the firm was sold to Vanduzen & Tift for $5,000.

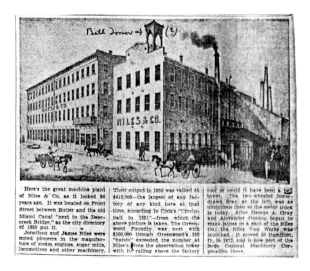

*Niles and Company Foundry*

# Norfolk Navy Yard

*Address:* Norfolk, Virginia; *Year Established:* No Data; *Year Closed:* No Data; *Years Known In Operation:* 1895; *Founder:* No Data; *Predecessor:* No Data; *Successor:* No Data; *Source: Bells Over Texas* by Bessie Lee Fitzhugh (Carl Hertzog, El Paso, Texas, Texas Western Press 1955) page 104; *Other Facts:* Picture of bell-inscription reads "U.S.S. Texas, Navy Yard Norfolk, 1895." Bell is 16 1/2" high and 21 1/4" diameter. Navy Yard made bells from 9" (20 lbs) to 34" (800lbs)-the latter for battleships.

# Northville Michigan Bell Foundry Company

*Address:* Northville, Michigan; *Year Established:* No Data; *Year Closed:* No Data; *Years Known In Operation:* ; *Founder:* No Data; *Predecessor:* No Data; *Successor:* No Data; *Source:* Bell belonging to Leonard Fleischer of Columbus, Nebraska; *Other Facts:* Mr. Fleischer bought a cast iron bell measuring 38 3/8" diameter with a cast iron wheel from the Mission Convent Church of Ogden, Iowa on November 20, 1982, when the church furnishings were being auctioned for sale.

# James Nuttall

*Address:* New Orleans, Louisiana; *Year Established:* No Data; *Year Closed:* No Data; *Years Known In Operation:* 1858; *Founder:* No Data; *Predecessor:* No Data; *Successor:* No Data; *Source:* Lois Springer letter, January 1992; *Other Facts:* No Data

# Odell & Ives

*Address:* Baltimore, Maryland; *Year Established:* No Data; *Year Closed:* No Data; *Years Known In Operation:* 1842 - 1856; *Founder:* No Data; *Predecessor:* No Data; *Successor:* No Data; *Source:* Research of city directories by Carl Scott Zimmerman of St Louis, Mo; *Other Facts:* No Data

## James H. Odell

*Address:* 29 South Frederick Street, Baltimore, Maryland; *Year Established:* No Data; *Year Closed:* No Data; *Years Known In Operation:* 1845; *Founder:* No Data; *Predecessor:* No Data; *Successor:* No Data; *Source:* L. Elsinore Springer letter of 1/22/1985; *Other Facts:* Brass and composition founder whose ad in the 1845 Baltimore Business Directory includes chruch and steamboat bells.

## Marcus O'Hara

*Address:* St Louis, Missouri; *Year Established:* No Data; *Year Closed:* No Data; *Years Known In Operation:* 1842 - 1847; *Founder:* No Data; *Predecessor:* No Data; *Successor:* No Data; *Source:* Carl Scott Zimmerman's inspection of city directories for 1842 - 1847 (not published every year); *Other Facts:* No bells have been found by this firm.

## Ohio Bell Foundry

*The Ohio Bell - Pre Civil War Shape*

*Address:* 204 Ludlow Street, Cincinnati, Ohio; *Year Established:* No Data; *Year Closed:* No Data; *Years Known In Operation:* 1904; *Founder:* George W. Vanduzen; *Predecessor:* E. W. Vanduzen; *Successor:* Ohio Brass & Bell Foundry; *Source:* 23" diameter cast iron bell belonging to Eve Brown of Lahaska, Pa. on Feb. 18, 1994, so it was probably considered to be a 24 inch bell, although it measured something less. This was common as the foundry measured the mold, and the metal shrank while cooling. Also research of Carl Scott Zimmerman of St. Louis area; *Other Facts:* The inscription is on the yoke with the word OH IO split between the H and I by the connecting bolt bulge in the center top-thus "The OH IO Bell". It has a running spoke iron wheel and inverted heart stands with fleur de lies-the same stands as used by a number of other large bell manufacturers, so they probably came from a bell stand supplier. "24" is marked on the skirt of the bell. George W. Vanduzen worked in his father's bell foundry, E. W. Vanduzen, and by 1904 had set up his own foundry at 207 Ludlow Street in Cincinnati. He advertised that year under Bell Manufacturers. In the years 1905 to 1909 he advertised under the name Ohio Brass Foundry.

## Ohio Brass & Bell Foundry

*Address:* 207 Ludlow Street, Cincinnati, Ohio; *Year Established:* No Data; *Year Closed:* No Data; *Years Known In Operation:* 1837 - 1905; *Founder:* George W. Vanduzen; *Predecessor:* Ohio Bell Foundry; *Successor:* No Data; *Source:* Bell inquiry received by Neil Goeppinger, and research of Carl Scott Zimmerman of St. Louis area; *Other Facts:* This was in regard to a 19" diameter, 140 lb bronze bell dated 1837 with a tang having two holes for mounting. This firm appeared as Ohio Brass Foundry in 1905 to 1909 directories. The 1837 bell used the name Ohio Brass & Bell Foundry.

# Onion Bell Foundry

***Address:*** Louisville, Kentucky; ***Year Established:*** No Data; ***Year Closed:*** No Data; ***Years Known In Operation:*** No Data; ***Founder:*** No Data; ***Predecessor:*** No Data; ***Successor:*** No Data; ***Source:*** Donald Feik of the I.T. Verdin Firm of Cincinnati, Ohio, and research of Carl Scott Zimmerman of St Louis, Mo.; ***Other Facts:*** No Data

# Parker & Company

***Address:*** Cincinnati, Ohio; ***Year Established:*** No Data; ***Year Closed:*** No Data; ***Years Known In Operation:*** 1904; ***Founder:*** No Data; ***Predecessor:*** No Data; ***Successor:*** No Data; ***Source:*** Bell in Pekin, Illinois; ***Other Facts:*** Above bell was in front of St Joseph's Catholic Church in Sept. 2000. It is approximately 18" in diameter, bronze, and the inscription "Parker & Co Cincinnati" is around the top of the bell. It is undated, but a plaque says it was installed in 1904. The only ornamentation besides the lettering is an indented band around the outside of the sound bow. The top has a rectangular tang with a hole for a cross bolt which fastens it into an iron yoke with matching rectangular hole. The arms of the yoke are square. This firm may be related to the J. P. Parker firm of Ripley, Ohio. Ripley is a good distance south east of Cincinnati, but they both are on the Ohio River.

# J.P. Parker

***Address:*** Ripley, Ohio; ***Year Established:*** No Data; ***Year Closed:*** No Data; ***Years Known In Operation:*** 1889; ***Founder:*** No Data; ***Predecessor:*** No Data; ***Successor:*** No Data; ***Source:*** Zell's U.S. Business Directory of 1889; ***Other Facts:*** No Data

# Abel Parmalee

***Address:*** New Haven, Connecticut; ***Year Established:*** 1736; ***Year Closed:*** No Data; ***Years Known In Operation:*** 1736; ***Founder:*** No Data; ***Predecessor:*** No Data; ***Successor:*** No Data; ***Source:*** History Cast in Metal; ***Other Facts:*** No Data

# John Pass

***Address:*** Philadelphia, Pennsylvania; ***Year Established:*** No Data; ***Year Closed:*** No Data; ***Years Known In Operation:*** 1749; ***Founder:*** John Pass; ***Predecessor:*** No Data; ***Successor:*** Pass & Stow; ***Source:*** That Vanishing Sound, and Cast in America by Justin Kramer; ***Other Facts:*** With Charles Stow Jr, in 1753 John Pass recast the Liberty Bell after it cracked while being hung. It was originally cast by Whitechapel of England. Pass later is thought to have cast other bells.

# Pass & Stow

***Address:*** Philadelphia, Pennsylvania; ***Year Established:*** No Data; ***Year Closed:*** No Data; ***Years Known In Operation:*** 1753; ***Founder:*** John Pass and Charles Stow, Jr; ***Predecessor:*** John Pass; ***Successor:*** No Data; ***Source:*** That Vanishing Sound, History Cast in Metal, and Cast in America by Justin Kramer; ***Other Facts:*** In 1753 they recast the Liberty Bell in America. It was originally cast in London, England by Whitechapel. It took them two tries to get a bell with a good sound.

# Paulson, Thomas & Son

*Address:* Brooklyn, New York; *Year Established:* No Data; *Year Closed:* No Data; *Years Known In Operation:* No Data; *Founder:* No Data; *Predecessor:* No Data; *Successor:* No Data; *Source:* List submitted by Roger Plaquet to ABAII website and posted November 14, 2008 from Sid Gelman's bell papers listing bells made by New York City firms; *Other Facts:* No Data

# Peck Stow & Wilcox Company

*Address:* Plantsville (later Southington in 1906), Connecticut; *Year Established:* No Data; *Year Closed:* No Data; *Years Known In Operation:* 1889 - 1906; *Founder:* No Data; *Predecessor:* No Data; *Successor:* No Data; *Source:* Zell's U.S. Business Directory of 1889, and Thomas' Register of 1905 - 1906; *Other Facts:* The Stow may have been related to John Stow of Pass & Stow who recast the Liberty Bell in this country.

# Perin & Gaff Mfg Company

*Address:* Cincinnati, Ohio; *Year Established:* 1875; *Year Closed:* 1882/83; *Years Known In Operation:* 1875 - 1882/83; *Founder:* No Data; *Predecessor:* No Data; *Successor:* No Data; *Source:* Carl Scott Zimmerman of St Louis, Missouri, and bell in collection of Leonard Fleisher of Columbus, Nebraska, and ABAII bell forum post of 10 - 23 - 2009 by M. Thompson with photos of a dinner bell; *Other Facts:* Zimmerman reports a small iron farm bell is located on a post outside the oldest church building remaining in St Louis County, and the yoke reads "Perin & Gaff, Cincinnati". The Fleisher bell is an 18" diameter iron dinner bell marked #2, and is the pre Civil War style with a small top. The Thompson bell is an 18" diameter iron dinner bell with the post Civil War shape. On the top is cast 16 - 5 - 90 which may have been the date. In the center of the yoke is a circle with the number 3 in it. Thus it was their #3 size dinner bell. I have also seen photos of a 16" bell by this firm.

# William Peters

*Address:* 8 West Pratt Street, near the bridge, Baltimore, Maryland; *Year Established:* No Data; *Year Closed:* No Data; *Years Known In Operation:* 1842 - 1856; *Founder:* No Data; *Predecessor:* No Data; *Successor:* No Data; *Source:* Research of city directories by Carl Scott Zimmerman of St Louis, Mo., and a courthouse bell dated 1848 referred to in an ABAII post of Feb 27, 2010; *Other Facts:* This firm advertised under the name "Wm Peters Brass & Bell Foundry".

# John Phillips

*Address:* New York City, New York; *Year Established:* No Data; *Year Closed:* No Data; *Years Known In Operation:* 1717; *Founder:* No Data; *Predecessor:* No Data; *Successor:* No Data; *Source:* *That Vanishing Sound*, and *Historic Bells in New Hampshire*, and list submitted by Roger Plaquet to ABAII website and posted November 14, 2008 from Sid Gelman's bell papers listing bells made by New York City firms. ; *Other Facts:* This is possibly the oldest bell foundry in what is now the United States.

# Phoenix Foundry

*Address:* Louisville, Kentucky; *Year Established:* No Data; *Year Closed:* No Data; *Years Known In Operation:* 1836 - 1846; *Founder:* William Grainger; *Predecessor:* No Data; *Successor:* No Data; *Source:* Research of city directories by Carl Scott Zimmerman of St Louis, Mo; *Other Facts:* Willaim Grainger, owner

# Samuel Powell

*Address:* Philadelphia, Pennsylvania; *Year Established:* No Data; *Year Closed:* No Data; *Years Known In Operation:* 1746; *Founder:* No Data; *Predecessor:* No Data; *Successor:* No Data; *Source:* L. Elsinore Springer letter of 1/22/1985; *Other Facts:* Brazier and bell founder who in 1746 cast a bell for Bethlehem Bell House, Bethlehem, Pennsylvania.

# Prindle Station

*Address:* 22 Prindle Station Road, Washougal, Washington; *Year Established:* No Data; *Year Closed:* No Data; *Years Known In Operation:* 1970's - 2015; *Founder:* No Data; *Predecessor:* C. S. Bell Co.; *Successor:* No Data; *Source:* C. S. Bell Co publication; *Other Facts:* This firm acquired the patterns to make bells from the C. S. Bell Co. of Hillsboro, Ohio sometime after the Bell family sold the firm in 1974. As of 2015 they continue to make dinner bells in several sizes, and dinner bell parts.

# Providence Brass Foundry

*Address:* 466 Eddy (in 1881) and 460 Eddy (in 1888 and 1889), Providence, Rhode Island; *Year Established:* No Data; *Year Closed:* No Data; *Years Known In Operation:* 1881 - 1889; *Founder:* A. H. Manchester, Jr. was the proprietor in 1881; *Predecessor:* No Data; *Successor:* No Data; *Source:* Zell's U.S. Business Directories of 1881 and 1888 - 1889; *Other Facts:* No Data

# Puget Sound Navel Shipyard

*Address:* Seattle, Washington; *Year Established:* No Data; *Year Closed:* No Data; *Years Known In Operation:* No Data; *Founder:* U.S. Navy; *Predecessor:* No Data; *Successor:* No Data; *Source:* *Bells Over Texas* by Bessie Lee Fitzhugh (Carl Hertzog, El Paso, Texas, Texas Western Press 1955); *Other Facts:* Puget Sound Naval Shipyard made bells from 9" (20 lbs) to 34" (800 lbs) for vessels built on the west coast.

# Pugh & Russell

*Address:* New York City, New York; *Year Established:* No Data; *Year Closed:* No Data; *Years Known In Operation:* No Data; *Founder:* No Data; *Predecessor:* No Data; *Successor:* No Data; *Source:* List submitted by Roger Plaquet to ABAII website and posted November 14, 2008 from Sid Gelman's bell papers listing bells made by New York City firms; *Other Facts:* No Data

# Thomas Pugh

*Address:* Maiden-Lane, New York, New York; *Year Established:* No Data; *Year Closed:* No Data; *Years Known In Operation:* 1768; *Founder:* No Data; *Predecessor:* No Data; *Successor:* No Data; *Source:* N.Y. Gazette, May 2, 1768 (research papers of Lois Springer). The Arts and Crafts in New York 1726 - 1776; *Other Facts:* House bells, Clock bells, Chiming Bells.

# Rankins Snyder H. Co

*Address:* No Data; *Year Established:* No Data; *Year Closed:* No Data; *Years Known In Operation:* No Data; *Founder:* No Data; *Predecessor:* No Data; *Successor:* No Data; *Source:* Bell located at Evergreen Farm, Eminence, Indiana; *Other Facts:* This was an iron bell, post Civil War shape. "D" is on the center of the yoke, and so it may have been a size designation, or the name may have been Rankins D. Snyder H. Co as Rankins was left of center and Snyder was right of center.

# R. B.

*Address:* No Data; *Year Established:* No Data; *Year Closed:* No Data; *Years Known In Operation:* 1773; *Founder:* No Data; *Predecessor:* No Data; *Successor:* No Data; *Source:* August 1974 Hobbies magazine advertisement by Plymouth Antique Centre, 26 Union St., Plymouth, Massachusetts. (research papers of Lois Springer); *Other Facts:* Photo of bell in advertisement mounted in white oak frame measuring 50" high, 32" wide, & 48" long. Photo showed wood wheel and yoke. Inscribed "R. B. 1773".

*RB Bell Advertisement*

# J. Regester & Sons

*Address:* 53 North Holliday Street in 1881, Holiday & Saratoga in 1889., Baltimore, Maryland; *Year Established:* No Data; *Year Closed:* No Data; *Years Known In Operation:* 1870 - 1906; *Founder:* Joshua Regester; *Predecessor:* No Data; *Successor:* No Data; *Source:* Zell's United States Business Directory of 1881 and 1889, and Thomas' Register 1905 - 1906; *Other Facts:* There is a 44" diameter bell inscribed Joshua Register & Sons 1870 Baltimore, MD. There may be a spelling question regarding the last name "Register" as a bell from Baltimore belonging to Neil Goeppinger has the inscription "Clampitt & Regester" (e instead of i)."

# J. Regester's Sons Company

*Address:* Baltimore, Maryland; *Year Established:* No Data; *Year Closed:* No Data; *Years Known In Operation:* 1899; *Founder:* No Data; *Predecessor:* J. Regester & Sons; *Successor:* No Data; *Source:* Letter from Ingo E. Rucker of Bel Air, Maryland, re: a 32 1/2" bell; *Other Facts:* Inscription on above bell reads Baltimore Bell Foundry, J. Register's Sons Co, Balt. MD, 1899 (note spelling difference of "i" for "e").

# Regester & Webb

*Address:* Baltimore, Maryland; *Year Established:* No Data; *Year Closed:* No Data; *Years Known In Operation:* 1858 - 1885; *Founder:* No Data; *Predecessor:* No Data; *Successor:* McShane Bell Foundry Company; *Source:* Iva May Long of Tarentum, Pennsylvania; *Other Facts:* Iva May Long says Russell McShane told her the owners of this firm were related to the McShanes and were probably the forerunners of the McShane foundry at Baltimore. Iva May Long of Pa. had a bell by this firm dated 1885.

# Paul Revere

*Address:* Boston & Canton, Massachusetts; *Year Established:* 1792; *Year Closed:* 1801; *Years Known In Operation:* 1792 - 1801; *Founder:* Paul Revere; *Predecessor:* Revere consulted Colonel Aaron Hobart before casting his first bell; *Successor:* Revere & Sons in 1801 and Revere & Son later in 1801; *Source: That Vanishing Sound*, Edward and Evelyn Stickney of Bedford, Massachusetts; *Other Facts:* He or the partnerships that succeeded him made 959 bells through 1828, of which 467 were church bells. A total of 137 church bells bearing the Revere inscription were known to be in existence in September of 1983 according to the Stickneys. One of Hobart's sons and a British Navy deserter, a foundry-man named Gilliam, showed Revere how to cast bells. A bell dated 1797 is in the People's Baptist Church of Boston. It weighs 1,125 pounds. Paul Revere consulted with Colonel Aaron Hobart before casting his first bell at age 57. See the text earlier in this book about the start of the bell foundry industry in the U. S. and the important part Revere played in it.

*Paul Revere - Painting by John Copley*

*Courtesy of Massachusetts Historical Society*

*Revere Advertisement Showing Bell and Cannon*

*Revere Bell with Heavy Reeds 2,2,3,2 plus 2 on top*

*Revere Bell With Iron Clamps For Wood Yoke*

*Revere Bell With Raised Top Above Top Reeds*

*Revere Bell With Square Cannons And Square Argent With Steps*

145

# Revere & Sons

*Address:* Boston, Massachusetts; *Year Established:* 1801; *Year Closed:* 1801; *Years Known In Operation:* 1801; *Founder:* Paul Revere and his 2 sons Joseph and Paul Jr; *Predecessor:* Paul Revere; *Successor:* Revere & Son; *Source:* Edward and Evelyn Stickney of Bedford, Massachusetts; *Other Facts:* The same year it was founded, Paul Revere Jr. left, reportedly to join George Holbrook. A bell weighing 997 lbs dated 1801 is in a Weston, Massachusetts, church.

# Revere & Son

*Address:* Boston (Canton), Massachusetts; *Year Established:* 1801; *Year Closed:* 1811; *Years Known In Operation:* 1801 - 1811; *Founder:* Paul Revere and son Joseph; *Predecessor:* Revere & Sons; *Successor:* Paul Revere & Son (Paul Revere's son Joseph and 2 grandsons, Paul Revere III and Thomas Eayres Jr); *Source:* Edward and Evelyn Stickney of Bedford, Massachusetts, and *That Vanishing Sound*; *Other Facts:* In 1801 Paul Revere brought his two sons Joseph and Paul Jr. in with him but that same year Paul Jr. is said to have left to cast bells with George Holbrook. The bell foundry was moved from Boston to Canton, Massachusetts, in 1804. Paul Revere retired from the bell manufacturing business when this firm ceased in 1811 (he was 76).

# Paul Revere & Son

*Address:* Canton (Bells read Boston), Massachusetts; *Year Established:* 1811; *Year Closed:* 1821; *Years Known In Operation:* 1811 - 1821; *Founder:* Joseph Revere (son of Paul Revere) and Paul Revere III and Thomas Eayres Jr. (both were grandsons of Paul Revere); *Predecessor:* Revere & Son; *Successor:* Revere Boston; *Source:* Edward and Evelyn Stickney of Bedford, Massachusetts; *Other Facts:* They used the "Paul Revere" name even though he died in 1818. Bells made by this firm had the inscription "Paul Revere & Son Boston" followed by the date. In 1816 they made two large bells-one weighs 2,437 lbs and is 49" in diameter (located at King's Chapel, Boston), and one weighs 2,488 lbs with a 51 lb clapper and is in the First Congregational Chruch in Providence, Rhode Island.

# Revere & Blake

*Address:* Boston, Massachusetts; *Year Established:* 1821; *Year Closed:* 1823; *Years Known In Operation:* 1821 - 1823; *Founder:* Paul Revere III and William Blake; *Predecessor:* Paul Revere & Son, William Blake; *Successor:* Paul Revere & Company (Paul Revere III, William Blake & John Sullivan); *Source:* Edward and Evelyn Stickney of Bedford, Massachusetts, and their booklet "The Bells of Paul Revere, His Sons, and Grandsons"; *Other Facts:* It isn't verified that this firm made bells, but since its immediate predecessors and successors did, and since its founders did the year before 1821 and the year after 1823, it seems a certainty that it did make bells. One of the founders, William Blake, apprenticed under Paul Revere according to the book, "*That Vanishing Sound*".

# Revere

*Address:* Canton (bells read Boston), Massachusetts; *Year Established:* 1821; *Year Closed:* 1828; *Years Known In Operation:* 1821 - 1828; *Founder:* Joseph Revere (?); *Predecessor:* Paul Revere & Son; *Successor:* Revere Copper Company; *Source:* Edward and Evelyn Stickney of Bedford, Massachusetts; *Other Facts:* From 1821 - 1824 bells read "Revere Boston" and were dated. From 1824 - 1828 they had the same inscription but were not dated. The successor firm, the Revere Copper Company used the same inscription but it wasn't incorporated until 1828. A bell made in 1827 is in a church in Portland, Maine and it weighs 1,827 lbs. A 36" diameter bell with this inscription but no date was offered for sale by Brosamers Bells in 2016 for $65,000.

# Paul Revere & Company

*Address:* Boston, Massachusetts; *Year Established:* 1823; *Year Closed:* 1825; *Years Known In Operation:* 1823 - 1825; *Founder:* Paul Revere III, William Blake, and John W. Sullivan; *Predecessor:* Revere & Blake 1821 - 1823 (not certain they made bells); *Successor:* Boston & Braintree Copper & Brass Manufactory; *Source:* Edward and Evelyn Stickney of Bedford, Massachusetts; *Other Facts:* One of the founders, Paul Revere III was the grandson of Paul Revere the patriot. He was earlier involved in "Paul Revere & Son" which was in existence from 1811 - 1821. Blake carried on a large bell foundry on his own later. The bells made by this firm were dated.

# Revere Copper Company

*Address:* Originally Lynn & Foster Streets, North Boston, Massachusetts (Revere Copper & Brass Co.), Canton, Massachusetts; *Year Established:* 1828; *Year Closed:* still in existence; *Years Known In Operation:* Made bells from 1828 into and perhaps through the 1830's; *Founder:* Joseph Revere (president until his death in 1868 at 91 years of age) and Frederick Walker Lincoln (who took over the presidency at that time); *Predecessor:* Paul Revere, Revere Copper and Brass Company; *Successor:* No Data; *Source:* Edward and Evelyn Stickney of Bedford, Massachusetts, and *History Cast in Metal*; *Other Facts:* Later, after the two founders were gone, Joseph's son John was president. The firm started in 1801 as the Revere Copper and Brass Company but didn't make bells. It was incorporated in 1828 and the name changed to Revere Copper Company, it then took over the production of the Revere bells. The bells were marked, "Revere Boston" and bore no date. Joseph Revere was Paul Revere's son and Frederick Lincoln his grandson. Paul Revere and Paul Revere Jr. had died before this (1818 and 1813 respectively). A 1,700 lb bell is in Covenant 1st Presbyterian Church of Cincinnati. A 39" diameter Revere bell sold by the Glad Tiding Church in St. Quincy, Ma., in April 2013 was undated, but the church records show it was cast in 1832.

# Richardson

*Address:* Boston, Massachusetts; *Year Established:* No Data; *Year Closed:* No Data; *Years Known In Operation:* No Data; *Founder:* No Data; *Predecessor:* No Data; *Successor:* No Data; *Source:* List of Sydney J. Shep, Mississauga, Ontario, Canada,; *Other Facts:* Carl Scott Zimmerman points out that in the absence of any evidence to the contrary, it would be reasonable to assume that this refers to one of the partners of Hooper, Blake and Richardson (also in Boston, Massachusetts). That partner's name was Thomas Richardson.

# H. W. Rincker Foundry

*Address:* Chicago, Illinois; *Year Established:* 1850; *Year Closed:* No Data; *Years Known In Operation:* 1850 - 1875; *Founder:* No Data; *Predecessor:* No Data; *Successor:* No Data; *Source:* *That Vanishing Sound*, 8 bells seen by Carl Scott Zimmerman of St Louis, Missouri, City of Chicago historical records, and list of bells in the St Louis area compiled by Carl Scott Zimmerman of St Louis; *Other Facts:* The first bell the firm cast was for a church in Oswego, Illinois. In December 1853 the City of Chicago contracted with this firm to cast an 8,000 lb bell. Mr. Rincker also made bells in Sigel, Shelby County, Illinois, and in Strasburg, Shelby County, Illinois. The two towns are just north of Effingham in central Illinois.

# John Robertson

*Address:* South Carolina; *Year Established:* No Data; *Year Closed:* No Data; *Years Known In Operation:* 1760; *Founder:* No Data; *Predecessor:* No Data; *Successor:* No Data; *Source:* *That Vanishing Sound*; *Other Facts:* No Data

# Charles T. Robinson & Company

*Address:* Brighton at Allen Streets, Boston, Massachusetts; *Year Established:* 1889; *Year Closed:* 1889; *Years Known In Operation:* 1889; *Founder:* William Blake; *Predecessor:* William Blake & Company; *Successor:* Blake Bell Company in 1890; *Source:* Zell's United States Business Directory of 1888 and 1889, *That Vanishing Sound* (for 1890 transition to Blake Bell company), Edward and Evelyn Stickney of Bedford, Massachusetts; *Other Facts:* A bell at the city hall in Haverhill, Massachuttets, states "cast by C.T. Robinson & Co. formerly Wm Blake & Co. Boston Mass. AD. 1889". Stickney states, "This would indicate that he had taken over the Blake business, but the latest Blake bell we've located is 1896, for the U. S. Lighthouse Establishment, and it is in Cutler, ME."

# Roland Farm Bells

*Address:* Baltimore, Maryland; *Year Established:* No Data; *Year Closed:* No Data; *Years Known In Operation:* No Data; *Founder:* No Data; *Predecessor:* No Data; *Successor:* No Data; *Source:* Todd Lower then of Toledo, Ohio; *Other Facts:* Lower had a bell by this firm and says they were made by the Baltimore Plow Company.

# S. E. Root

*Address:* Bristol, Connecticut; *Year Established:* No Data; *Year Closed:* No Data; *Years Known In Operation:* 1888, 1889; *Founder:* No Data; *Predecessor:* No Data; *Successor:* No Data; *Source:* Zell's United States Business Directories of 1888 and 1889; *Other Facts:* In above directories listed under "Cathedral Bells".

# David Ross

*Address:* Elizabeth Town, New Jersey; *Year Established:* No Data; *Year Closed:* No Data; *Years Known In Operation:* 1774; *Founder:* No Data; *Predecessor:* No Data; *Successor:* No Data; *Source:* The Arts & Crafts in New York 1777 - 1799 (New York Gazetteer and the Country Journal, Dec 10, 1783); *Other Facts:* He stated in an advertisement on December 10, 1783 that he "intends to erect a Furnace early in the spring for making bells from fifty to one thousand weight or upwards which he will warrant to be equal to any imported, he having followed the business previous.."

# Ross Meehan Foundries

*Address:* Chattanooga, Tennessee; *Year Established:* No Data; *Year Closed:* No Data; *Years Known In Operation:* Late 1800's to some time in the 1980's; *Founder:* No Data; *Predecessor:* No Data; *Successor:* No Data; *Source:* Bell owned by Clarence Kline of RR Prescott, Iowa (94 in 1985) & Lois Springer research papers, Thomas' Register 1905 - 1906, and ABAII website post in the big bells forum by nightflier51 on May 5, 2015; *Other Facts:* The above bell is cast iron and has a cast iron wheel. Also listed as Ross-Meechan Foundries in letter from Chattanooga Public Library of 7/23/1974 to Lois Springer. Likely a typographical error. Listed as Ross Meehan Foundry Co in 1905 - 1906. They made iron farm and dinner bells, but may have made other sizes as well.

# Rumley & Company

*Address:* Seneca Falls, New York; *Year Established:* No Data; *Year Closed:* No Data; *Years Known In Operation:* No Data; *Founder:* No Data; *Predecessor:* No Data; *Successor:* No Data; *Source:* A 23 3/4 inch diameter bell belonging to Elsie Sawyers of Winterset, Iowa; *Other Facts:* Made cast iron bells.

# Rumsey & Company (Limited)

*Address:* 19 Dey. Factory, Seneca Falls (later New York City), New York; *Year Established:* No Data; *Year Closed:* No Data; *Years Known In Operation:* 1865 - 1919; *Founder:* No Data; *Predecessor:* No Data; *Successor:* No Data;

*Source:* Wayne E. Morrison Sr of Ovid, New York, and Zell's United States Business Directory of 1888 / New York State Directory 1870 (New York Historical Association), Thomas' Register 1905 - 1906, and a bell owned by Neil Goeppinger of Boone, Iowa; *Other Facts:* They listed their bells in their general pump catalogue, but may have had a separate catalogue as well as they advertised their bells separately in Zell's. The firm moved from the above address to (or opened an office at) 93 Liberty, New York City, New York, sometime between 1882 and 1887. In 1870 they advertised 13" diameter to 42" diameter (980 lbs, 1,276 lbs with yoke and frame) Steel Amalgam Bells. Church bell sizes 30", 34", 38", 42", Fire Alarm bell sizes 25", 27", 30", 34", 38", 42", School & Factory bell sizes 25", 27". In 1870 the name was "Rumsey & Co"

# Rumsey Manufacturing Company

*Address:* 806 - 820 N. 2nd in 1880 - 1900  (610 N. 2nd in 1867), St. Louis, Missouri; *Year Established:* 1865; *Year Closed:* No Data; *Years Known In Operation:* 1865 - 1919; *Founder:* No Data; *Predecessor:* No Data; *Successor:* No Data; *Source:* A 39" bronze bell dated 1882 was in Winston Jones collection. A 29" bronze is in front of Assembly of God Church Corning, Iowa, dated 1891. Bells owned by Neil Goeppinger of Boone, Iowa, and Don P. Moreland of Farrar, Iowa, and Gould's 1867 & 1900 Directories for St. Louis, research by Carl Scott Zimmerman of St Louis, Missouri., and 1968 letter from the Saint Louis Public Library; *Other Facts:* Bells in Boone, Tiffin, and Farrar, Iowa are all bronze but in the Gould's 1900 Directory they advertised "Steel Amalgam Bells" so they made (or had made for them) both steel and bronze bells. In that directory they advertised bells and bathtubs. In 1867 and 1880 Gould's City Directories the Steel Amagam Bell Co was listed at the same address as Rumsey Mfg. Co. so they may have made steel bells earlier under a separate name which they later dropped. Most of their bells were made by McShane of Baltimore and were identical in shape, finish, reeds, etc, but the above bell in Corning, Iowa was similar in shape, finish and reeds to Stuckstede bells, so they may have had both McShane and Stuckstede make bells for them. They did business as L. M. Rumsey & Co from 1865 - 1880 at 141 N. 2nd, 610 N. 2nd, 811 N Main, 804 - 820 N. 2nd. They did business as L. M. Rumsey Mnfg. Co from 1881 - 1917 at 806 - 820 N. 2nd. They advertised bells (brass and amalgam) from 1867 to 1910.

*Rumsey M'F'G Company Bell 1884*

# Jacob Ruppenthal

***Address:*** 804 N. Main, St. Louis, Missouri; ***Year Established:*** 1870; ***Year Closed:*** 1876; ***Years Known In Operation:*** 1870 - 1876; ***Founder:*** Jacob Ruppenthal; ***Predecessor:*** Mayer & Ruppenthal; ***Successor:*** No Data; ***Source:*** 1870 Edwards City Directory and 1875 Gould's City Directory (thru Missouri Historical Society), and Carl Scott Zimmerman of St Louis, Missouri; ***Other Facts:*** This firm was identified as a "bell and brass foundry" only in the 1870 city directory. Thereafter it was listed as "brass foundry" or "brass" or "finisher".

# James Russell

***Address:*** Baltimore, Maryland; ***Year Established:*** No Data; ***Year Closed:*** No Data; ***Years Known In Operation:*** 1837 - 1856; ***Founder:*** No Data; ***Predecessor:*** No Data; ***Successor:*** No Data; ***Source:*** Research of city directories by Carl Scott Zimmerman of St Louis, Mo; ***Other Facts:*** No Data

# Sayre Force

***Address:*** New York, New York; ***Year Established:*** No Data; ***Year Closed:*** No Data; ***Years Known In Operation:*** 1821; ***Founder:*** No Data; ***Predecessor:*** Possibly Ephraim Force; ***Successor:*** Possibly C. B. Force & Co; ***Source:*** Emails from Carl Scott Zimmerman dated 12/15/2004 regarding inquiry from either Denise Gillies or "Matt" about a bell by this firm; ***Other Facts:*** The inscription on the above bell read "Sayre Force New York 1821". This may have been a partnership of Ephraim Force who was already in the bronze bell foundry business in New York, and whoever Mr. Sayre was. The website www.handtubs.com shows the firm Force & Sayre New York, NY 1821-. If they were in business together to make fire fighting handtubs, they must have also made bells since one exists.

# C. Scheidler

***Address:*** Cedar Lake, Indiana; ***Year Established:*** 1903; ***Year Closed:*** No Data; ***Years Known In Operation:*** 1903; ***Founder:*** C. Scheidler; ***Predecessor:*** No Data; ***Successor:*** No Data; ***Source:*** Pioneer History by Richard C. Schmal, Bells of History, from the May 25, 1994 Lowell Tribune, page 7, and posted on the Internet by the Lowell public library; ***Other Facts:*** The above post quotes "Reports of the Old Settler and Historical Assn. of Lake County, 1905" as stating "On Feb. 13th, 1903, C. Scheidler, having started at Cedar Lake a bell foundry, made the first cast of a nine-inch bell, called a fine piece of work, and he had then underway three large bells. He claims to be able to make superior bells."

# Schmidt & Wilson Brass Foundry

***Address:*** Near Market Square, Houston, Texas; ***Year Established:*** No Data; ***Year Closed:*** No Data; ***Years Known In Operation:*** 1843; ***Founder:*** No Data; ***Predecessor:*** No Data; ***Successor:*** No Data; ***Source:*** *Bells Over Texas* by Bessie Lee Fitzhugh (Carl Hertzog, El Paso, Texas, Texas Western Press, 1955), and *That Vanishing Sound*; ***Other Facts:*** In 1843 they cast a 218 lb bell for Sain Vincent de Paul church of Houston (bell is now in vestibule of Annunciation Catholic Church of Houston, Texas), and another for a catholic church in Galveston weighing about 300 lbs. Scroll work around top, have crowns, and have a cross on the side. Inscription on Saint Vincent bell, on one side "Houston Texas 1843", on other side "Ste Vincente ORA. PRO. NOBIS"

# Schmieding & Witte

*Address:* St Louis, Missouri; *Year Established:* No Data; *Year Closed:* No Data; *Years Known In Operation:* 1867 - 1873; *Founder:* No Data; *Predecessor:* No Data; *Successor:* F. A. Witte; *Source:* City directories of the St Louis area reviewed by Carl Scott Zimmerman of St Louis, Mo; *Other Facts:* There is no proof this firm made bells, although its successors did (F. A Witte & Co, and Witte Hardware Co., both of St Louis, Mo.).

# L. H. & G. C. Schneider

*Address:* Washington City, ; *Year Established:* No Data; *Year Closed:* No Data; *Years Known In Operation:* 1851; *Founder:* No Data; *Predecessor:* No Data; *Successor:* No Data; *Source:* Email from a member of St. Mary's Catholic Church of Piscataway, Clinton,. Maryland; *Other Facts:* The above church has a bell marked "L. H. & G. C. Schneider, Washington City, 1851". Since the church is in Maryland, Washington City may refer to Washington D.C.

# Charles Schoening

*Address:* Louisville, Kentucky; *Year Established:* No Data; *Year Closed:* No Data; *Years Known In Operation:* 1855; *Founder:* No Data; *Predecessor:* No Data; *Successor:* No Data; *Source:* Research of city directories by Carl Scott Zimmerman of St Louis, Mo; *Other Facts:* No Data

# Schulmerich

*Address:* Sellersville, Pennsylvania; *Year Established:* No Data; *Year Closed:* No Data; *Years Known In Operation:* 1976; *Founder:* No Data; *Predecessor:* No Data; *Successor:* No Data; *Source:* Photo of bell; *Other Facts:* This firm normally makes hand bells, but in 1976 as part of the bicentennial of the United States, they made a replica of the Liberty Bell, complete with a simulated crack. It is 10" to 12" tall and has a crown.

*Schulmarich Bell in Foreground*

# Conrad Seibel Copper and Sheet Iron Company

***Address:*** St Louis, Missouri; ***Year Established:*** No Data; ***Year Closed:*** No Data; ***Years Known In Operation:*** 1881 - 1884; ***Founder:*** No Data; ***Predecessor:*** Conrad Seibel; ***Successor:*** No Data; ***Source:*** Carl Scott Zimmerman review of business directories for the St Louis area; ***Other Facts:*** In the state directory for 1883, Conrad Seibel's company was classified under "Bell and Brass Founders".

# Conrad Seibel

***Address:*** 810 S. 2nd, St Louis, Missouri; ***Year Established:*** No Data; ***Year Closed:*** No Data; ***Years Known In Operation:*** 1857 - 1879; ***Founder:*** No Data; ***Predecessor:*** No Data; ***Successor:*** No Data; ***Source:*** Business directories reviewed by Carl Scott Zimmerman for the St Louis area; ***Other Facts:*** Seibel was a coppersmith and sheet iron worker. In the state directory for 1883, his company was classified under "Bell and Brass Founders". No bells by this firm have been found.

# Louis Seibel & Bro.

***Address:*** 623 S. 2nd, St Louis, Missouri; ***Year Established:*** No Data; ***Year Closed:*** No Data; ***Years Known In Operation:*** 1888 - 1902; ***Founder:*** Louis Seibel and his brother Alexander Seibel; ***Predecessor:*** No Data; ***Successor:*** No Data; ***Source:*** St Louis area business directories reviewed by Carl Scott Zimmerman of St Louis; ***Other Facts:*** These brothers operated a brass foundry. In 1888 they advertised "Brass, Pattern and Bell Castings, Light work a specialty."

# Sellew & Company

***Address:*** St Louis, Missouri; ***Year Established:*** No Data; ***Year Closed:*** No Data; ***Years Known In Operation:*** 1848 - 1883; ***Founder:*** No Data; ***Predecessor:*** No Data; ***Successor:*** No Data; ***Source:*** Business directories reviewed by Carl Scott Zimmerman of St Louis, Mo; ***Other Facts:*** Sellew was mainly a dealer in plate and sheet iron and other metals, but in the 1850 directory his display advertisement included "church, steam boat and tavern bells". He may simply have been a dealer or agent for a bell foundry.

# Semple, Birge & Co.

***Address:*** 910 & 912 Washington Ave., St Louis, Missouri; ***Year Established:*** No Data; ***Year Closed:*** No Data; ***Years Known In Operation:*** 1868 - 1879; ***Founder:*** No Data; ***Predecessor:*** No Data; ***Successor:*** No Data; ***Source:*** Business directories of the St Louis area reviewed by Carl Scott Zimmerman of St Louis and by L. Elsinore Springer; ***Other Facts:*** This firm also did business under Semple & Birge Mnfg Co in 1879. They were classified under "Bells (Brass and Amalgam)" from 1872 - 1879.

# Sheriffs & Loughrey

***Address:*** Pittsburgh, Pennsylvania; ***Year Established:*** No Data; ***Year Closed:*** No Data; ***Years Known In Operation:*** No Data; ***Founder:*** No Data; ***Predecessor:*** No Data; ***Successor:*** No Data; ***Source:*** Bell belonging to Robert Cowie of Paris, Ark; ***Other Facts:*** Cowie bell is bronze and well finished, 14" in diameter, undated with a tang on top for mounting, and a heavy tin patina.

*Sheriffs And Loughrey 14 Inch Bell*

# Simons Brothers

*Address:* Cambridge, Ohio; *Year Established:* No Data; *Year Closed:* No Data; *Years Known In Operation:* 1889; *Founder:* No Data; *Predecessor:* No Data; *Successor:* No Data; *Source:* Zell's U.S. Business Directory of 1889; *Other Facts:* No Data

# Richard Skellorn

*Address:* Beaver St, near the King's Statue, New York, New York; *Year Established:* No Data; *Year Closed:* No Data; *Years Known In Operation:* 1775; *Founder:* No Data; *Predecessor:* No Data; *Successor:* No Data; *Source:* Rivington's New York Gazetteer, May 18, 1775, The Arts and Crafts of N.Y. 1726 - 1776; *Other Facts:* No Data

# R. Skinner

*Address:* No Data; *Year Established:* No Data; *Year Closed:* No Data; *Years Known In Operation:* No Data; *Founder:* No Data; *Predecessor:* No Data; *Successor:* No Data; *Source:* Email and photo sent to Carl Scott Zimmerman 12/21/2009 inquiring about a bell purchased; *Other Facts:* The bell referred to above is bronze with a tang on top, curved center arm with a hole for a pull rope, an iron yoke, and is undated. The weight of the bell was estimated at 100 to 130 lbs. Zimmerman thought the bell was made around the 2nd quarter of the 1800's.

# C H Slocomb & Company

*Address:* New Orleans, Louisiana; *Year Established:* No Data; *Year Closed:* No Data; *Years Known In Operation:* 1860; *Founder:* No Data; *Predecessor:* No Data; *Successor:* No Data; *Source:* *Bells Over Texas* by Bessie Lee Fitzhugh (Carl Hertzog, El Paso, Texas, Texas Western Press, 1955) pages 114 - 115, and Lois Springer records; *Other Facts:* Bell used at George A. Kelly cow bell foundry to call workers in Kellyville, Texas. 200 lbs, 22" diameter, 17" high, tapered cone mount like Meneely bells. The inscription is all in caps and the C & H are close so they may be an abbreviation for Charles. CH SLOCOMB & CO, NEW ORLEANS, 1860.

# Smith & Beggs

***Address:*** 800 N. Main, St Louis, Missouri; ***Year Established:*** No Data; ***Year Closed:*** No Data; ***Years Known In Operation:*** 1866 - 1878; ***Founder:*** No Data; ***Predecessor:*** No Data; ***Successor:*** No Data; ***Source:*** Business directories for the St Louis area reviewed by Carl Scott Zimmerman; ***Other Facts:*** This firm also did business as Smith, Beggs & Co. (1871 - 1879, and as Lafayette Foundry (1868 - 1878). In the Edwards 1868 city directory they were classified under "Bell Founders".

# Henry M. Snyder

***Address:*** St Louis, Missouri; ***Year Established:*** No Data; ***Year Closed:*** No Data; ***Years Known In Operation:*** 1840 - 1848; ***Founder:*** No Data; ***Predecessor:*** No Data; ***Successor:*** No Data; ***Source:*** Business directories of 1840 - 1848 for St Louis area reviewed by Carl Scott Zimmerman of St Louis, Mo; ***Other Facts:*** The above directories list him as a bell and brass founder. He may have been in the city earlier as a partner in Snyder & Knight (Foundry 1836 - 1837), or Snyder & Price (brass founders and blacksmiths 1838 - 1839).

# Sommerset

***Address:*** No Data; ***Year Established:*** No Data; ***Year Closed:*** No Data; ***Years Known In Operation:*** No Data; ***Founder:*** No Data; ***Predecessor:*** No Data; ***Successor:*** No Data; ***Source:*** Inquiry on ABAII website by Pete in Lousiana dated August 27, 2007; ***Other Facts:*** The above individual states they purchased a 16" diameter bell with "Sommerset" cast in the "pull bar" across the top.

# South Bay Bronze/Aluminum Foundry Inc.

***Address:*** P.O. Box 3254, San Jose, California; ***Year Established:*** No Data; ***Year Closed:*** No Data; ***Years Known In Operation:*** 1990 - 1992; ***Founder:*** Owner in 1990, Gil Hernandy; ***Predecessor:*** Eagle Pitcher Bearing, Kingwell Bros, Ltd, Weed & Kingwell; ***Successor:*** No Data; ***Source:*** Letter dated 3/29/1990 from owner to Charles Blake of ABAII; ***Other Facts:*** Excerpt from the letter, " I own and operate South Bay Bronze, which was purchased from Eagle Pitcher Bearing, previously known as Kingwell Bros, Ltd., formerly Weed & Kingwell of San Francisco, a very old bell Foundry, 1854. I cast bells..." They bought the old Weed & Kingwell patterns. They made a 10" bell with pine cone decorations around the sound bow for Winston Jones of Evergreen, Colorado.

# Southland Bell Co

***Address:*** Natchez, Mississippi; ***Year Established:*** No Data; ***Year Closed:*** No Data; ***Years Known In Operation:*** No Data; ***Founder:*** No Data; ***Predecessor:*** No Data; ***Successor:*** No Data; ***Source:*** Inquiry made to ABAII wibsite moderator on 1/10/2011; ***Other Facts:*** The bell inquired of was a 20" diameter school bell.

# Square Deal Bronze Foundry

***Address:*** Bellview Ave., Detroit, Michigan; ***Year Established:*** 1966; ***Year Closed:*** 1966; ***Years Known In Operation:*** 1966; ***Founder:*** Steven Gergely owned the foundry, but John Gergely who worked in it made the bells; ***Predecessor:*** No Data; ***Successor:*** No Data; ***Source:*** Mary Gergely, wife of John Gergely who died in 1972. She lived in East Detroit, Michigan; ***Other Facts:*** The foundry ran at above location for many years, but only made bells in 1966. That year a man brought in a large bell which was broken. They melted it down and cast three bells from it. The customer got one of them, and John Gergely kept the other two.

# Charles Stanley

*Address:* Walnut St. between Front and Second, Cincinnati, Ohio; *Year Established:* No Data; *Year Closed:* No Data; *Years Known In Operation:* 1839-1849; *Founder:* Charles Stanley; *Predecessor:* No Data; *Successor:* No Data; *Source:* Cincinnati in 1841 in Early Annals section of Cincinnati Library - copy supplied by Russell F. Frehse, Kendallville, Indiana and Cincinnati directories of 1839-1849 researched by Carl Scott Zimmerman of St. Louis, Mo.; *Other Facts:* Advertised "Bells and Brass Fossets of every description on hand". This firm obviously worked in bronze, not iron, as they advertised other bronze items.

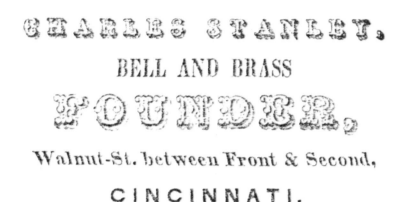

*Charles Stanley Advertisement*

# The Starr Brothers Bell Company

*Address:* East Hampton, Connecticut; *Year Established:* 1882; *Year Closed:* No Data; *Years Known In Operation:* 1882 - 1906; *Founder:* No Data; *Predecessor:* Veasey & White; *Successor:* No Data; *Source:* *That Vanishing Sound,* Zell's U.S. Business Directories of 1888 and 1889, and Thomas' Register 1905 - 1906; *Other Facts:* They bought out Veasey and White. In 1906 they advertised Engine, Locomotive and Church bells.

# J. G. Stuckstede & Company

*Address:* 201 S. 3rd Street (2735 Lyon St.), St. Louis, Missouri; *Year Established:* 1855; *Year Closed:* 1862; *Years Known In Operation:* 1855 - 1862; *Founder:* John Gerhardt Stuckstede, who emigrated from Germany via New Orleans in the 1840's; *Predecessor:* No Data; *Successor:* J. G. Stuckstede, as sole proprietor 1863-1864; *Source:* Correspondence with 1990's generation of Stuckstede family, and research of Carl Scott Zimmerman of St Louis, Mo; *Other Facts:* Bells are labeled "J. G. Stuckstede & Co." The "& Co" referred to Henry Bloemker (formally Heinrich Bloemker). John Stuckstede and Henry Bloemker married sisters. Zimmerman reports that based on their early bells, Stuckstede may have learned bell-making from Francis Mayer who came to St. Louis in 1852.

# John G. Stuckstede

*Address:* Saint Louis, Missouri; *Year Established:* 1863; *Year Closed:* 1864; *Years Known In Operation:* 1863 - 1864; *Founder:* John G. Stuckstede; *Predecessor:* John G. Stuckstede & Company; *Successor:* John G. Stuckstede & Bro; *Source:* Research of Carl Scott Zimmerman of Saint Louis, Mo; *Other Facts:* For only one year did John G. Stuckstede operate under just his name. He died in 1901.

# J. G. Stuckstede & Brother

*Address:* 201 S. 3rd, 1000 S. 3rd, 1312 Columbus, St Louis, Missouri; *Year Established:* 1863; *Year Closed:* 1883; *Years Known In Operation:* 1863 - 1883; *Founder:* John Gerhardt Stuckstede and his younger brother, Henry Stuckstede; *Predecessor:* No Data; *Successor:* No Data; *Source:* Research of Carl Scott Zimmerman of St Louis; *Other Facts:* Bells were labeled "J. G. Stuckstede & Bro."

# Henry Stuckstede & Company

*Address:* 1312 -1314 S. 2nd Street, St. Louis, Missouri; *Year Established:* 1884; *Year Closed:* 1891; *Years Known In Operation:* 1884 - 1891; *Founder:* No Data; *Predecessor:* J. G. Stuckstede & Bro; *Successor:* Henry Stuckstede Bell Foundry Co; *Source:* Bells and 1900 Gould's City Directory (thru Missouri Historical Society), and research of Carl Scott Zimmerman of St Louis, Mo; *Other Facts:* See John G. Stuckstede & Bro. for more information. Many bells from this firm are in Iowa churches. Most of them have a rather harsh tone which is recognizable and unique. Hy is the abbreviation for Henry and is found on many of their bells. They are made with the Germanic shape which means there is a sharp ridge on the outside and inside of the sound bow. Henry used little ornamentation on his bells.

*H. Stuckstede Bell 1890*

# The Henry Stuckstede Bell Foundry Company

*Address:* St. Louis, Missouri; *Year Established:* 1892; *Year Closed:* 1931; *Years Known In Operation:* 1892 - 1931; *Founder:* No Data; *Predecessor:* Henry Stuckstede & Co; *Successor:* No Data; *Source:* 2 Bells owned by Leonard Fleischer of Columbus, Nebraska, Zell's U. S. Business Directory of 1888, and research of Carl Scott Zimmerman of St Louis, Mo; *Other Facts:* "The" was part of the name. The above referenced two bronze bells are as follows: Approximately a 38" diameter bell dated 1909 from the St. Johannes Church in Omaha, Nebraska, the other is approximately 36" in diameter and dated 1901. Some of their bells were marked "Hy Stuckstede". Also appearing on their bells was the simplified inscription "Hy Stuckstede B. F. Co". They made a 65" diameter bell in 1891 for the St. Peter and Paul's Church of St Louis which stood 8' high and weighed 6,000 lbs. Their bells had the Germanic shape with a ridge around the outside and inside of the sound bow. Western Bell & Metal Co was at the same address in the 1888 Zell's U.S. Business Directory. Henry Stuckstede ran the business along with two nephews of Henry Bloemker. After Stuckstede died in 1911, the Bloemker brothers ran the foundry until 1931, but the name did not change.

# Stuckstede & Brother

*Address:* 1200 S. 7th, 2836 S. 3rd, 2735 Lyon, St. Louis, Missouri; *Year Established:* 1890; *Year Closed:* 1961; *Years Known In Operation:* 1890 - 1961; *Founder:* Herman and Henry Stuckstede, the sons of John G. Stuckstede (nephews of Henry Stuckstede); *Predecessor:* No Data; *Successor:* No Data; *Source:* Individual bells, *That Vanishing Sound*, The Missouri Republican of Jan. 26, 1873, and Gould's 1900 Directory (thru the Missouri Historical Society), and the research of Carl Scott Zimmerman of St Louis, Mo; *Other Facts:* This is a separate foundry from the one run by John G. Stuckstede first and then Henry Stuckstede. This firm also did business as H. Stuckstede and as Stuckstede & Bro (1908). This firm cast many bells. The last few years of the firm's operation only 10 to 15 bells were cast per year. In 1890 they advertised as Stucksted & Bro. at 1200 S. 7th. These advertisements were in Gould's Directories. Most bells were poorly finished, but one of Fleischer's dated 1908 is well finished. In 1893 they used the name Saint Louis Bell Foundry, Stuckstede & Bro, proprietors. There was a period during WWII and the Korean War when the foundry was closed, but Joseph Stuckstede started it up again from 1957 - 1961. Their bells were better finished than those of the Henry Stuckstede foundry. This is a separate foundry from the J. G. Stuckstede & Brother foundry.

*Joseph Stuckstede and Worker Pouring a Bell*

*Joseph Stuckstede and Worker Fitting Bell Moulds*

*Stuckstede and Brother Foundry*

*Stuckstede and Brother Bell 1908*

*Stuckstede and Brother Catalogue*

# Sutton Brothers Bell Company

*Address:* Indiana, Pennsylvania; *Year Established:* No Data; *Year Closed:* No Data; *Years Known In Operation:* No Data; *Founder:* No Data; *Predecessor:* No Data; *Successor:* No Data; *Source:* Bell in Ben Tuck collection in Lebanon, Pa; *Other Facts:* This iron dinner bell was 18" in diameter and was their size #4.

# Ezra B. Sweet

*Address:* 249 Water, New York, New York; *Year Established:* No Data; *Year Closed:* No Data; *Years Known In Operation:* 1840 - 1841; *Founder:* No Data; *Predecessor:* No Data; *Successor:* No Data; *Source:* N.Y. Business Directory 1840/1841 (research papers of Lois Springer); *Other Facts:* No Data

# B C Taylor

*Address:* Davton, Ohio; *Year Established:* No Data; *Year Closed:* No Data; *Years Known In Operation:* No Data; *Founder:* No Data; *Predecessor:* No Data; *Successor:* No Data; *Source:* 28" diameter bell at Evergreen Farm, Eminence, Indiana; *Other Facts:* Iron bell, pre Civil War shape, yoke made of bent square bar with name of firm on it. Unusual straight horizontal yoke-drops down just before gudgeons. Examined by Neil Goeppinger of Boone, Iowa. The "V" in the word DAVTON didn't quite come as far down as the other letters, so it may be that the letter was supposed to be a "Y" and the bottom vertical leg dropped out of the mold. If that is the case, the city is Dayton, not Davton.

# Thomas

*Address:* Oxford, Alabama; *Year Established:* No Data; *Year Closed:* No Data; *Years Known In Operation:* No Data; *Founder:* No Data; *Predecessor:* No Data; *Successor:* No Data; *Source:* Carl Scott Zimmerman of St. Louis, Mo; *Other Facts:* An iron dinner bell by this firm was seen by Mr. Zimmerman prior to January 20, 1999.

# J. H. Thompson

*Address:* New York, New York; *Year Established:* No Data; *Year Closed:* No Data; *Years Known In Operation:* 1838 - 1839; *Founder:* No Data; *Predecessor:* No Data; *Successor:* No Data; *Source:* Bell owned by J. D. Miles of Maine on 6/1997, and by Micky & Marie Varian of Maine; *Other Facts:* Above bell is bronze with old iron yoke, top of bronze bell has heavy tang for attaching yoke with a horizontal bolt. From the photo, the bell appears to be nicely finished. It is 18' in diameter and dated. The middle initial "H" could be an "M". The Varian bell is dated 1839.

# Edgar Thomson Foundry

*Address:* Pittsburgh, Pennsylvania; *Year Established:* No Data; *Year Closed:* No Data; *Years Known In Operation:* 1870's into the 1900's; *Founder:* Edgar Thomson; *Predecessor:* No Data; *Successor:* No Data; *Source:* Louise Springer letter of 3/4/1985, her source: program folder from U.S. Steel's Sixth Christmas Choral Festival; *Other Facts:* Letter quote: "St. Michael's church in nearby Braddock is credited with a Thomson bell inscribed with founder's name but no date. *Source:* Program folder from U.S. Steel's Sixth Christmas Choral Festival, where a huge 1878 wooden bell pattern unearthed at the Edgar Thomson plant (no longer casting bells) was on display. St. Michael's bell is 40" high and 50" in diameter.

# Matthias Tommerup

*Address:* Bethlehem, Pennsylvania; *Year Established:* 1768; *Year Closed:* No Data; *Years Known In Operation:* 1768 - 1776; *Founder:* No Data; *Predecessor:* No Data; *Successor:* No Data; *Source:* *That Vanishing Sound*, The Morning Call (newspaper) of Allentown, Pennsylvania, 11/25/74, and 1974 letter from Historic Bethlehem, Inc. to Lois Springer; *Other Facts:* He made at least 6 bells, 2 in existence in 1974. One is in lobby of the Easton, Pennsylvania. Courthouse, and other in Moravian Bell House, Church St., Bethlehem, Pennsylvania.

# J. G. Torrey & Sons

*Address:* Rockland, Maine; *Year Established:* No Data; *Year Closed:* No Data; *Years Known In Operation:* 1881 - 1889; *Founder:* No Data; *Predecessor:* No Data; *Successor:* No Data; *Source:* Zell's United States Business Directories of 1881 and 1889; *Other Facts:* No Data

# S. S. Tuttle & Co.

*Address:* Fredericktown, Ohio; *Year Established:* No Data; *Year Closed:* No Data; *Years Known In Operation:* 1881; *Founder:* No Data; *Predecessor:* No Data; *Successor:* No Data; *Source:* Peggy Mershon of Bellville, Ohio quotes an 1881 history of Knox county, Ohio in an email to Neil Goeppinger of 12/27/2006; *Other Facts:* No Data

# The U.S. Supply Company (Limited)

*Address:* 51 John, New York, New York; *Year Established:* No Data; *Year Closed:* No Data; *Years Known In Operation:* 1888, 1889; *Founder:* No Data; *Predecessor:* No Data; *Successor:* No Data; *Source:* Zell's U.S. Business Directories of 1888 and 1889, and list submitted by Roger Plaquet to ABAII website and posted November 14, 2008 from Sid Gelman's bell papers listing bells made by New York City firms, and bell belonging to Micky & Marie Varian of Maine in 2001; *Other Facts:* Varian bell is 17" in diameter and dated 1889. It is bronze and has an iron yoke.

# Van Bergen Bell Foundry

*Address:* Greenwood, South Carolina; *Year Established:* 1953; *Year Closed:* 1978; *Years Known In Operation:* 1953 - 1978; *Founder:* Harmannus T. (Harry) van Bergen; *Predecessor:* Van Bergen Bell Foundry of Heiligerlee, Netherlands; *Successor:* No Data; *Source:* George Matthew, Jr., carillonneur, 1st Presbyterian Church, Bedford St., Stamford, Connecticut, and Carl Scott Zimmerman of St Louis, Mo; *Other Facts:* This was a branch of the bell foundry listed above in the Netherlands, Van Bergen Bell Foundry. This branch produced about 700 bells including a number of chimes and carillons.

*Harry van Bergen with U.S. Bells*

# W. A. Vanduzen (Buckeye Bell Foundry)

*Address:* 164 East 2nd, Cincinnati, Ohio; *Year Established:* 1865; *Year Closed:* 1869; *Years Known In Operation:* 1865, name changed by 1869 (Mary Noe); *Founder:* No Data; *Predecessor:* G. W. Coffin; *Successor:* Vanduzen & Tift (Buckeye Bell Foundry); *Source:* Mrs. G. Lyle Ringland, Mary Noe of Iowa, and many bells; *Other Facts:* This firm took over from the G. W. Coffin bell firm and made some very ornate bells for a short time. Mr. Coffin was the guardian of a child named W. A. Vanduzen who, at the age of 14, started to work in his foundry. By the age of 20, he owned a fifth interest in the foundry and later, with a Mr. Tift, took over and renamed the foundry "Vanduzen and Tift Buckeye Bell Foundry". An ornate 48" diameter bell dated 1867 with a large cross on the waist was offered for sale by Brosamers Bells in 2016.

# Vanduzen & Tift (Buckeye Bell Foundry)

*Address:* 164 E. 2nd (in 1889), Cincinnati, Ohio; *Year Established:* 1865; *Year Closed:* 1894; *Years Known In Operation:* 1865 - 1894; *Founder:* W. A. Vanduzen and a Mr. Tift; *Predecessor:* G. W. Coffin & Co, and C. A. Coffin Foundry "Buckeye Bell Foundry", G. W. Coffin & Company "Buckeye Bell Foundry"; *Successor:* E. W. Vanduzen; *Source:* Mrs. G. Lyle Ringland, research papers of Lois Springer, and many bells; *Other Facts:* This firm manufactured volumes of bells, all bronze to my knowledge, and used a large opening at the top of the bell (usually about 4 to 5 inches in diameter) which was gripped by a pair of cast iron discs used for hanging the bell. They claimed to have invented the rotary yoke. G. W. Coffin was the guardian of W. A. Vanduzen as a boy, and Vanduzen learned bell founding in the G. W. Coffin foundry starting at age 14.

*Early Vanduzen and Tift Bell with Ornamentation*

*Vanduzen and Tift Church Bell 1888*

*Vanduzen and Tift 1894 Advertisement*

# The E.W. Vanduzen Company

***Address:*** Cincinnati, Ohio; ***Year Established:*** 1894; ***Year Closed:*** 1950; ***Years Known In Operation:*** 1894 - 1950; ***Founder:*** Ezra Williams Vanduzen; ***Predecessor:*** Vanduzen & Tift (Buckeye Bell Foundry), and G. W. Coffin (Buckeye Bell Foundry); ***Successor:*** James Homan Co; ***Source:*** Mrs. G. Lyle Ringland, many bells, Thomas' Register, and Carl Scott Zimmerman of St. Louis, Mo; ***Other Facts:*** This firm, with name changes, was one of the seven major bronze bell foundries of the U. S., making thousands of bells. They advertised car, gong, chime, church, engine, alarm, fire alarm, mule, school, ship, steamboat and tower clock bells. On October 30, 1895 this firm cast the 9 foot diameter, 35,000 pound bell for St Francis De Sales Church in Cincinnati, Ohio. The bell strikes the note E Flat and is mounted 125 feet above the ground in the 230 foot tall steeple. The clapper weighs 640 pounds. E. W. Vanduzen's name was originally Van Duzen, but according to Carl Scott Zimmerman, he changed the spelling. E. W. Vanduzen might have operated as part of Vanduzen & Tift as well before changing the foundry name to E. W. Vanduzen, because "Vanduzen" appears as one word in both these foundry names.

*E. W. Vanduzen Bell on Tuning Table*

*Vanduzen Bell Foundry Making Core Mould*

*E. W. Vanduzen Company Fire Bell 1898*

# H. H. Vansands

*Address:* 733 Broadway, New York, New York; *Year Established:* No Data; *Year Closed:* No Data; *Years Known In Operation:* 1888; *Founder:* No Data; *Predecessor:* No Data; *Successor:* No Data; *Source:* Zell's U.S. Business Directory of 1888, and list submitted by Roger Plaquet to ABAII website and posted November 14, 2008 from Sid Gelman's bell papers listing bells made by New York City firms; *Other Facts:* No Data

# Veazey & White

*Address:* East Hampton, Connecticut; *Year Established:* 1859; *Year Closed:* 1882; *Years Known In Operation:* 1859 - 1882; *Founder:* Hiram Veazey & Alfred B. White; *Predecessor:* Harrison and Davis; *Successor:* Starr Brothers; *Source: That Vanishing Sound* / Verified by Eugene Burns, Winthrop Warren of Fairfield, Connecticut, and The Connecticut Magazine of June 1899, article The Town of Chatham by Isreal Foote Loomis; *Other Facts:* One of this firms bells is in the chapel of Weslyan University at Middletown, Connecticut, another is in the Congregational Church in Farmington, and one is in the Asylum Hill Cong. Church of Hartford, Conn. The Farmington bell has an unusually thick lip, and a novel geared wheel on the top to rotate the bell so the clapper will hit a new place.

*Hiram Veazey of Veazey and White*

# The Verdin Company

*Address:* 2021 Eastern Ave., Cincinnati, Ohio; *Year Established:* 2003; *Year Closed:* No Data; *Years Known In Operation:* 2003 - present (2016); *Founder:* No Data; *Predecessor:* Meneely & Company (sort of, see other facts below); *Successor:* No Data; *Source:* Eugene P. Burns of Troy, N.Y. and The Verdin Co Pamphlets, conversations with Bob Verdin Sr., and Carl Scott Zimmerman of St Louis, Mo. regarding bell inscriptions; *Other Facts:* This firm never made its own bells until 2003 when it started casting bells using a mobil foundry to cast a bell in each county of Ohio to celebrate that state's bicentennial. For many years they had them made by Meneely & Co of West Troy, N.Y., until 1950 when that firm closed. Verdin then bought all that firms equipment, bells, and records. Verdin also bought the Vanduzen firm's equipment, bells, and records when it closed in the early 1950's after being owned and run for a short time as the James Homan Foundry. In 1984 their bells were being made by the Petit & Fritsen Bell Foundry of Aarle-Rixtel Holland, which was partially owned by them. The Petit & Fritsen bells typically carried both the name of Petit and Fritsen and the I. T. Verdin Co (as it was known then). Petit & Fritsen was in business until the end of 2014. Starting in 2015 The Verdin Company has it's bells over 1,000 lbs made by Eisbouts of the Netherlands. Verdin casts their own bells in Cincinnati in several sizes with the largest being 1,000 lbs.

# V-M Bell Co

*Address:* Waynesboro, Virginia; *Year Established:* No Data; *Year Closed:* No Data; *Years Known In Operation:* 1886; *Founder:* No Data; *Predecessor:* No Data; *Successor:* No Data; *Source:* Sept. 30, 2009 post at the ABAII website from Novice regarding a bell they own, another post of April 26, 2003 by Paul Fagan regarding another bell, another American Bell Assoc inquiry dated Aug. 1, 2002 regarding a bell with the yoke inscriptions "V-M Bell Co." on one side and "No. 2, 1886" on the other side, and dinner bell outside Iowa Machine Shed Restaurant in West Des Moines, Iowa; *Other Facts:* The above person in 2009 postulated the bell might have been made by Virginia Metalcrafters of Waynesboro, VA. They thought it was either iron or steel. The Fagan bell had a date of 1886. That may have been a patent date as these are iron or steel bells. The Iowa Machine Shed bell says Crystal Metal on it, and appeared to be new in 1995. This bell reads V. M. Bell Company without the hyphen.

# The Wall Manufacturing Company

*Address:* Cobalt, Connecticut; *Year Established:* No Data; *Year Closed:* No Data; *Years Known In Operation:* 1888 - 1889; *Founder:* No Data; *Predecessor:* No Data; *Successor:* No Data; *Source:* Zell's U.S. Business Directories of 1888 and 1889; *Other Facts:* No Data

# Ward, Bartholomew & Brainard

*Address:* 238 Main Street, Hartford, Massachusetts; *Year Established:* No Data; *Year Closed:* No Data; *Years Known In Operation:* 1828; *Founder:* No Data; *Predecessor:* No Data; *Successor:* No Data; *Source:* No Data; *Other Facts:* No Data

# Watkin Free & Company

*Address:* Cincinnati, Ohio; *Year Established:* No Data; *Year Closed:* No Data; *Years Known In Operation:* No Data; *Founder:* No Data; *Predecessor:* No Data; *Successor:* No Data; *Source:* ABAII website inquiry of December 19, 2003 by Matt Ferguson; *Other Facts:* Mr. Ferguson stated he had his grandfather's farm bell, and that it was a #6. He emailed that it measured 32" in diameter.

# Watrous & Company

*Address:* East Hampton, Connecticut; *Year Established:* 1857; *Year Closed:* No Data; *Years Known In Operation:* 1857 - 1889; *Founder:* D. W. Watrous; *Predecessor:* No Data; *Successor:* No Data; *Source:* Zell's U.S. Business Directories of 1888 and 1889, and East Hampton Connecticut Bicentennial Celebration 1967 pamphlet; *Other Facts:* No Data

# J. Webb

*Address:* Boston, Massachusetts; *Year Established:* No Data; *Year Closed:* No Data; *Years Known In Operation:* No Data; *Founder:* Joseph Webb; *Predecessor:* No Data; *Successor:* No Data; *Source:* Carl Scott Zimmerman of St Louis, Mo., and *Paul Revere and the World He Lived In* by Esther Forbes; *Other Facts:* No bells have been located made by this firm. They advertised bells for sale, but the Revere biography referred to above states "The few bells [Gillimore] and Hobart managed to make before the Revolution were sold in Boston by Revere's friend, Joseph Webb". This was pointed out by Carl Scott Zimmerman, so it may be that Webb made no bells himself, but had them made by the Aaron Hobart foundry in Abington, Mass.

# John Webb & Son

*Address:* Boston, Massachusetts; *Year Established:* No Data; *Year Closed:* No Data; *Years Known In Operation:* No Data; *Founder:* No Data; *Predecessor:* No Data; *Successor:* No Data; *Source:* An advertisement sent from Carl Scott Zimmerman of St Louis, Mo. with a drawing of a bell standing in front of a cannon and a mortar; *Other Facts:* The above advertisement had a drawing of a bell standing in front of a cannon and a mortar, with the words: "John Webb & Son, at their BELL & CANNON foundry, at the North Port of BOSTON".

# Weed & Kingwell

*Address:* 125 First Street, San Francisco, California; *Year Established:* No Data; *Year Closed:* No Data; *Years Known In Operation:* 1881 - 1889; *Founder:* No Data; *Predecessor:* No Data; *Successor:* Eagle Pitcher Bearing, Kingwell Brothers Ltd., South Bay Bronze/Aluminum Foundry Inc; *Source: That Vanishing Sound*, and Zell's U.S. Business Directories of 1881 and 1889, and letter of 3 - 29 - 90 from Gil Hernandy, owner South Bay Bronze/Aluminum Foundry Inc; *Other Facts:* No Data

# A. A. Weeks

*Address:* 11 Gold, New York, New York; *Year Established:* No Data; *Year Closed:* No Data; *Years Known In Operation:* 1888 - 1889; *Founder:* No Data; *Predecessor:* No Data; *Successor:* No Data; *Source:* Zell's U.S. Business Directories of 1888 and 1889, and list submitted by Roger Plaquet to ABAII website and posted November 14, 2008 from Sid Gelman's bell papers listing bells made by New York City firms; *Other Facts:* No Data

# Weir Mach and Foundry

*Address:* Plano, Illinois; *Year Established:* No Data; *Year Closed:* No Data; *Years Known In Operation:* No Data; *Founder:* No Data; *Predecessor:* No Data; *Successor:* No Data; *Source:* Carl Scott Zimmerman of St Louis, Mo. Inquiry; *Other Facts:* Mr Zimmerman received an Internet inquiry on July 4, 2015 from a man who had a bell inscribed "WEIR MACH AND FOUNDRY, PLANO, ILL.

# Western Bell & Metal Company

*Address:* 1312 -1314 S. 2nd, St. Louis, Missouri; *Year Established:* No Data; *Year Closed:* 1888; *Years Known In Operation:* 1885 - 1888; *Founder:* No Data; *Predecessor:* No Data; *Successor:* No Data; *Source:* Zell's U.S. Business Directories of 1888 and 1889, and research of Carl Scott Zimmerman; *Other Facts:* This name appears in the Zell's U. S. Business Directory above, and Zimmerman says it was in an 1885 St Louis city directory, but not in any other city directories, nor has he found it on any bells. It was obviously a name used by Henry Stuckstede as it is listed at the same address. The St Peter's United Church of Christ, Oakkton Street at Laramie Ave., Skokie, Illinois issued a sheet "The Story Of Our Bells" which states "...two new bells were installed in a new tower in 1887. These bells were purchased from the Western Bell and Metal Company of St. Louis, Missouri. The firm was also known has (sic) H. Stuckstede & Company. They furnished a large bell forty three inches in diameter weighing 1500 pounds that was pitched to F-natural. The small bell was 35 inches in diameter weighing 900 pounds and tuned to the pitch of G-sharp. The total cost for the bells installed was $422.25 as indicated by the invoice dated November 7, 1887. These bells still serve our church..." The article was written sometime after 1966.

# West Troy Bell Foundry

*Address:* West Troy, New York; *Year Established:* 1827; *Year Closed:* No Data; *Years Known In Operation:* 1827; *Founder:* A. Meneely & Sons; *Predecessor:* No Data; *Successor:* No Data; *Source:* *History Cast in Metal* - 1976 by Sanders & Gould - Cast Metals Institute, American Foundrymen's Society; *Other Facts:* These bells were made of "blister bar steel" rather than bronze and thus the Meneelys set up a separate company to manufacture them.

# Wheeler Foundry

*Address:* Troy, New York; *Year Established:* No Data; *Year Closed:* No Data; *Years Known In Operation:* active in 1980s, closed by 1994; *Founder:* No Data; *Predecessor:* No Data; *Successor:* No Data; *Source:* Joe Connors of Albany, N.Y. on 2 - 12 - 94; *Other Facts:* They made yacht bells.

# Benjamin Whitear

*Address:* Sharon, Connecticut; *Year Established:* No Data; *Year Closed:* No Data; *Years Known In Operation:* 1743; *Founder:* No Data; *Predecessor:* No Data; *Successor:* No Data; *Source:* Steven Martin of Platsburg, N.Y., auctioneer, whose brother belongs to a church in Saratoga County, N.Y. which has a bell (information dated April 6, 1998); *Other Facts:* The above referenced bell is 25 1/2" in diameter, has a wooden yoke, an outside clapper, but not an internal clapper. The inscription reads "Benjamin Whitear Sharon 1743". I assume it was Sharon, Connecticut as John Whitear operated in Fairfield, Connecticut, and there is a town of Sharon in Connecticut. The bell came to the present church from the High German Reformed Church in Albany, N.Y.

# John Whitear

*Address:* Fairfield, Connecticut; *Year Established:* No Data; *Year Closed:* 1774; *Years Known In Operation:* 1738 - 1774; *Founder:* John Whitear; *Predecessor:* No Data; *Successor:* Issac Doolittle; *Source:* *That Vanishing Sound*, Winthrop Warren of Fairfield, Connecticut, including his paper "Early New England Bell Founders"; *Other Facts:* Whitear made bells up to 2,000 pounds. His son, John Whitear Jr. ran the business under the same name and when he died the equipment was sold to Isaac Doolittle.

# Taylor Whitehouse

*Address:* Ohio; *Year Established:* No Data; *Year Closed:* No Data; *Years Known In Operation:* No Data; *Founder:* No Data; *Predecessor:* No Data; *Successor:* No Data; *Source:* Gary Childress of ABAII; *Other Facts:* Gary Childress saw a 28" diameter school bell with the above inscription.

# E. Whitman & Sons

*Address:* Baltimore, Maryland; *Year Established:* No Data; *Year Closed:* No Data; *Years Known In Operation:* No Data; *Founder:* No Data; *Predecessor:* No Data; *Successor:* No Data; *Source:* ABAII posting of 4 - 8 - 2010 by Joseph Biddlecomb of Reedville, Va; *Other Facts:* The above individual ownes a bell by this firm made of iron, which has a ratcheting device on top to rotate the bell.

# Whyte & DeRome

*Address:* 137 Beale, San Francisco, California; *Year Established:* No Data; *Year Closed:* No Data; *Years Known In Operation:* 1889; *Founder:* No Data; *Predecessor:* No Data; *Successor:* No Data; *Source:* Zell's U.S. Business Directories of 1889; *Other Facts:* No Data

# Wilbank Foundry

*Address:* 262 Market Street, Philadelphia (Germantown), Pennsylvania; *Year Established:* No Data; *Year Closed:* No Data; *Years Known In Operation:* 1822 - 1837; *Founder:* John Von Wilbank; *Predecessor:* No Data; *Successor:* No Data; *Source: That Vanishing Sound,* name John Wilbank from Sydney J. Shep of Mississauga, Ontario, the Daily News, Huntingdon, Pennsylvania, March 24, 1990, and Dr. Harry Long of Rochester, Minnesota in the large bells section of the ABA website forum on May 18, 2009; *Other Facts:* A bell inscribed J. Wilbank, 1837 is in Abbey Reformed Church, UCC, 6th and Church Street, Huntingdon, Pennsylvania. A 14" diameter bell inscribed J. Wilbank Philada 1836 sold in March 2012, and a 17" diameter bell dated 1833 from the ship Susquehanna was offered for sale by Brosamers Bells in 2016. Wilbank and Isaiah Ludens and Joseph Saxton (latter 2 were clock makers) bid on and got contracts for a new bell and clock in Independence Hall in Philadelphia, to replace the cracked Liberty Bell (1828). These remained operational until 1874 when they were moved to the Germantown Town Hall where they were still operational as of March 24, 1990. Dr. Long contributed the following: "John Wilbank was a Bronze Founder in Germantown, Philadelphia, PA. His greatest claim to fame was his ownership of the cracked Liberty Bell. In 1828, in preparation for a visit to Philadelphia by the Marquis de Lafayette, the city fathers renovated the old State House where the Marquis 'held court'. The Pass & Stow Statehouse Bell was cracked and had a poor tone. The city fathers contracted with John Wilbank to cast a new bell for the clock tower at the Old State House (Independence Hall). In order to reduce cost, they gave the Liberty Bell to Wilbank for scrap value ($400). When Wilbank saw it in the clock tower, he felt that it would cost him more than $400 to remove and cart it to his foundry. The city sued him, and the Judge gave him ownership of the bell, but allowed him to leave it with the city on permanent loan. Subsequently, the Liberty Bell became the centerpiece of the Abolition Movement because of its inscription. In recent years, Wilbank's heirs sued in court to take possession of the Liberty Bell. The original court records could not be found, and the Liberty Bell remains in possession of the National Park Service... The current bell in the clock tower of Independence Hall is the Wilbank Bell." The suit was brought by Wilbank's great-great-great grandson in 1984. Wilbanks' bells were all bronze, and there are a number of them still in existence.

# J. W. Wilbank & Son

*Address:* Philadelphia, Pennsylvania; *Year Established:* No Data; *Year Closed:* No Data; *Years Known In Operation:* 1833 - 1838; *Founder:* No Data; *Predecessor:* No Data; *Successor:* No Data; *Source:* Bell owned by Iva Mae Long of Tarentum, Pennsylvania, and bell sold by Bob Brasamer of Brooklyn, Mich.; *Other Facts:* No Data

# Williams Bell Foundry

*Address:* 107 - 111 Plymouth, Jersey City, New Jersey; *Year Established:* 1889; *Year Closed:* No Data; *Years Known In Operation:* 1889; *Founder:* No Data; *Predecessor:* E. G. Williams & Son in 1881, E. A. Williams & Son Until 1888; *Successor:* No Data; *Source:* Zell's U.S. Business Directories of 1881, 1888, 1889; *Other Facts:* No Data

*J. Wilbank Bell 1838*

# E. A. Williams & Son

*Address:* 107 - 111 Plymouth, Jersey City, New Jersey; *Year Established:* 1888; *Year Closed:* No Data; *Years Known In Operation:* 1888 - 1915; *Founder:* No Data; *Predecessor:* E. G. Williams & Son; *Successor:* Williams Bell Foundry; *Source:* Zell's U.S. Business Directories of 1881, 1888, and 1889, and Joe Duffy of Church Specialties, Inc, Norwalk, Conn; *Other Facts:* A 44" buoy bell is located at the Great Lakes Marine Hall of Fame in Sault Ste. Marie, Michigan dated 1910. Mr Duffy says this company's bells were made by Meneely of Troy, N. Y. and McShane of Baltimore, Md. Another bell belongs to Neil Goeppinger of Boone, Ia. and has the inscription U.S.L.H.S. on one side for United States Light House Service, and the founder and year (1915) in small letters on the reverse side. This bell resembles neither Meneely nor McShane bells, but may have been made to the Light House Service specifications as it has very thick walls to withstand years of constant ringing by the movement of waves on a bouy. It originally had four outside clappers and the bell shows wear spots on four locations. This bell had been fired upon by navy men with a 50 caliber machine gun as there are 1/2" diameter pocks and one hole in a straight line. The hole would have been caused by the armor piercing bullet (1 of every 5).

*USLHS 1915 E. A. Williams And Son (USLHS: United States Light House Service)*

# E. G. Williams & Son

*Address:* 107 - 111 Plymouth, Jersey City, New Jersey; *Year Established:* No Data; *Year Closed:* No Data; *Years Known In Operation:* 1881; *Founder:* No Data; *Predecessor:* No Data; *Successor:* E. A. Williams & Son, Williams Bell Foundry; *Source:* Zell's U.S. Business Directories of 1881; *Other Facts:* No Data

# H. C. Williams & Company

*Address:* New Britain, Connecticut; *Year Established:* No Data; *Year Closed:* No Data; *Years Known In Operation:* 1889; *Founder:* No Data; *Predecessor:* No Data; *Successor:* No Data; *Source:* Zell's U.S. Business Directory of 1889; *Other Facts:* No Data

# The Wilmot & Hobbs Manufacturing Company

*Address:* Railroad at Hancock, Bridgeport, Connecticut; *Year Established:* No Data; *Year Closed:* No Data; *Years Known In Operation:* 1888 - 1889; *Founder:* No Data; *Predecessor:* No Data; *Successor:* No Data; *Source:* Zell's U.S. Business Directories of 1888 and 1889; *Other Facts:* No Data

# O. B. Wilson Mfg Company

*Address:* Barth Ave & Sanders, Indianapolis, Indiana; *Year Established:* No Data; *Year Closed:* No Data; *Years Known In Operation:* 1905 - 1906; *Founder:* No Data; *Predecessor:* No Data; *Successor:* No Data; *Source:* Thomas' Register 1905 - 1906; *Other Facts:* No Data

# O. O. Wings

*Address:* Seneca Falls, New York; *Year Established:* No Data; *Year Closed:* No Data; *Years Known In Operation:* 1802; *Founder:* No Data; *Predecessor:* No Data; *Successor:* No Data; *Source:* Jim Williams of Columbus, Ohio; *Other Facts:* There is a cast iron bell in the town of Shell Rock. I believe Shell Rock is in Indiana. Inside the bell it reads "O. O. Wings Seneca Falls, N.Y. Pat Nov. 18, 1802 and is approximately 18" in diameter.

# F. A. Witte

*Address:* St. Louis, Mo.; *Year Established:* 1873; *Year Closed:* 1874; *Years Known In Operation:* 1873 - 1874; *Founder:* Frederick A. Witte; *Predecessor:* Schmieding & Witte; *Successor:* F. A. Witte & Co; *Source:* Carl Scott Zimmerman of St Louis, Mo; *Other Facts:* Zimmerman says "the primary business of this company and its successors was wholesale and retail hardware and cutlery. Bells were not mentioned in any city directory entry for any name of this firm." Never the less, bells have been found in north Kansas City (Riverside) and in Labadie, Mo., near St Louis.

# F. A. Witte & Company

*Address:* St. Louis, Missouri; *Year Established:* 1875; *Year Closed:* 1880; *Years Known In Operation:* 1875 - 1880; *Founder:* No Data; *Predecessor:* F. A. Witte; *Successor:* Witte Hardware Co; *Source:* Bell belonging to Ed Young of Riverside (Kansas City) Missouri, and St Louis city directories reviewed by Carl Scott Zimmerman; *Other Facts:* Ed Young bell is cast iron and is inscribed "Witte & Co".

# Witte Hardware Company

*Address:* St. Louis, Mo.; *Year Established:* No Data; *Year Closed:* No Data; *Years Known In Operation:* 1886; *Founder:* Earnest & Otto Witte (brothers) who formed the hardward company upon the death of Frederick Witte; *Predecessor:* F. A. Witte & Co; *Successor:* No Data; *Source:* Carl Scott Zimmerman letter of May 6, 1996; *Other Facts:* Zimmerman reports a "smallish iron bell in an open but unreachable roofridge cupola", "what I saw through my binoculars on both A-frames is Witte Hdwe Co. 1886". The bell was at the Bethel Methodist Church, Labadie, Missouri, outside St Louis.

# Z. T. Wright

*Address:* Portland, Oregon; *Year Established:* No Data; *Year Closed:* No Data; *Years Known In Operation:* 1927; *Founder:* No Data; *Predecessor:* No Data; *Successor:* No Data; *Source:* ABAII website inquiry by William Scholla of Bensenville, Illinois regarding bell in Glide, Oregon church; *Other Facts:* Above bell is inscribed "Z. T. Wright, Portland Oregon #40 Bell 1927"

# MANUFACTURERS LISTED BY STATE

## Alabama

American Casting Company
Thomas

## California

Bay City Foundry
California Bell Company
Eagle Pitcher Bearing
Mrs. A. S. C. Forbes Manufacturer
Garratt & Company
W. T. Garrett & Son
Globe Bell & Brass Foundry
Greenberg & Company
Kingwell Brothers Ltd.
Vincent Kingwell
Justin Kramer
South Bay Bronze/Aluminum Foundry Inc.
Weed & Kingwell
Whyte & DeRome

## Colorado

Denver Brass Works

## Connecticut

Bartholomew & Brainard
The Barton Bell Company
Bevin Brothers
C. & A. G. Bevin
Bevin Brothers Manufacturing Company
Blake, Lamb & Company
Bradley & Cochran
J. C. Clark
R. S. Clark & Company
James Cochran
Fenton & Cochran
Bradley & Cochran
J.P. Connell
Enos Doolittle
Doolittle & Goodyear
Isaac Doolittle
James Doolittle

East Hampton Bell Company
Fenton & Cochran
Gong Bell Manufacturing Company
Jesse Goodyear
N. N. Hill Brass Company
Holmes, Booth & Haydens
G. M. Hotchkiss & Company
R. Ives
New Departure Bell Company
Abel Parmalee
Peck Stow & Wilcox Company
S. E. Root
The Starr Brothers Bell Company
Veazey & White
The Wall Manufacturing Company
Watrous & Company
Benjamin Whitear
John Whitear
H. C. Williams & Company
The Wilmot & Hobbs Manufacturing Company

## Georgia

G. R. Meneely & Company

## Illinois

Bogue & Mills Manufacturing Company
Chicago Bell Foundry
R. T. Crane Brass & Bell Foundry
J. C. Deagan, Inc.
Everhardt & Company
Hibbard, Spencer, Bartlett & Company
Frederick A. Jensch
John Deere Plow Company
Tho's Kane & Company
Lakeside Foundry Company
Montgomery Ward
H. W. Rincker Foundry
Weir Mach and Foundry

## Indiana

Over Ewald

Joseph Garratt & Son
C. Scheidler
O. B. Wilson Mfg Company

## Iowa

J. C. Harrington
Dennis Liebus

## Kentucky

Joseph Collingridge
Collingridge, Lawson & Co.
Kaye & Company
William Kaye
Kentucky Bell Company
Kentucky Brass & Bell Foundry
Lawson & Frank
Louisville Foundry
Onion Bell Foundry
Phoenix Foundry
Charles Schoening

## Louisiana

Durand & Thiac
A. Hissler
Samuel Ives
James Nuttall
C H Slocomb & Company

## Maine

G. T. Allamby & Son
J. G. Torrey & Sons

## Maryland

Baker, Holmes & Brown
Baltimore Plow Company
Clampitt & Regester
Coast Guard Yard Foundry
Godfrey & Meyer
Henry McShane & Company
McShane Bell Foundry Company
McShane and Bailey
John Meneely
Odell & Ives
James H. Odell
William Peters
J. Regester & Sons
J. Regester's Sons Company
Regester & Webb

Roland Farm Bells
James Russell
E. Whitman & Sons

## Massachusetts

Cyrus Alger
Ames Company
Ames Manufacturing Company
William Blake
Blake Bell Company
William Blake & Company
Boston & Braintree
Boston Copper Company
E. Field
Field & Macy
Colonel Aaron Hobart
Major George Holbrook
Edwin H. Holbrook
Holbrook & Son
Hooper, Blake & Richardson
Henry N. Hooper & Company
Paul Revere
Revere & Sons
Revere & Son
Paul Revere & Son
Revere & Blake
Revere
Paul Revere & Company
Revere Copper Company
Richardson
Charles T. Robinson & Company
Ward, Bartholomew & Brainard
J. Webb
John Webb & Son

## Michigan

American Bell Foundry Company
G. W. Arnold & Sons
S. Davis
Fulton Iron & Engine Works
Globe Furniture Company
Northville Michigan Bell Foundry Company
Square Deal Bronze Foundry

## Minnesota

W. Bleedorn

## Mississippi

Southland Bell Co

## Missouri

M. C. Bignall & Company
Bignall & Ostrander
Henry Bloemker
Burd & Tilden
Burd, Tilden & Burd
Burd, Rucker & Company
John W. Burd
John R. Calhoun & Co.
Caughlan Bell & Brass Founders
Caughlan & Bro.
Caughlan & Dauernheim
David Caughlan
Caughlan & Piquette
Central Bell & Brass Foundry
Central Union Brass Co.
Cordry Caughlin Co.
Eagle Bell & Brass Foundry
J. W. Garratt Brass Foundry Co.
J. W. Garratt & Co
Goulds and Ostrander
George W. Gregg
William Harpke
Harpke & Dauernheim
Harpke Manufacturing Company
Hewitt Mfg. Co.
A. J. Hunt
George S. Hunt
Jackson Bell and Brass Foundry
William Koennker
Kupferle & Boisselier
Kupferle, Boisselier & Company
John Kupferle
John Kupferle & Bro.
John C. Kupferle
John C. Kupferle
Lafayette Foundry
P. P. Manion Blacksmith & Wrecking Company
Manny & Company
Emil C. Mayer
Francis Mayer & Company
Mayer & Ruppenthal
More, Jones & Company
N. O. Nelson Mfg Copmpany

N. O. Nelson & Company
Marcus O'Hara
Rumsey Manufacturing Company
Jacob Ruppenthal
Schmieding & Witte
Conrad Seibel
Conrad Seibel Copper and Sheet Iron Company
Louis Seibel & Bro.
Sellew & Company
Semple, Birge & Co.
Smith & Beggs
Henry M. Snyder
J. G. Stuckstede & Company
John G. Stuckstede
J. G. Stuckstede & Brother
Henry Stuckstede & Company
The Henry Stuckstede Bell Foundry Company
Stuckstede & Brother
Western Bell & Metal Company
F.A. Witte
F. A. Witte & Company
Witte Hardware Company

## New Hampshire

Gamaliel Fenton

## New Jersey

Arthur Lynds Bigelow
Howell Works Company
Aaron Miller
David Ross
Williams Bell Foundry
E. A. Williams & Son
E. G. Williams & Son

## New York

Alcor & Company
James P. Allaire
American Bell Company
Aspinwall
John Bailey
Barton Beelzebub
John Benson
Alex. Borrowman
Bradley & Hubbard Manufacturing Company
C. Brinkerhoff
William Buckley
Charles Cory & Sons

Cowing & Company
Curtis
William L. Dodd
Downs & Company
C. B. Force & Company
Ephraim Force
James Gallagher
John A. Gifford & Sons
Good & Moores
Gould's Manufacturing Company
James Gregory
Hall & Whittermore
Benjamin Hanks Foundry
Julius Hanks
Hanks & Meneely Company
A & T Hanks
O. Hanks
William Hedderly
Bailey & Hedderly
Holly Manufacturing Company
Alfred Ivers & Company
Jones & Company Troy Bell Foundry
Jones & Hitchcock Troy Bell Foundry
George H. Kimberly
Wm. McKenna & Son
Andrew Meneely
Meneely & Oothout
Andrew Meneely & Son
Andrew Meneely 's Sons
E. A. & G. R. Meneely
Meneely & Company
Meneely & Kimberly, Founders
Meneely Bell Company
Clinton H. Meneely Bell Company
Morgan Iron Works
Thornton N. Motley
New York Bell Foundry
Paulson, Thomas & Son
John Phillips
Pugh & Russell
Thomas Pugh
Rumley & Company
Rumsey & Company (Limited)
Sayre Force
Richard Skellorn
Ezra B. Sweet
J. H. Thompson

The U.S. Supply Company (Limited)
H. H. Vansands
A. A. Weeks
West Troy Bell Foundry
Wheeler Foundry
O. O. Wings

## North Carolina

Hardy & Newsom

## Ohio

Bates & Blymyer Co.
Beecher Gibbs
Bell & Brass Founder
C. S. Bell
C. S. Bell Company
C. S. Bell & Company
Bleymeyer Foundry
Blymyer & Brothers Company
Blymyer Day & Company
Blymyer Manufacturing Company
Blymyer Norton & Company
B. N. & Company
Brass & Bell Foundry
Bucker-Gibbs
Buckeye Bell Foundry
C & D
Cincinnati Bell, Brass & Iron Foundry
Cincinnati Bell Company
Cincinnati Bell Foundry Company
Clark & Elliot
The Cleveland Bell Mfg & Foundry Company
C. A. Coffin "Buckeye Bell Foundry"
G. W. Coffin & Company "Buckeye Bell Foundry"
Commings & Hosack
C. Dockray
William C. Downey & Company
Foote Foundry
Frank and Johnston
Frederick Town Bell Company
Free & Company
J. Garrett
Hall & Allen
Hanks & McGraw
George L. Hanks
W. S. Harrington
James L. Haven Company

Haven Malleable Castings Company
Hedges, Free & Company
Henry-Bonnard Company
Hillsboro Ohio Bell Company
James Homan Foundry
Jenny & Manning
Peter & Benjamine Keith
Wm. Kirkup & Son Foundry
The Ktown Bell Company
Laird & Company
Lehr Agricul. Company
Meeks & Watson
The Miller Company
John Millers Foundry
National Bell Foundry
Niles Bell Foundry
Ohio Bell Foundry
Ohio Brass & Bell Foundry
Parker & Company
J. P. Parker
Perin & Gaff Mfg Company
Simons Brothers
Charles Stanley
B C Taylor
S. S. Tuttle & Co.
W. A. Vanduzen (Buckeye Bell Foundry)
Vanduzen & Tift (Buckeye Bell Foundry)
The E.W. Vanduzen Company
The Verdin Company
Watkin Free & Company
Taylor Whitehouse

## Oregon

Z. T. Wright

## Pennsylvania

Joseph Bernhard
Carbon Bronze Company Limited
Chaplin - Fulton Manufacturing Company
Lewis Debozear
T. I. Dyre Jr
Eagle Bell Co
Fredricktown
Fulton Brass & Bell Foundry
A. Fulton & M. McDonald Brass Foundry
A. Fulton's Son & Company
Fulton & Reno Company
Andrew Fulton

J. Gallagher
George Hedderly
Edwin Hedderly
Daniel King
Daniel King, Jr.
Lebanon Manufacturing Company
John S. Lee & Company
T. W. Levering
A. Major & Brother
M. M'Donald
Messinger Mfg Company
Millbank Foundry Company
Mish Brothers
Charles Mousley
John Pass
Pass & Stow
Samuel Powell
Schulmerich
Sheriffs & Loughrey
Sutton Brothers Bell Company
Edgar Thomson Foundry
Matthias Tommerup
Wilbank Foundry
J. W. Wilbank & Son

## Rhode Island

F. Fuller
Fuller Iron Works
S. & J. T. Jackson
A. H. Manchester
Providence Brass Foundry

## South Carolina

John Robertson

van Bergen Bell Foundry

## Tennessee

Ross Meehan Foundries

## Texas

Giron
Schmidt & Wilson Brass Foundry

## Virginia

Loudoun Manufacturing Company
Norfolk Navy Yard
V-M Bell Co

## Washington

Duncan McKiernan
Prindle Station
Puget Sound Navel Shipyard

## Wisconsin

Gardiner Campbell & Sons
Centennial Bell Foundry
B.W. Felthousen Company
Milwaukee Foundry

## Unknown

C. W. Arnold
Basler-Goe
C.H. Bell Co.
The Bowlden Bell
Edward M. Brown
Concordia
Melvin C. Corbett
Derby
Gallagher, Long & Miller
Gilbert & Meredith
Harrison and Davis
Hish Brothers
Cyril Johnston
LEB Mfg Company
Lusk & Company
Rankins Snyder H. Co
R.B.
L. H. & G. C. Schneider
R. Skinner
Sommerset

# BIBLIOGRAPHY

Denton, William Richard — *BELLS AND THEIR USE AS A MEANS OF CHRISTIAN EDUCATION*, San Anselmo, California, Thesis for Master of Arts degree, San Francisco Theological Seminary 1961

Forbes, Esther — *PAUL REVERE & THE WORLD HE LIVED IN*, Boston, Massachusetts, Houghton Mifflin Company, 1942

Jennings, Trevor S. — *BELLFOUNDING*, Merlins Bridge, Haverfordwest, Dyfed, England, Shire Publications Ltd., 1988

Kramer, Justin — *CAST IN AMERICA*, Los Angeles, California, Justin Kramer Incorporated, 1975

Price, Percival — *BELLS & MAN*, New York, Oxford University Press, 1983

*CAMPANOLOGY EUROPE 1945 - 47*, Ann Arbor, Michigan, The University of Michigan Press, 1948

Rossing, Thomas D. — *ACOUSTICS OF BELLS*, New York, Van Nostrand Reinhold Company, 1984

Spear, Nathaniel Jr. — *A TREASURY OF ARCHAEOLOGICAL BELLS*, New York, Hastings House Publishers, Inc. 1978

Springer, L. Elsinore — *THAT VANISHING SOUND*, New York, Crown Publishers, 1976

*THE COLLECTOR'S BOOK OF BELLS*, New York, Crown Publishers, 1972

Stickney, Edward & Evelyn, — *THE BELLS OF PAUL REVERE, HIS SONS AND GRANDSONS*, Bedford, Massachusetts, The Stickneys, 1976

Triber, Jayne E. — *A TRUE REPUBLICAN, THE LIFE OF PAUL REVERE,* Amherst, Massachusetts, University of Massachusetts Press, 1998

*THE BELL TOWER* — Magazine of The American Bell Association International, Inc. various articles from 1950 to 2016.

# ABOUT THE AUTHOR

Neil Goeppinger grew up on an Iowa farm where his parents taught him not just a work ethic, but the enjoyment that comes from a job well done.

While managing farms in two states, Neil picked up an appreciation for the sound of church bells in 1978 and started to collect them. He also became interested in church bell foundries and started to research those as well. In the early years, his research was done by phone and correspondence with state historical societies, often hiring a researcher to go through the records and mail photocopies. Around 1983, Neil found and joined the American Bell Association, Int'l Inc. (ABAII), which gave him access to the knowledge its members had of large bells and foundries. Soon Neil was answering all the Association's inquiries on large bells, including requests from the Smithsonian and the National Park Service.

The advent of the Internet helped research efforts, but much of the information on early foundries was still in old foundry catalogs which were not on the Internet. During 38 years of collecting and researching, Neil amassed a large amount of information which he wanted to pass along to future bell collectors and researchers. The result is this book.

Neil personally collected over 60 large bells. In 2001 – 2002, he served as President of the ABAII, wrote many articles for the association's magazine, The Bell Tower, and traveled to Japan several times to visit fellow bell collectors. This book solves a common frustration among collectors, providing one single source to check for the origin of an American-made large bell.

Today, Neil lives with Ginny, his college sweetheart and wife of 49 years, enjoying summers in Iowa, and winters in Florida. His daughter, her husband and four grandchildren are an hour away, and his son and wife live in California. At 71, Neil still manages a few farms, and still answers a few large bell inquiries.

Made in the USA
Columbia, SC
26 December 2021

52744629R00111